D0059305

TRANSFORMING
YOUR
DRAGONS

Other Books by José Stevens, Ph.D.

EARTH TO TAO
Michael's Guide to Healing and Spiritual Awakening

MICHAEL ON ICELAND
(coauthored with Lena Stevens)
(*available in Iceland only*)

THE MICHAEL HANDBOOK
(coauthored with S. Warwick-Smith)
A Channeled System of Self-Understanding

THE PERSONALITY PUZZLE
(coauthored with J.P. Van Hulle)
Solving the Mystery of Who You Are

SECRETS OF SHAMANISM
(coauthored with Lena Stevens)
Tapping the Spirit Power Within You

TAO TO EARTH
Michael's Guide to Relationships and Growth

TRANSFORMING YOUR DRAGONS

HOW TO TURN FEAR PATTERNS INTO PERSONAL POWER

JOSÉ STEVENS, PH.D.

BEAR & COMPANY

PUBLISHING

SANTA FE, NEW MEXICO

LIBRARY OF CONGRESS CATALOGING-IN-PUBLICATION

Stevens, José.
Transforming your dragons : how to turn fear patterns into
personal power / José Stevens.
    p. cm.
Includes bibliographical references.
ISBN 1-879181-17-7
1. Self-actualization (Psychology) 2. Interpersonal relations—
Miscellanea. 3. Maturation (Psychology)—Miscellanea.
4. Fear-Case studies. I. Title.
BF637.S4S82 1994
158—dc20   94-16002
                                                                CIP

Copyright © 1994 by José Stevens

All rights reserved. No part of this book may be reproduced by any
means or in any form whatsoever without written permisssion from
the publisher, except for brief quotations embodied in
literary articles or reviews.

Bear & Company, Inc.
Santa Fe, NM 87504-2860

Cover Design: Lightbourne
Editor: Gail Vivino
Typography and interior design: Marilyn Hager
Printed in the United States of America by R.R. Donnelley

3 5 7 9 8 6 4

This book is dedicated to my friend Jan McNeal—skydiver, counselor, and teacher—who contributed her knowledge to this book before her final jump; and to all of us who are remembering we are free.

Contents

Acknowledgments

I extend a heartfelt thanks to all my clients who, for over twenty years have struggled and made an effort to transform their own dragons, sometimes with great success. Without their sacrifices this book could never have been written. I wish to thank as well, all my friends and colleagues who allowed themselves to be interviewed in depth regarding their own dragons. Their candidness and honesty contributed to a much more thorough book. I send my gratitude to all my teachers both ancient and modern who have guided me to the insights about human suffering and its transformation to joy.

Special thanks go to Gail Vivino for her invaluable editing skills, Karen Moye for her long labors at the computer, Carol Bowles for her creative interpretation of the dragons, and the fine folks at Bear and Company for their support in getting this book out. Finally I thank you the reader for having the courage to pick this book up. May your journey lead to freedom, satisfaction, and happiness. Blessings.

Preface

Over a period of more than twenty years, I had the privilege of working with a great variety of people—some in crisis, some dysfunctional, and some seeking to meet their greater potential. These clients were my most profound teachers.

Although I was trained in traditional theories of human behavior and was taught to think according to the psychotherapist's diagnostic manual, I noticed seven basic patterns of behavior amongst my clients that were not mentioned in the psychological literature. I began to see these patterns repeated over and over again, no matter what race, culture, gender, or age of client appeared in my office. These seven patterns corresponded to personality complexes mentioned, not in the mental health literature, but in the writings of philosophers, mystics, and spiritual teachers.

In the course of my studies, I found that there was something critical missing from contemporary psychology—something ancient and valuable. In our rush to embrace new technology and science, we modern professionals had turned our backs on ancient wisdom. We had forgotten that there had been astute psychologists throughout the ages who had pointed the way to an understanding of human nature.

I began a search that took me far afield from psychology. I studied ancient myths and fairy tales. I read sacred books related to various spiritual traditions. I began to sense a thread of knowledge that was woven throughout the ages—an understanding of the challenges and obstacles a human being meets on the heroic journey of life. I saw that these ancient teachings could be related to modern psychological theory in a way that would balance and support it, not displace it.

The writings of the Russian mystic G. I. Gurdjieff and his

students P. D. Ouspensky and J. Gordon Bennett, were perhaps the best accessible sources for the historical material in *Transforming Your Dragons*. Gurdjieff called the seven fear patterns Chief Features, because he said they were the most noticeable features visible upon first meeting people.

As I learned more and more about the seven patterns from my work with myself and my clients, I began to teach graduate students in supervision with me, as well as other experienced counselors, the basics of the seven styles. I called them simply obstacles or more formally, Personality Fear Patterns. I discovered that my students' understanding of their clients and their subsequent work with them dramatically improved with this knowledge.

In this book, I have chosen to call the fear patterns dragons, because I believe this is a more interesting and fun way to learn about them in a book. Thus, the focus of this book is the Seven Dragons, how they block your growth, and how you can transform them to gain maturity and meet your potential.

Many people notice the similarity between the Personality Fear Patterns system and the Enneagram, another ancient but recently popular approach to understanding human behavior. Within the Enneagram are the influences of the Personality Fear Patterns. There are similarities in the systems but there are also significant differences. The Personality Fear Patterns system is part of a much greater body of knowledge, too vast for this book. I have referred to the rest of this system in both *The Personality Puzzle: Solving the Mystery of Who You Are*, by J. Stevens and J.P. Van Hulle (Affinity Press) and in *The Michael Handbook* by J. Stevens and S. Warwick-Smith (Warwick Press).

Transforming Your Dragons was written not only for counselors and psychotherapists but for anyone with an interest in transforming human behavior. I hope that you, in reading this book, will be inspired to take on the challenge of facing your own dragons and that you will emerge successful and joyful, ready to live—really live.

Introduction

Humankind is poised on the brink of massive planetary change. The next hundred years will determine whether life on Earth is transformed into a global community with cooperation among all peoples or whether it disintegrates into a chaos of destruction and becomes an unlivable garbage dump. The choice for positive change will not be made by government, science, or business interests, but by individual human beings engaged in personal transformation. These individuals will then influence governments, business, and the sciences to conduct their affairs in ways that are conducive to greater happiness on this planet.

You as an individual cannot transform yourself unless you personally face your own fears. This is no easy task, but it is absolutely required for any personal breakthrough. Facing fear often means looking at the dark, shadowy side of yourself—not to feel guilty or shameful or to punish yourself, but to release the potential vitality locked up therein.

This book is a guide to facing your fears in the forms of the seven personal dragons. In fairy tales, the dragons must be confronted and slain for the heroes to gain rights of passage. Yet this dynamic, masculine, Western notion of slaying dragons needs to be balanced with the more magnetic, feminine, Eastern approach to transforming the dragons. In martial arts, it is a well-known fact that if you resist or struggle with your opponent, you risk injury and possibly death. Therefore, the best strategy is to know your opponents, anticipate their moves, and let your opponents defeat themselves by denying them a target. This does not mean that you avoid confronting your antagonists. You still face your enemies but you transform the energy of combat into a dance of learning.

The dragons are the most worthy opponents you will ever face. Yet only by meeting such worthy adversaries will you ever realize your full potential. The dragons exist to make you strong. They are the vehicles of transformation. Nothing of great value in life is attained without some kind of test. This book is about recognizing those transforming tests that you have the special opportunity to face, and pass, each day of your life.

The Dragon as Metaphor

I have chosen to use the metaphor of the dragon throughout this book for several reasons. The first is that it takes you out of your everyday mind set and redirects you toward your imagination, where all problems are ultimately solved. A dragon is a visible, concrete being, not an abstract theory. Secondly, the dragon links you with your ancient past, the source of much forgotten knowledge. Thirdly, the dragon connects you with your inner child, that part of yourself that knows the simple truth.

There are several main ideas I hope to communicate throughout the book. The first is that no one is to blame for any dysfunction. No good comes from blaming parents, siblings, guardians, friends, enemies, or even yourself for pain and dysfunction. In one respect, all those people who caused us problems are victims of a heritage of dysfunction that goes back to the distant past. In another respect, the characters that we sometimes blame for our misfortunes are actually our hidden teachers. Without them we would have little to challenge us, and life would not be so interesting.

The dragons themselves have been around for eons. Fairy tales, myths, and human experience tell us that each one of us is responsible for making changes and enlightening ourselves. We can do something about our own dragons. We can do nothing about someone else's dragon. We can merely support the other person's efforts at becoming free.

Secondly, I want to draw a clear distinction between our dragons or dysfunctions and ourselves. No person is a dragon.

The dragon is like a parasite or a virus that lives with us but is not who we are. Too often in Western psychology we get the idea that it is we who are damaged at the core. This is not so. We human beings are not and have never been damaged goods. We are magical and wonderful beings when we know who we are. Our task now and throughout the ages is to fight the dragons that beset us and become the liberated heroes and heroines of our own lives that we were meant to be. The myth of Saint George slaying the dragon is a metaphor for everyone in every life. Our challenge is to transform the dragons that try to live with us and take over our power. Blaming is a waste of time. We are responsible for our freedom, and we are not our dragons.

TRANSFORMING
YOUR
DRAGONS

Chapter One

THE
SEVEN
DRAGONS

Seven mighty dragons appear to block the path of all human beings. They bellow and roar and paralyze us with their sheer size and might. They lie in wait with lures and seductions. They use their magic to transform themselves into enticing and breathtaking distractions, all the while hiding from us their soul-killing poisonous breath.

A dragon is merely an icon, a powerful image that represents danger and fear, and of course lies in wait on our path to roar out a terrible challenge to our progress. The dragon when first encountered represents fear itself. It is only later, with familiarity, that the dragon may actually give us clues to redemption—the necessary information to transform defeat at its claws to victory and passage. With victory, fear and separation are overcome. Fear flies, and the path leads to a greater reality encompassing unity, knowledge, wisdom, truth, and beauty.

The seven dragons are the most familiar of all human limitations. Throughout the ages they have been called many names: the seven deadly sins; the seven vices; bad blood; original sin; base human nature; plagues; the fall of man; Satan; evil spirits; and so on. These notions of dragons have suggested that evil is visited upon human beings by the devil, demons, or humankind's own innate wickedness and sinfulness. According to these views, people are helpless in the face of these dragons

4 TRANSFORMING YOUR DRAGONS

and it is only by crying out to the gods through prayer, ritual, or sacrifice that these demons can be avoided. While they create temporary relief, in the long run these perspectives are disempowering and offer little in the way of effective solutions to the problems.

In modern times, we call the seven dragons by more scientific names: dysfunctions, psychopathologies, defense mechanisms, addictions, abnormal and aberrant behaviors, neuroses, and antisocial behaviors. We attribute these modern demons to familial conditioning, poor social conditions, chemical imbalances, and genetic makeup. However, with all the modern science in the world, we have not come one step closer to slaying the age-old dragons that continue to plague us. Why? Because we do not understand the fundamental nature of the dragons we seek to slay. The dragons are swift and sly and entice us on wild goose chases that lead to a false sense of security. They continue to reign supreme on the world scene. In fact, more commonly we call the dragons ordinary, everyday behavior. We not only regard destructive, callous, insensitive, self-defeating behavior as ordinary, but we reward it socially with fame, fortune, and social status.

Truly, the seven dragons lie at the heart of every major dysfunction and addiction known to humankind. They are the addictions underlying every addiction. They are the dragons behind every obstacle to human potential. They are the dragons that masquerade as power, brilliance, modesty, strength, colorfulness, sacrifice, and fortitude.

For the purposes of this book, the dragons will be called by simple, blunt names: arrogance, self-deprecation, impatience, martyrdom, self-destruction, greed, and stubbornness. These are seven familiar words to describe the cause of all human-created suffering. Judging by human history, there would seem to be no hope of erasing these scourges that erode the best intentions of even the most developed humans. And yet, it is possible to defeat the seven dragons if you are armed with accurate infor-

mation, intense desire, perseverance, the courage to admit difficulty, and the humility to ask for help. This book is dedicated to
arming you with the tools to eradicate these seven obstacles.

Your first challenge is to identify the primary dragon that
blocks your path. Next, you must identify the secondary dragon
that lurches forward when the first is at bay. When you can
identify your dragons, you have made a quantum leap toward
defeating them. Dragons rarely permit themselves to be seen,
and under scrutiny they disappear and change into something
that looks more seductive. That is why most people are in the
dark about their dragons. When the dragons are in charge, it is
much easier to see them in someone else. So, if you are in doubt
about what your dragons are, ask your friends. They can usually
see yours clearly.

In this book you will find complete descriptions of how all
the dragons operate, how they hide, and the tricks they use to
seduce you. You will gain insights into their devastating impact
on life. You will see, in real life scenarios, the various forms the
dragons take in the lives of everyday, ordinary people. In addition, you will discover the methods to gradually erase your dragons and prevent their further encroachment on your personality.
However, no book can ever do the actual work for you. You may
be armed with knowledge, but information is not enough to
tackle these massive creatures. You must take definitive actions
to defeat them. You will find such actions included in this book
so that it will be easier for you to know what steps to take. Then
you are on your own.

There is always a paradox at the heart of challenges. As in
all fairy tales, the basic task of defeating the dragons must be
undertaken by the hero or heroine—in this case you and you
alone. No one can do this for you, no matter how much they
care about you. And yet, there is always hidden help.
Sometimes the help is right in front of your face, but you
haven't noticed it. The paradox is that you cannot defeat the
dragon alone. You do not exist as an island, but rather as a

swimmer in the ocean of humanity. There are those who have gone down your path before. There are those whose purpose includes assisting you on your way. Liberation from tyranny is both an individual feat and a group-sponsored endeavor. It is a lot like growing up. You have to do it by yourself, but much help is available.

The Origin and Purpose of the Dragons

Just where did the dragons come from and why do people choose to live amongst them? Since dragons are an archetypal symbol of menace and transformation, the answer to these questions can be discovered metaphorically. Life is a kind of mythic tale for each person. A tale has to be interesting and exciting or else it bores us. Without dragons, monsters, demons, and evil sorcerers, the fairy tale of life loses its punch. Without some kind of dragon, there is no drama. Dragons and evil magicians fill our fairy tales and appear in our dreams. They give us challenges and obstacles that, through heroic effort, can be overcome. This heroic effort is what makes life fascinating and worth living. If you think of life as an elaborate, cosmic game, then you can see that there are always challenges and obstacles to make the game more interesting. If the game is too easy, it is not fun. Think of the dragons as the elements that make life more interesting. Transforming them is one of the primary goals of life's game.

Why, specifically, are dragons historically so riveting? Because they at once entrance us and terrify us. Unlike the one-dimensional villains of Westerns or cops-and-robbers dramas, dragons are shapechangers; they can be beautiful one moment and menacing the next. They are infinitely more interesting to us because we have ambivalent feelings about them. The nature of dragons can be learned by examining their secret components.

In mythology, the fish, who is related to the element of water, symbolizes the origin of life and the powers of rebirth.

The snake, the reptile with belly to the ground, represents the regenerative powers of the earth element. The bird, with winged flight, represents air, the breath of life and spirit. The warm-blooded lion represents fire—vitality, light, and transformation. The mythic dragon, however, is special, because it operates in every element. It walks on the land, flies in the air, lives in the sea, and breathes fire. This ability of the dragon to exist simulta-neously in every element makes it a powerful adversary indeed. It is capable of influencing your thoughts (air), altering your actions (earth), disrupting your emotions (water), and altering your personality (fire) in fundamental ways. Because the dragon can shift so easily among the elements, it becomes sneaky and has the ability to hide from your notice for extended periods of time. The dragon, being magical, occupies the hypnogogic state between waking and sleeping—that land between physicality and the formless subconscious.

As they are neither male nor female, all seven dragons have the ability to affect men and women equally. Additionally, since dragons are ageless, they can impact you at any time of your life. However, they do develop over the course of a lifetime, and impact you in different ways at different developmental stages. You can begin to see them at work when you are a very young child. Later, the dragons take advantage of the raging hormones of adolescence to run wild through your personality. In adult-hood, a specific dragon or pair of dragons takes over the job of tormenting you until you wake up and take action. Waking up is actually remembering who you are at the essence level. When that happens, the dragons begin to flee.

Weapons to Fight the Dragons

If you are interested in defeating your dragons, you must become like the legendary Saint George, and be the potential hero or heroine of your own tale. All dragon slayers need weapons to do battle against what appear to be overwhelming odds. Your masculine weapons are the magical sword and staff, representing truth and knowledge. The way you slay any one of the seven dragons is by the sword of truth and the staff of knowledge. It is up to you to use the sword to tell the truth to yourself. In this book, you will find the staff of knowledge to assist you in transforming your dragons. Your female weapons are the magical chalice of intuition and love and the pentacle representing tangible experience and awareness. When you drink from the magical chalice your deeper perception and feeling guide your actions toward victory. When you use the magical coin you become more aware of the actions needed to transform the dragons on your journey.

As you study each of the dragons, you will learn specific techniques to neutralize them in their vulnerable spots. The dragons are not invincible, even though they appear to be, just as in any game the obstacles are not meant to defeat you, only to challenge you. You can rid yourself of every trace of the dragons. In a way, however, they do live forever by moving on to new generations of human beings for as long as they continue to be tolerated.

You will not be able to transform the dragons by running away or hiding from them. As in all tales of old, you can only defeat them by doing what is most frightening of all: facing them directly and challenging them.

Dragons as Allies

Although I speak of slaying dragons, in fairy tales, dragons live forever and cannot be slain. Throughout this book, to slay dragons means to stop them from controlling your life. When you ultimately slay dragons once and for all, they become your allies. Dragons are actually master teachers, and in the end you will have their wisdom to use to help others. That is why this book is called Transforming Your Dragons.

Discovering Your Dragons

This section contains a simple checklist that will help you identify your personal dragons. As you read the rest of this book, pay particular attention to the dragons you have identified that you want to transform.

Check the group of statements that most resembles your habitual responses, especially to stressful situations in your life. In particular, think about how you respond when you are trying to learn something new that is difficult for you. All statements need not apply to you for the group of statements to be generally true. Think about what is generally true of your behavior under stressful conditions because that is the time when the dragons are most likely to emerge. If a couple of the groups apply, then go through the groups and check the statements that are most true of you. Establish a primary and a secondary group. The dragon numbers are translated into names at the end of the checklist. Don't read this until you've finished your check.

Be as honest as possible. You may not like to admit being a certain way or holding a certain attitude. If you are in doubt, ask your friends what they would say about you. They are usually more objective and accurate about you.

Dragon One

I become quiet and a bit distant with people I don't know.
Some people say I am hard to get to know.
To be embarrassed in public is like dying a thousand
     deaths.
I like to feel special.
I appear to others to have everything under control.
I have to work hard to overcome my shyness.
I hate to be judged and compared.
I feel that if people really knew me they would think I'm
     great.

It's hard for me to admit I'm wrong.

Apologizing is difficult for me.

I am very critical of myself and I am often secretly critical of others.

I worry about how I look.

I try to catch glimpses of myself in store windows and mirrors to see if I look OK.

Winning is very important to me.

Dragon Two

I often doubt my abilities and feel inadequate.

If I think I've done something wrong, I apologize profusely.

If something goes wrong, I usually feel that it was my fault somehow.

People often tell me to stand up straight and not to slump.

I am very hard on myself.

There are many things I would like to do but I doubt myself and am afraid to take the risks.

People say that I lack confidence.

I often feel that a new car or new clothes are too nice for me.

I typically think others can do things better than I can.

I often talk with my hand covering my mouth.

Sometimes people ask me to speak up because I'm inaudible to them.

I find that I often breathe shallowly.

When I am uncomfortable, I look at my feet.

Dragon Three

I often feel that the grass is greener and things are better somewhere else.

I often feel like I'll never find what I'm looking for.
When something goes wrong, I feel like shopping to
    make myself feel better.
When something goes wrong, I feel like eating and I can't
    seem to stop.
I often deprive myself when I feel a craving. I try to
    control myself, but it's so hard.
Often I lose the battle and indulge myself. Later I feel bad
    and guilty.
I love material things. Even if I don't need something, I
    may buy it.
I often dream of having all I want of something.
I worry that I will end up with nothing.
Sometimes I can't decide among all the things I want and
    I end up with none of them. Then I feel really bad.
I have addictions.
I often gamble on high-risk enterprises.
I have been known to overprice what I am selling.
Coming down in price is painful.
I often blame my partner for my lack of satisfaction.

Dragon Four

When things go wrong, I take several drinks to feel better.
I like to be in control, but I find I often lose control of
    situations.
I often feel really desperate.
Sometimes I think of killing myself because life is too
    painful.
I take drugs to numb the pain of living.
I often take big risks with my life—driving fast, trusting
    people I shouldn't, or ending up in dangerous places.
Sometimes I think others would be better off if I weren't
    around any more.
I often think I won't live very long.

I feel out of control much of the time.

I have left a trail of damaged relationships and broken agreements behind me.

I frequently move to start my life over, but it doesn't work.

I am worried I could hurt someone badly.

I like to prove that I can overcome danger.

I have violent outbursts.

Dragon Five

I often feel there is too little time to get everything done.

Sometimes I break or jam things in my haste to get going.

I worry that life will pass me by before I do everything I want to do.

I find myself rushing my kids, friends, or employees because they move too slowly.

People say I'm intolerant and I guess they are right.

I often interrupt people or finish their sentences for them.

I hate to wait, and I sometimes blow my top if something takes too long.

People in this world are too damn slow.

In my rush to get everything done, I often get to my appointments late.

I often run late and forget things along the way.

I find it hard to slow down even on vacation.

I find myself rushing for no reason at all.

My lists are long and my time is short.

I feel fatigued and stressed much of the time.

Dragon Six

I often feel trapped by circumstances.

People say I complain a lot, but they just don't understand.

I feel that I don't often have a choice.

If it weren't for certain people, my life would be better.

It makes me angry when people say I'm free to do what I want. They don't know my situation.

In life, you just can't just do what you want. There are many things that stop you.

I often feel taken for granted. People just don't know how much I do for them.

When people make helpful suggestions, I can usually think of reasons why they won't work.

I can't seem to find someone who will help me.

No one can ever right the wrongs done to me in my life.

I feel I do a lot for people, and they pay me back by making me do even more work.

Most children just aren't grateful for what they get anymore.

I find it difficult to say no to requests.

I often feel that I must be jinxed; things go wrong for me more than for other people.

Dragon Seven

When I'm in doubt, I usually say no.

I hate it when someone tries to tell me what to do or tells me how to be.

When I make a plan, nothing can prevent me from carrying it out.

Rapid changes scare me.

Sometimes I'll do the opposite of what someone tells me to do just to show them who is boss.

I can be very obstinate when I want to be.

Nobody can change my mind. If anybody changes it, it will be me.

People say I can really dig in my heels.

Nobody can make me do what I don't want to do.

Nobody. That's a promise.

Sometimes I dig in my heels and block even my own progress.

I can argue my way out of anything.

If I decide I'm not going anywhere, nobody can budge me.

It's hard for me to give in, even when I know I'm wrong.

Nobody can stop me from doing what I plan.

What Dragons Have You by the Throat?

The sets of statements represent the following dragons:

Dragon one: arrogance
Dragon two: self-deprecation
Dragon three: greed
Dragon four: self-destruction
Dragon five: impatience
Dragon six: martyrdom
Dragon seven: stubbornness

Most people have a primary and a secondary dragon. The list you most agreed with is your primary dragon and the list you agreed with next most frequently is your secondary dragon. If you saw yourself in all of the lists, you are probably plagued by the stubbornness dragon. If you could not figure yourself out at all, then you are probably blinded by your dragons and cannot see them. Ask your trusted friends, if you dare. Try not to punish them when they tell you the truth!

The Dragons' Hidden Treasure

There is a hidden power that comes from defeating your dragons. When Saint George defeated his dragon, it became his servant forever. He became the master of its powers. Traditionally, dragons hoard great treasures in their hidden lairs. These treasures represent knowledge and truth, kept captive by the monster dragons. When you, the dragon slayer, defeat your dragons, you liberate the jewels of truth and knowledge. When you transform your dragons, you gain the powerful knowledge of their ways from your own experience. You discover a powerful secret. You learn that much of your behavior that causes your suffering is not who you are.

The dragons have nothing to do with your essence-self. They are merely parasites intent on taking over your personality by living on your energy. Like other parasites, once they have a grip on you, they are tenacious and will not want to let go without a fight. If you do nothing to stop the dragons' encroachment, they will gradually intrude into every part of your social, business, family, and spiritual life, as well as into your health. Ancient lore describes dragons eating humans whole and dining on human blood. Nothing could be more true of the seven deadly dragons. They truly dine on you.

Among the elderly there are generally two types of people. One kind is cantankerous and difficult. No one wants to be around them because they seem to display, in an exaggerated way, the worst traits of their personalities. These people have, over the years, allowed the dragons to inexorably take over their lives. Now, they are difficult for their families and distinctly unpleasant for almost anyone to deal with. They are miserable and unhappy. In keeping with their worst fears and expectations, they are often abandoned in old age.

The second type of elderly person is wonderful. It is as if they have become ripe with age and now display their most admirable traits. They are a pleasure to be around, and the relatives fight over who will have them over for the holidays. These elders have a unique charm. They are, in a word, happy. As a whole, these people are healthier than their dragon-run counterparts. Even when they have health problems, they manage to keep their special attractiveness. These are people who have managed to rid themselves of unwanted dragons over the years. They have cast off the parasites and now display their essence-selves. They are wise and have much to offer younger people.

You have a choice. What kind of older person do you want to be? Do you want to be miserable or do you want to take your place as a contributing and respected elder? The answer depends on whether you clear your dragons now.

When you defeat your dragons, you will:

—be more present.
—have all of your energy available to you to make choices.
—take actions that are evolutionary in nature.
—have the power that comes from being truly at peace for the first time.
—be happy.
—be a magnet and role model for the people around you.
—be a genuinely attractive human being, not attractive simply because of your dramas.
—no longer attract those people who are compulsively drawn to your weaknesses.
—find compassion for others still in the grip of their own dragons.
—be able to assist others without becoming entrapped yourself.
—be truly powerful for the first time in your life.

The Order of the Dragons

The first and most important thing to know about the seven dragons is that there is no hierarchy among them. One is not worse or better than another. Greed is not better than arrogance, nor is martyrdom worse than stubbornness. All are equal in their ultimate consequences. They soak up the vital juices of your life, leaving you an empty husk, stifled and unable to pursue your dreams. The reason that there is no hierarchy among them is that they are all based on one thing and one thing only: fear. Fear is their food, and it feeds them until they grow large. So all human-created suffering essentially comes down to one thing alone: the illusion of irrational fear. This fear takes many forms and subforms. The seven dragons are the main forms of unfounded fear, and to know them is the first step in eliminating fear. Without irrational fear, there is ultimately no human suffering.

What is irrational fear?

Fear is created by the illusion of separateness.
Fear is the illusion of the absence of love.
Fear is ignorance.
Fear is self-made.
Fear is a blinder to vision.
Fear twists and distorts reality.
Fear is painful and supports all suffering.
Fear, if indulged, breeds more of itself.
Fear limits experience.
Fear begets unhappiness.
Fear paralyzes.
Fear moves in when love is forgotten.

Bear in mind that there are legitimate forms of fear that help humans to survive. Fear of an avalanche causes you to avoid a dangerous area. This is not an irrational fear but a real and positive form of fear. The dragons are about irrational fear, but they masquerade as sensible fears.

Although the dragons have no hierarchy, they do have an order that provides valuable clues to how they operate:

ARROGANCE—SELF-DEPRECATION
IMPATIENCE—MARTYRDOM
GREED—SELF-DESTRUCTION
STUBBORNNESS

The pairs of dragons are sets of twins. The members of a pair have much in common with one another, and indeed their roots are based in similar dynamics. In surface appearance, they seem like opposites. However, each dragon of a pair has within it the seed and shadow of its partner. Within arrogance there is always self-deprecation, and within self-deprecation there is always the shadow of arrogance.

Stubbornness is a dragon that stands alone. It does not have a twin or opposite form. In that sense, it is considered neutral because it is not allied. Stubbornness can, however, be paired with any of the other six dragons. For example, a person may not only be stubborn, but stubbornly greedy, or perhaps stubbornly arrogant. Stubbornness also has a hint of each of the other dragons within it. Too much stubbornness can be self-destructive. It also can mean that a person fears being victimized by an authority, so it has a bit of martyrdom within it. And so on.

The next four sections will briefly describe each pair of dragons, as well as the neutral one, to illustrate the geography of the land of dragons. Following this, the book will go into much greater depth on each dragon so that you can learn how to defeat them. It is only through knowledge of each dragon's habits and characteristics that you have any hope of outsmarting them. They flourish on human ignorance of their weaknesses and limitations. And yet, each dragon has a vulnerable spot, a place where it can be weakened and eventually transformed. The first step in this archetypal battle with the dragons is to arm yourself with knowledge.

Dragons One and Two: Arrogance and Self-Deprecation

Arrogance and self-deprecation are both based on faulty notions of self-esteem. Arrogance overinflates the ego and self-deprecation undermines the basic sense of self-worth.

In the stereotypical sense, arrogant people appear to be puffed up with too much air. They seem to have puffed-out chests and to put their noses up in the air. They are said to be overinflated. In response to arrogant people, others often feel a desire to puncture their balloons and deflate them; to bring them down to size, so to speak.

On the other hand, people suffering from strong self-deprecation often present the image of being deflated. They have rounded shoulders, bowed heads, and caved-in chests. They appear to be like deflated balloons. Other people's response to them is to want to help them to stand up straight and tall, hold their heads up, and stick their chests out.

These two dragons, arrogance and self-deprecation, disturb the natural flow of the inhalation-expiration breathing process. They inhibit inspiration. If people breathe in all the way without exhaling, they cannot breathe in any more. However, if they are totally deflated, they may have a hard time beginning the inhalation process. It is difficult to put more air into balloons that are fully inflated or to fill those that are completely empty. When breathing is interrupted, oxygen to the brain is diminished. When oxygen to the brain is curtailed, people are no longer capable of higher mental functioning. How can they be inspired with new creative ideas if they are starving for air?

These two dragons, then, are classified as the inspiration dragons. When these twin dragons are defeated, breathing improves and inspiration flows. Inspiration is restored.

Each dragon may slide to the other at times. Self-deprecating people may suddenly become rather inflated or arrogant. By the same token, arrogant people can suddenly deflate after a humiliating experience.

Dragons Three and Four: Impatience and Martyrdom

The impatience and martyrdom dragons are both based on faulty notions of time and space. Each comes from the fear of being restricted by time or by circumstances. In the case of impatience, the restriction people fear is the lack of time. They fear there will not be enough time to get somewhere or to get a job done. Their response to this fear is to rush to finish something before time runs out.

In the case of martyrdom, the restriction people fear is "hampering circumstances." The feeling and belief is that if it were not for other people or situations, they would be free to exercise choice. With all avenues of choice apparently blocked, all they can do is whine or complain, since action has halted.

Both of these dragons are based on fears of lack of mobility or restricted movement. That is why impatience and martyrdom are classified as the dragons blocking action, just as arrogance and self-deprecation are the dragons blocking inspiration.

Paradoxically, impatience and martyrdom are both actions taken that block more effective action. These two dragons can also slide into each other. If people are impatient, they find that they are actually feeling martyred or victimized by the frustration of time limitations. Likewise people feeling trapped in martyrdom also become exceptionally impatient as their frustration mounts.

Dragons Five and Six: Greed and Self-Destruction

Greed and self-destruction are both based on faulty notions about self-expression. Each involves fear of loss of control over behavior and appetite. People experiencing self-destruction concerns fear losing control over their behavior. In an effort to gain control over lives that appear to be spinning wildly out of control, these people engage in desperate measures to regain control. Their addictions and efforts to deaden pain then can result in premature loss of life. This form of self-expression leads to the end of expression.

In the case of greed, the ultimate fear is that there will never be enough of anything in life to fulfill personal satisfaction and happiness. Love, money, power, and affection are always somewhere else rather than at home. People confronted by this dragon go on endless wild goose chases, looking in all the wrong places for what they so desperately seek. At the same time, they attempt to control their voracious appetites by depriving themselves and others of what they want.

Since these two dragons undermine true self-expression, they are classified as blocking expression. Paradoxically, these two dragons appear to others as forms of self-expression.

Self-destruction may slide into greed in that self-destructive activity often takes the form of greedy behavior such as consuming too much food or alcohol. Likewise, greed can lead to self-destructive behavior as people overindulge or neglect their safety while pursuing the object of their greed.

Dragon Number Seven: Stubbornness

The final dragon is stubbornness. This dragon is based on faulty beliefs about authority. People confronted by this dragon resist authority or anyone trying to make them do something they do not feel ready to do. Their stubbornness is a way of buying time, of slowing down the pace of events so they do not have to confront change. These people literally fear change and try to stop it by saying no even when they might like to say yes.

Because of its tendency to slow action and buy time, this dragon can be classified as an issue with assimilation. People afflicted with stubbornness hope to be able to assimilate everything about situations before making a move. However, in point of fact, these stubborn people block assimilation and close the doors to all new input in a desperate attempt to maintain their integrity.

Recall that the dragon of stubbornness stands alone and does not have a partner or opposite. It tends to slide to any of the other dragons. For example, stubborn people can become so entrenched in their point of view that their behavior becomes self-destructive. An example is the people who refuse to evacuate their homes in the face of an impending volcanic eruption, flood, or fire.

The Appearance of Dragons

Fat or skinny dragons

There are further metaphorical characteristics of the dragon pairs. Some dragons tend to be fat or broad, while others are long and narrow. Each dragon is built for its own sinister purpose. There are three dragons whose eyes are set wide apart and who have a broad range of vision. These three fat, wide-focused dragons are greed, arrogance, and impatience. Three other dragons have eyes set close together to produce a narrow focus. These three skinny, narrow-focused dragons are self-destruction, self-deprecation, and martyrdom.

Fat, wide-focused dragons

The greed, arrogance, and impatience dragons lead people to take actions that are worldly and impactive on the social level. Greed, arrogance, and impatience can each influence people to embark on campaigns to take over countries, corporations, or other people's spouses. They tend to expand people's behavior outwardly. A greedy person will often amass a great material fortune and, with just as much flair, lose that fortune. An arrogant person will overstep flamboyantly into politics only to be brought down by a humiliating public scandal. An impatient general will impulsively cross a border to attack without waiting for necessary supplies, only to be repelled after sustaining heavy losses.

If the dragon of greed is upon you, you are driven to satisfy that greed in the outside world. The world is directly impacted by your greed. If the dragon of arrogance has you cornered, you are driven to demonstrate to others your superiority. Your arrogance propels you into the public arena. If the dragon of impatience has you by the throat, you are driven to rush out to accomplish what you are afraid you won't have time for. This impatience directly impacts on the environment and at times destroys it.

These three are the fat dragons, the ones with sweeping effects on the environment. When they walk, the Earth shakes, and their range across the landscape is vast. They are very noticeable and tend to draw attention to themselves. This is a part of their deadly seduction, for they can camouflage themselves as capability, courage, and daring. Only too late do you discover their true natures, at which point they are already consuming you.

Skinny, narrow-focused dragons

By contrast, the three dragons of self-destruction, self-deprecation, and martyrdom are narrow in their focus. These dragons cause people to take actions that gradually lead them away from society. People with these dragons have an impact that is felt within a more immediate circle of friends and associates.

If people are self-destructive, their self-sabotage undermines their worldly endeavors and leads to isolation and even suicide. They often do not live long enough to have a major impact on society. Although self-destructive behavior may impact people's immediate families, it affects their own lives most of all.

When people are self-deprecating, they tend to avoid situations that would carry them outward into society. Their self-deprecation tends to isolate them, and it mostly impacts themselves. Seldom, if ever, is there a Hitler or a Stalin with a self-deprecating behavior.

Martyrdom leads people to complaining rather than acting and therefore moves them out of the public arena quickly. The martyr more often seeks the quiet desperation of an abusive spouse rather than public office.

If the emaciated dragon of self-destruction is running your life, you are destroying yourself either slowly or quickly. The greatest damage is inflicted upon yourself, a rather narrow focus indeed.

When the self-deprecation runt dragon has taken control of

your personality, you feel too inadequate to take charge. The narrow focus of this dragon has you looking mostly at your feet.

When the forlorn dragon of martyrdom has harnessed you, your choices disappear and you are trapped in the little world of excuses and whining.

While these narrow, skinny dragons are less impressive-looking than their wide-bellied counterparts, they are no less deadly. In fact, they can be even more poisonous, just as the tiny adder can be more quick to kill than the mighty python. These thin dragons, with their close-set eyes, are not to be underestimated. In fact, it is their very appearance that is so disarming and deceiving. As you shall see, they can create as much suffering as any impressive fat dragon.

The dragon in the middle

The stubbornness dragon can fool you because it seems to elude categorization. You have to get to know it to find out what nastiness it hides. Because the stubbornness dragon has elements of each other dragon within it, it can appear as either fat or skinny.

The Best and the Worst of each Dragon

Each dragon has a positive pole and a negative pole. When the dragon has flames and sulfuric smoke pouring from its mouth and nostrils, and its sharpened claws are tearing at your throat, and its ear-splitting roaring is in your ears, it is at its nastiest. The dragon is in the negative pole when it has full control over your personality.

When you begin to defeat the dragon, you see its positive pole. The dragon senses that it is losing its power over you, and it attempts to compromise. It figures that perhaps by compromising with you it can distract you momentarily and regain its powerful grip.

The positive pole of each dragon represents a dicey situation. When you experience the positive aspect, both you and the dragon are in a state of dynamic tension in which neither one of you is in control. The contest can go either way. So, while the positive pole does not truly reflect complete freedom from the clutches of the dragon for you, it is definitely a step forward. The positive pole reflects a positive step to loosen the dragon's death grip on your life. However, you cannot let up for one second or you will be overcome once more by whichever wily dragon you are in combat with. Following is a summary of the positive and negative poles of each dragon.

The best and worst of the arrogance dragon

The negative pole of the arrogance dragon is *vanity*.

The dictator shamelessly flaunts his wealth at the expense of the people. The starring actress snubs the bit players and technicians on her set. The dragon is firmly in control.

The positive pole of the arrogance dragon is *pride*.

Proud of his latest film, the director talks of nothing else on the talk show circuit. Is the dragon in charge of him, or does he have a natural ebullience about a creative project? Proud of winning, the tennis star shows off her trophies to all her friends. Is she using them for her own aggrandizement, or is she genuinely enthusiastic about her accomplishments?

The best and worst of the self-deprecation dragon

The negative pole of the self-deprecation dragon is *abasement*.

With downcast eyes, the disheveled, reeking hobo shuffles through the back alleyways. After receiving a low mark, the college student lacks the courage to ask the professor how to improve the grade. The dragon wins.

The positive pole of the self-deprecation dragon is *humility*.

The modest cook refuses credit for beautifully decorating the cake. Is she simply modest or is the dragon of low self-esteem hovering? The author of the outstanding short story remains anonymous. Is this fear of success or an understandable need for privacy? The dragon lurks.

The best and worst of the impatience dragon

The negative pole of the impatience dragon is *intolerance*, that nasty flareup that alienates everyone.

The cab driver screeches his car around the crippled old woman, making an obscene gesture at her while pressing the horn. The teacher yells and strikes the child's fingers as she fumbles with the piano keys. The dragon smiles.

The positive pole of the impatience dragon is *daring*, an audacious act of freedom.

Tiring of his slow, roundabout progress on the shore, the hiker plunges into the frigid water and begins to swim across the lake. Is this a foolhardy maneuver or a brilliant decision? Refusing to wait any longer for the letter, the broker books a plane for New York to see the client. Is this the business decision of a power salesman or a foolish, money-wasting gambit? The scent of sulfur is in the air.

The best and worst of the martyrdom dragon

The negative pole of the martyrdom dragon is *victimization*, the reproachful complaining that engenders guilt in even the most stalwart of souls.

In yet another poor decision, the owner of a string of failed restaurants opens a white elephant in an unproductive location. He blames the disaster on bad luck, his wife, his children, the IRS, and the weather. The divorcee, fresh out of two disastrous marriages to alcoholics, finds an ex-con (on parole for drug dealing) to become involved with. The dragon roars its approval.

The positive pole of the martyrdom dragon is *selflessness*.

She gives up her scholarship to medical school to put her new husband through law school. Hmmmm. Is this love or a setup for later resentment? He sends his children to the best private schools and works two jobs to make ends meet. Is this sacrifice, or are there heavy strings making this love conditional and a setup for later emotional blackmail? The dragon is restless.

The best and the worst of the greed dragon

The negative pole of the greed dragon is *voracity*, the insatiable lust for something that promises pleasure but fails to deliver.

The greedy bully person spills all the rice in a mad rush to grab the distributed food. Scrooge hoards all the money, deprives others, and enjoys none of it.

The positive pole of the greed dragon is *appetite*, the desire for something pleasurable.

A person develops an appetite for collecting fine cars, fine wines, and fine lovers. Another wants to have many experiences that others seem to have. Are these natural desires for life's experiences or is the greed dragon secretly tempting these people with never-ending searches?

The best and worst of the self-destruction dragon

The negative pole of the self-destruction dragon is *suicide*— behavior that leads eventually to certain death, whether quickly by a gun to the temple or more gradually through drugs and wild living.

After popping a handful of pills and drinking a six-pack of beer, Ted climbs into his Porsche for a fast drive.

The positive pole of the self-destruction dragon is *sacrifice*.

The soldier volunteers for a suicidal mission with the possibility that he may accomplish something useful with his death. The young athlete allows someone else to win a race by withdrawing. Are these examples of altruism or self-sabotage? The motives are questionable. Is the dragon in charge or not?

The best and the worst of the stubbornness dragon

The negative pole of the stubbornness dragon is *obstinacy*, a refusal to cooperate, and a complete shutdown of the flow of communication.

An obstinate person refuses to be flexible in negotiations, a stance that kills a potentially constructive partnership. The obstinacy of the bigot results in a breakdown in race relations and the development of armed camps.

The positive pole of the stubbornness dragon is *determination*.

The general facing overwhelming firepower is determined never to give up. Is this courage or terribly poor judgment? The young athlete is determined to play in the big game although recovering from a bad sprain. Is the dragon of stubbornness running the show or is there a streak of independence here?

The following chart displays the complete set of dragons.

THE INSPIRATION DRAGONS

wide focus	*narrow focus*
+ pride	+ humility
ARROGANCE	SELF-DEPRECATION
– vanity	– abasement

THE ACTION DRAGONS

wide focus	*narrow focus*
+ daring	+ selflessness
IMPATIENCE	MARTYRDOM
– intolerance	– victimization

THE EXPRESSION DRAGONS

wide focus	*narrow focus*
+ appetite	+ sacrifice
GREED	SELF-DESTRUCTION
– voracity	– suicide

THE ASSIMILATION DRAGON

wide or narrow focus
+ determination
STUBBORNNESS
– obstinacy

Chapter Two

STAGES OF MATURITY

Although the seven dragons have distinct appearances and fall into a specific order, each person has a different response to his or her dragon. For example, one person operating under the dragon of impatience will act quite differently from another impatient person. One impatient father may beat his children for being so slow. Another impatient man may be kind to his children but may demonstrate major impatience with himself.

Myriad forces are at play to create people's responses to their dragons, perhaps more than anyone can fully comprehend. However, one primary factor affecting the dragon's behavior for each person is the person's level of maturity.

Levels of Maturity

There is no question that human beings display varying levels of maturity in their behavior. We expect that people will behave according to the levels of maturity of their years. That is, we expect a forty-year-old to display behavior appropriate to a forty-year-old and not a two-year-old. However, a quick glance at the news tells us that this is not so. Not only do adults act like two-year-olds with regularity, but nations display immature behavior toward each other as well. "I won't let you play with my toy because you called me a name" becomes "trade sanctions for failed diplomacy."

The reality is that many adults never develop beyond a childhood level of functioning. They are fixated at earlier stages of development. The problem is that they can fool us because of their adult size and appearance. They can even learn the basics of how to pass for adults in society without ever actually developing the maturity of adults.

Following is a checklist, similar to the previous one but more challenging, to assist you in determining the level of maturity from which you usually operate. Again, choose the set of statements with which you most identify. Try to be honest and objective as you were before. The sets of statements are presented in mixed order to help you answer objectively.

Level A

I feel most comfortable being around other folks just like me.

Strangers and foreigners make me uncomfortable.

What this country needs is more law and order.

Wild animals make me nervous. I feel better when they are caged.

You have to watch out for germs and viruses. They are everywhere.

I clean and sterilize everything. You can't be too clean.

People should know their place.

The old ways are the best ways.

I do what the doctor says. Doctors know best.

I usually do what I'm told.

If you don't follow the rules, God will punish you.

I believe in right and wrong and good and evil.

I believe in Satan or the devil as a powerful force of temptation.

I like the old traditions and values.

I do not like foreign or unfamiliar foods.

My country, right or wrong.

Animals carry a lot of germs.

Spare the rod and spoil the child, I always say.

You can't be too careful. Strangers can't be trusted. Better stick with your own kind.

Level B

I feel it is my duty to help the poor in this world.

Life is very hard much of the time.

My heart goes out to other people.

I want to understand myself more.

I like to understand people and why they do things.

I am often confused and I seek answers.

I am interested in many different religions. They seem to all
    have some truth.

I like many different foods.

I believe that ultimately we are all brothers and sisters on
    this planet.

I have not completely made up my mind about the meaning
    of life.

My emotional relationships are intensely involving.

When I have problems, I almost always seek help.

I have had moments when I wondered if I was crazy or
    something.

I have often been with people who did not understand me.

I love animals. Sometimes they seem like better friends
    than people.

I believe in animal rights.

I believe that the environment has to be protected from
    ruthless plundering.

I will gladly march in protest for what I feel is right.

Sometimes I feel confused and misunderstood.

I believe there is much unfairness in the world and that I
    should work to correct it.

Level C

I am very superstitious about everything.

It's me against the world.

Everything in life feels so new and overwhelming to me.

My tribe, clan, or gang is everything to me. I couldn't exist
    without them.

Life is so complicated I don't understand most of it.
I feel lost without direction and people telliong me what
    to do.
I am a survivalist. I stockpile guns to survive in the future.
As far as I am concerned, no behavior is out of bounds
    for me.
Torturing people is sometimes necessary.
It's every man for himself.
If someone gets in your way, get rid of them.
People that play fair are suckers.
I seem to be scared all the time.
There are certain ethnic groups that cause all the trouble.
    They should be eliminated.
Threatening people is the only way to get what you want.

Level D

You do your thing and I'll do mine.
Nature is our teacher. Wild land is important to the soul.
I believe that all humans are connected by a deeper spiritual
    bond.
I cannot harm others without harming myself.
Everything will work out in the long run.
I believe in the spirit of the law rather than the letter of it.
    It is something that has to be seen in the individual
    context.
I like my leisure time to pursue my own interests.
People sometimes see me as an eccentric. I have my own
    beliefs that are sometimes counter to the main culture.
I value being as much as doing.
Sometimes I notice I am very intuitive—perhaps even
    psychic.
I cut the mold from cheese and bread before eating it.
Others see me as compassionate and kind.
I feel a deep spirituality that is not necessarily related to
    religion.

I have a great affinity for nature and animals.

I'm not too worried about germs. I believe that emotions
  and beliefs are responsible for illness in many cases.

Appearance is not so important. Internal qualities are what
count in life.

I seem to be able to move among social classes with relative
  ease.

I enjoy the food and customs of most countries of the world.

I do not believe in arms for peace.

I like to work hard and then relax with my friends.

There is much more to life than getting ahead.

I am basically philosophical about life.

I would give up a fortune to preserve the forests, lakes, and
  animals.

There is nothing like spending time with my family and
  friends.

Level E

Life is about competition. You have to be better than the
  next guy.

I like to work very hard to get ahead.

I want to succeed more than anything.

I can always think of a way to turn something into a profit.

People think too much about themselves. Better to get to
  work.

There are a lot of lazy people around who will never get
  ahead.

A fool and his money are soon parted. They deserve what
  they get.

I believe in progress. Commercial development should be
  encouraged.

People should be free to exploit natural resources for profit.

Free enterprise is good. Nothing should interfere with it.

I believe my ideas are best for the world. People should be
  more like me.

People that see psychiatrists are crazy. I'm not.

It is important to put on a good show. It will get you far.

First impressions are everything. You have to put the best foot forward.

Clothes make the man/woman.

I don't have much sympathy for losers in life.

Life is survival of the fittest. The strong win. The weak lose.

There is a sucker born every minute.

Maintaining a powerful reputation is primary.

The tough win in business. I don't respect those that show weakness.

Someday we will conquer all of nature. We will control the weather.

If you're going to see a doctor, pay top dollar and see the best.

The sets of statements represent the following levels of maturity:

Level A: Toddler
Level B: Adolescent
Level C: Infant
Level D: Adult
Level E: Child

Following is a practical and obvious set of developmental steps that lead a person from infancy to adulthood. These steps illustrate the behavior of the child, the adolescent, and the adult at each basic developmental stage of life. They also describe adult behaviors that reflect fixations at all the steps along the way; for example, how fully grown people appear when they behave like toddlers, adolescents, or adults.

Understanding the levels of maturity creates a foundation for better understanding of how the dragons work and what form they take in people. These levels of maturity seem obvious, but they are also obscure. Otherwise they would already have been written about extensively . Additionally, some of the information in this chapter is controversial. Perhaps this is also why maturity levels have been neglected in other literature. Read through and consider the material and see if it matches your experience. This information will be incorporated with that on the dragons in later chapters.

The Seven Principles of Maturity

Infants are magical, dynamic human beings who learn at an accelerated pace in multiple dimensions at once. However, practically speaking, because of their size and undeveloped physical condition, infants display restricted mobility and lack sophistication in everything external to them. As infants develop and grow into toddlers and then into children, their scope of activity widens by quantum leaps. As adults, they display infinitely more capacity in almost every dimension in contrast to when they were infants.

There are seven basic principles that apply to the maturation process. Trying to evaluate maturity can be a minefield, so keep in mind these are only general principles that may be altered by special circumstances. Remember that being a fully grown person does not equal being a mature person. Likewise being a young person does not mean being immature.

Principle one: The basic trend in maturation is toward wider and wider experiences and greater and greater capacity to digest the events and situations that life offers. Flexibility grows as people mature.

Principle two: As people mature, they show more and more capacity to find peaceful solutions to their differences with others.

Principle three: As people mature, they demonstrate greater independence of thought.

Principle four: As people mature, they develop more kindness and compassion toward all creatures of the world.

Principle five: As people mature, they develop ever greater self-confidence and clarity about their purpose.

Principle six: As people mature, they grow ever more respectful of the rights of others to freedom of expression and personal happiness.

Principle seven: As people mature, they demonstrate less and less fear of the unknown.

This may appear to be a short list of maturity principles, but they apply to a great many circumstances. Following is a discussion of the basic stages of development in the human being. This is an outline only. These stages represent a range of years, and there are many steps within each stage that are not addressed here.

The Seven Stages of Human Development

> **Stage One.** Infant
> **Stage Two.** Toddler
> **Stage Three.** Child
> **Stage Four.** Adolescent
> **Stage Five.** Adult
> **Stage Six.** Elder
> **Stage Seven.** Master

Stage One: Infant

Characteristics:

Age: Approximately birth to six months

Viewpoint: "Me" and "not me"; "not me" may be seen as either friendly or dangerous.

Ability: Helplessness. Needing the total care and attention of parent.

Thought and Emotion: Cosmic feeling; no abstract thought; primitive emotions govern all activity. Screaming, crying, gurgling, smiling.

Focus: Survival. Wanting food, warmth, nurturing, safety.

Activity: Exploring self and not-self in the immediate vicinity.

Values: None

Relationships: Others are objects to manipulate; presexual. Eat what is thrust in their mouths.

Adults fixated at the infant stage

Viewpoint: "Me" and "not me"; "not me" may be seen as either friendly or dangerous.

If these people often perceive "not me" as dangerous or frightening, they can be extremely dangerous. Their tendency is to attack and destroy whatever they don't understand. Or, they might do so just for the sake of simple curiosity.

Ability: No sophistication. They need guidance and structure from others. They often prefer prison to the scary outside world. They act helpless.

Thought and Emotion: Adult infants usually don't know why they do things. "Why did you kill that family?" or "Why did you rob that store?" the judge asks. "I don't know," the infantile adult replies. "I just felt like it." No abstract thinking. Thinking is rote and concrete. Primitive emotions drive all actions: rage, lust, and fear drive most activities. They seek pleasure and avoid pain.

Focus: Survival is primary. They eat basics to survive. "Me first" in everything.

Activity: Simple life at outskirts of society. Simple tasks and routines. They often get into trouble without guidance. There is criminal behavior if no structure is provided.

Values: None

What would it be like to kill someone and dismember them? These people might say, "Let's find out. Perhaps it would even be interesting to eat them." Just as infants put body parts into their mouths, including Mom's fingers, so do cannibals.

In a spiritual context, adult infants engage in superstitious, fear-based practices such as black magic, devil worship, or satanism. They are fascinated with death and sometimes kill animals or people out of curiosity. They are known for torturing people and animals. It is interesting to them.

Relationships: Co-survival. Sex is merely lust. They use others as objects for their own ends. No real shared communication. They only communicate their own needs. No eye contact. They do not relate in the true sense.

Examples: Members of death squads; torturers, cannibals, the criminally insane; members of satanic cults that sacrifice babies; backward and simple members of society; many harmless autistic people.

Examples of countries with a noticeable percentage of adult infants in their populations: El Salvador, Guatemala, New Guinea, Peru, Romania, Somalia, Uganda, Campuchea. This is not a comprehensive list.

Keep in mind that this list represents conditions in the world at this time. These conditions do change, and with them the maturity of their populations. These people represent a minority of the world's population. They probably make up only about one-twentieth of the overall population of the planet.

Stage Two: Toddler

Although this stage can also be broken down into many specific developmental steps, the following categories pertain only to the basic general appearance of the child at this age.

Age: Six months to four years.

Viewpoint: "Me" and "other me's"; parallel play. "I am separate from Mom but dependent on her."

Ability: Toddlers are able to explore immediate surroundings by crawling or walking. They need constant guidance and support by adults. They can manipulate objects to test parental authority.

Thought and Emotion: They are able to consider dichotomies like yes and no, good and bad, black and white. Abstract thought has not yet developed. For example, the concept of death is not a reality. Emotions are strong and in the forefront.

Focus: Testing personal independence; testing authority; learning the rules; breaking the rules.

Activity: They learn language, explore within sight or hearing of Mom and Dad, and play at being adult. They repeat and introject the rules and beliefs of their parents. "Hot, hot, stove is hot. Musn't touch!" They seek the safety and comfort of the home structure.

Values: No independent values; only the introjected values of Mom and Dad. "Boys are bad. Girls are good" (or vice versa). Being white is better than being black. Boys don't cry. Girls are helpless."

Relationships: Parallel play with peers. They always look to authority for modeling and for rules of behavior. Authority is always right because that is where love, approval, and punishment ultimately come from. They are presexual.

Adults Fixated at the Toddler Stage

Viewpoint: "Me" and "other me's." Adults fixated at this level want to be like everyone else. They want to fit in, drive the same cars, wear the same clothes, and eat the same foods as their neighbors. They want to be good citizens of their communities. They like the safe structure of known foods and people who are just like themselves. They are afraid of those who are different and therefore they make poor travelers. This results in bigotry and prejudice against the feared "others" who look or act differently. When taken out of their familiar surroundings, they become confused, forget their codes of conduct, and can be quite savage. The colonizing Dutch in Indonesia and South Africa, the Spanish and Portuguese colonizers of America, the British colonialists in India, and some U.S. soldiers in Vietnam are good examples of this.

Ability: Adult toddlers are able to follow basic instructions. They are good at enforcing the letter of the law but don't understand the spirit of the law. They prefer their local communities and are intimidated by the world at large. They are able to perform many basic tasks but avoid anything that requires independent thinking.

Thought and Emotion: Adult toddlers tend to follow the thoughts of authority without question. "I was just following orders when I shot the civilians." They become confused when presented with ideas that are different from the ones they grew up with. "What's wrong with slavery? We've always done it that way." They are famous for paradoxical thinking such as, "Love your neighbor or I'll beat you to a pulp." Their thinking is extremely rigid, orthodox, and traditional. They think only in terms of good or bad, heaven or hell, right or wrong, with no shades of gray.

If they are confronted with beliefs different from their own, these different customs or thoughts are inevitably considered bad or evil. New thoughts are suspect and feared, seen as temptation by evil spirits or the devil and something that should be banished. Logic is usually nothing more than strong emotional attachments or sentiments that masquerade as ideas.

Focus: The focus for these adults is to learn the rules and test them. They spout rules and regulations and quote authority, whether it be a holy book, minister, medical doctor, policeman, general, or leader. However, they just as readily break the rules and test authority. This is the policeman who takes protection money, the minister who embezzles church money, the corrupt official who takes bribes. They demand structure but just as easily bend that structure and arrange to get caught for their crimes. They usually do not take responsibility for their crimes but blame something or someone else: "The devil made me do it." Their focus is always the paradox of learning what the rules are and then testing them.

Activity: These people like to be the big fish in very small ponds. They prefer to live life in the confines of their local belief systems, their churches, clubs, or social groups. Travel is stressful and they usually complain about the customs and foods of the places they are visiting. They strive to prevent any kind of change or reform, and would rather roll back the clock to the good old days "when men were men and women knew their place." They can be proficient in many kinds of work, but they do not think creatively. They like to work in bureaucracies.

Values: Adult toddlers without question carry the values that were given to them by authority. "If you commit sin, then you must be stoned to death. There is no other way." They value authority, yet tend to see authority as punitive and unforgiving. They value structure, order, and sterile safe environments where there are no surprises. They do not examine or question, nor are they philosophers in the true meaning of the word.

Spiritually, these adults do not examine or question the faith they were brought up with. They understand religion from a rule-oriented perspective. They follow church authority to the letter and cast out heretics. Religious conversion of heathens is considered a legitimate reason to go to war. They wish to either exterminate heathens or convert them.

These people are terrified by the prospect of death and basically do anything in their power to deny it or pretend it does not happen. In their opinion, getting old is terrifying and brings with it infirmity, illness, and total dependency. Interestingly, as old people they usually become helpless and dependent.

Relationships: Adults fixated at the toddler stage are not good at maintaining eye contact and are often afraid of other people, especially if they are not known. They cannot conceive of their children being any different from themselves.

They are afraid of their environments, and that includes their own bodies. They tend to see their bodies as not their own responsibility, and they strive to "be good" by taking their medicines and doing without question what their doctors say. They are not able to see that their emotions and beliefs might have something to do with their illnesses.

Wilderness is scary to these people, and they prefer the predictability of paved, trimmed, and mowed environments. "The only safe animals are in zoos or on farms." Environments have to be spotlessly clean of all dangerous germs or dirt that could be contaminating.

Sex is seen as a necessary duty to be performed for procreation only. This stage is presexual, therefore any sexual behavior is infantile in nature. Sex is fun if it is naughty, and it is usually very immature. Sex is not about communication at this stage of development.

Their relationship to food is the same every day; they prefer it over-cooked and under-spiced. Foreign foods are disdained. These people eat what is good for them, not what they like.

Examples: Members of rigid orthodox religions or philosophies; racial bigots; government bureaucrats; corrupt officials; small village folks who consider outsiders bad; people who are terrified that the devil is lurking; people who feel heaven is up and hell is down; people who believe that only they and their group will be saved; scientists, academics, and professors who display paradoxical behavior such as making weapons for peace, or producing nerve gas and then going to church; gurus and cult leaders who demand total obedience and punish those who break rules; many people living conservative, ordinary lives who do what they are told and follow like sheep. Modern examples are: Idi Amin, Papa Doc Duvalier, Mohammar Khadafy, Joseph McCarthy, David Koresh, and Jim Jones.

Examples of countries with a noticeable percentage of adult toddlers in their population: Iran, Iraq, the United States (especially the deep South and Midwest), Colombia, Morocco, Nepal, India, China, South Africa. However, these people are found all over the world. They probably represent about one-fifth of the world's population at this time. As mentioned, they like to cluster together in their own communities.

Stage Three: Child

Age: Anywhere from five to twelve years.

Viewpoint: "Me" and "You" and "I'm going to win." Children in these years relate to others directly, but usually with an agenda. They want to control situations and test the new-found abilities that go with greater independence. Their normal point of view is, "Life is fun, and I'm going to live it to the limit."

Ability: During these years children expand their worlds even more. They explore the world beyond parental vision and hearing. They are able to have adventures on their own with a minimum of surveillance and supervision by Mom and Dad. Their bodies strengthen, and they compete with other children in footraces, tests of strength, and all types of athletics. With increased sophistication, they compete with one another to demonstrate their social prowess. Their mental powers develop, and they compare themselves with other children in terms of academic ability. As they gain independence, they begin to notice their own appearance and the appearance of others in general.

Thought and Emotion: During these years children attain the ability to think abstractly. For example, at about age nine,

children understand the finality of death. With abstract thinking comes the ability to have thoughts that are independent
from those of parents or other authority figures. Children
become more cunning and sophisticated in their attempts to
control their worlds. Rather than be completely controlled by
their emotions, older children associate thoughts with feelings
and can understand such things as delayed gratification: "If I
save my money, I can buy a bike."

Focus: The focus of older children is mastery over the
environment. These children want to compete and participate in the bigger world of school and neighborhood. They
want to win.

Activity: These children demonstrate creative skills and
talents not seen in younger children. They make things, play
music, sing, participate in athletics, and begin to shine. They
acquire things like clothes, athletic equipment, and sophisticated toys. They notice if they don't have a bicycle like the other
children, and it matters to them if they are not as cool as some
of their peers. They want to belong by being the best.

Values: Children in these ages begin to form their own values. They are still heavily dependent on their parents and other
authorities for their beliefs. Yet, because they can now think
abstractly, they can try out an opinion now and then. Their
peers sometimes force them to change their loyalty from their
parents to gangs or social groups. Then they try these new values out on their parents to test them.

Children in these years learn how to lie effectively. Whereas
very young children lack the sophistication that it takes to pull
off a lie, older children, with new mental abilities, can be masters of deceit. This gives them a sense of power. However, many
children only flirt with this power.

Relationships: At this age, relationships become extremely
important. However, the relationships have an agenda connected with them—the comparison of actions, beliefs, feelings, and

values. Relationships are also about competing and strengthening the sense of self in reference to others. There is a new sense of exploring relationships outside of home base. These relationships are often complex and interesting, yet they do not include much compassion or understanding. Children of these years can be notoriously cruel to one another.

Adults Fixated at the Child Stage

Viewpoint: Adults fixated at the child level are highly competitive and out to win. They like to go head to head with other people and emerge victorious. They firmly believe that in every game there is a loser—and it's not going to be them. They see the world in terms of winners and losers, the strong and the weak, and the rich and the poor. They are vociferous and ambitious, and are willing to pull any strings to get ahead. For them, it is reasonable to cheat to get ahead. Life is seen as challenging, and winning is great fun.

Ability: These people can be highly competent at many tasks and have a good sense of the politics of any situation. They can be masters of manipulation, and they usually get their way by telling people what they want to hear.

Thought and Emotion: Adults fixated at the child level are much more rational than their counterparts fixated at younger levels. These people know how to deliver convincing, well-thought-out arguments. They know how to avoid distasteful topics, and they like to control conversations. They are calculating. Sometimes it seems that they lack heart or compassion; everything seems to have a price tag on it. They seldom have insight into their own emotional dynamics and concentrate their attention outwardly instead. If in personal confusion or difficulty, they usually want a quick fix instead of an overall cure. They prefer to work things out on their own and to not ask for help from others. Asking for help makes them feel like losers. They tend to believe psychotherapy is only for crazy people, and if they do see a therapist it has to be a high-status one.

Their theories and philosophies are laced with difficult jargon, are complex, and are hard to understand. This is meant to impress others.

Focus: The focus for adult children is winning at any cost. At this age fixation, people try to win converts to their own points of view by bullying, persuading, manipulating, conquering, or whatever seems to work. Their focus is on fame, fortune, glory, status, and power.

Activity: Adult children court the rich and famous and put appearance before substance. If they are not rich, then it is important to them that they look rich or move up the social ladder through marriage or other means. Much energy and attention is placed on personal appearance, driving the right cars, living in the right neighborhoods, and being seen with the right crowds. These people may be willing to work very hard, perhaps sixty to eighty hours a week, to get ahead, even if it is at the expense of family time.

Adult children are exploratory in everything they do. They like travel, especially if it has something to do with conquering or status. They are fairly flexible in their eating habits and in their sexual preferences. They sometimes examine a different culture or religion for the sake of curiosity. They don't mind change if it benefits themselves or if it furthers what they are trying to accomplish.

Values: Adults at the child level value what can be seen and counted. Their motto might be, "He who dies with the most toys wins." Their values include hard work in order to get ahead at all costs, appearance before substance, and productivity in a material sense. The inner life is not valued; the outer life is. Spiritually speaking, these people may have several points of view. One is: "Since there is no God and this life is all there is, it's every man/woman for him/herself." A second is: "God loves a winner. Winners are saved. May the fittest win." A third is: "In case there is a God, I'd better go to church once in a while for insurance; besides, it's good for business to be seen there."

Adult children are uncomfortable with conversations about death. They perceive death as losing, and they cover up death with euphemistic denials such as demands for beautiful views from grave sites or requests that their bodies look as they did in life. These people are very attached to the way they look, and they like their bodies to look young at all costs. Getting old is losing. Balding and graying is losing. Plastic surgery becomes a way to keep the illusion of youth.

Relationships: Adults fixated as children form relationships with agendas. "This husband (or wife) will improve my status. This friend will further my career." Relationships are seldom equal because someone has to be a winner and someone has to be a loser or, at best, a follower. Eye contact is maintained longer than with adult toddlers but more for the purpose of dominating or persuading. If the topic changes to something of a more personal nature, eye contact is often broken.

Animals, plants, and the natural environment are seen as resources to be exploited. Nature is something to be conquered and overpowered by technology and human ingenuity. The basic relationship with the land is exploitation. Adult children exploit it, take the cash, and leave for the good life somewhere else.

Examples: Yuppies; many ordinary people who want to make a buck and get ahead; tycoons; fortune hunters; golddiggers; conquerors; missionaries; many politicians and world leaders; media personalities who crave publicity; professionals who put income and status as the highest priorities in life; empire builders; some strong conservatives and ideologues; scientists, academics, and professors with a reputation to uphold, who feud over their pet theories; gurus who seek personal power and control; many cult leaders who have sex with their followers and take advantage of them financially and otherwise.

Examples of countries with a noticeable percentage of adult children in their populations: Germany, Japan, the United States (especially southern California, Washington, DC, and much of the East Coast), Spain, France, Korea, Philippines, Venezuela, and Kuwait. These people are found in every country of the world, but they prefer the capitalistic and influencial ones. They represent about one-third of the world's population.

Stage Four: Adolescent

Age: Thirteen to nineteen. (Can be up to age thirty-five; adolescence is often prolonged.)

Viewpoint: "Me" and "you." "I know how you feel. I know how you feel about me." The adolescent point of view is, "Life is more difficult now, and I have a million unanswered questions. I am looking for answers, and I am going to question everything to find out. I don't really feel understood by anyone, and I don't understand myself."

Ability: Teenagers are highly capable, and they are fully mature physically in the sense that they can be sexually active. They can perform at advanced levels mentally and can be talented artists and musicians as well as capable cooks. When they are healthy, they can make decisions for themselves without much parental guidance. They are capable of living independently of their parents when necessary. They are fully able to form their own opinions and frequently oppose their parents in order to more fully achieve independence.

Thought and Emotion: Teenagers are capable of complex and advanced abstract thought. They are fully functional mentally and are quite philosophical. Their thoughts are geared toward questioning and are heavily influenced by their emotions, which are driven by hormones. These emotion-based thoughts are often highly idealistic in nature. At times, the intensity of emotion overwhelms the reasoning process, and to their own chagrin, teenagers regress momentarily to early childhood. This makes teenagers unstable and difficult to understand.

Adolescents' thoughts are often turned toward trying to understand their own emotions and those of others. They often ask for guidance from adults other than their parents when they are stuck.

Focus: The focus of adolescence is advanced emotional expression and the drive for independence, experimentation, and the satisfaction of curiosity. The primary focus is emotional development synthesized with rational thought. When this is achieved, adolescents can be considered adults. In addition, adolescents focus on developing their sexual identities.

Activity: Adolescent activities include dating, advanced athletics, intellectual development, the beginning of responsible jobs, creative expression, and idealistic social reform.

Values: Teenagers value the following: questioning and challenging authority, idealistic reform, idealistic concern for others, taking risks, the environment and nature, discussion and argument, sex, relationships, alone time, new ideas, food, art, music, and philosophy. They either overvalue or undervalue their bodies and usually struggle with them.

Relationships: Adolescents relate to one another in an emotionally sophisticated way. They create deep bonds with each other that can become lifelong relationships. When not flooded by emotion, teenagers make very good eye contact. They value relationships that have a strong emotional component and a soap-opera quality of intensity. Their relationships also have an unstable quality and swing heavily according to emotions of the moment. Adolescents overidentify with the problems of the world and feel a commitment to reform and fix them to make life better for others. They try out their wings in the sexual arena. They are often committed to environmental concerns, animal rights, and human rights because they can identify with suffering so acutely.

Adults Fixated at the Adolescent Stage

Viewpoint: Adults fixated as adolescents are sensitive to how other people feel. They identify with others emotionally, which facilitates their developing deep, long-lasting relationships. However, their relationships are often confusing because they don't always know who is feeling what about whom. Their point of view is, "life is difficult and not a lot of fun. There is much injustice in the world and, to make matters worse, nobody seems to understand me. Maybe I'm crazy, since nobody gets who I am or validates me for my point of view. Well, there are answers out there somewhere, and I'm going to look until I find them." These adult adolescents often have self-esteem difficulties because they don't know their place in the world.

Ability: Adults acting as teenagers are highly capable individuals who can excel in many fields and often make major contributions to the human race. Their abilities are facilitated by their keen perceptions and their commitments to progressive solutions and reform. They are not afraid to take exception to the policies of their governments, companies, or religions. They are not afraid of the big arena and readily enter politics or tackle problems at the global level. They work hard for the principles they believe in, often for little monetary gain. Money is not a high priority and is often deeply suspect.

Thought and Emotion: These adults are quite idealistic in their thoughts and are the creators of new philosophies and ideologies intended to fix the injustices of the world. The social reforms they create are complex and highly developed but usually include a fatal flaw that undermines them in the final outcome. The adult adolescent creators and believers are emotionally attached to their ideas and often lay down their lives for them. Nevertheless, they are oriented to understanding the ideas and feelings of other people.

The emotional lives of adult adolescents are intense, and these people often seek psychotherapy and other methods to help them sort things out. They welcome assistance if it promises them answers. Confusion often reigns supreme in their lives, which makes them hard to understand. They are impossible to understand for adults fixated at younger ages.

Focus: The focus of adult adolescents is to understand themselves and others. Therefore, their focus is primarily on the development of relationships and emotional expression within them. Their focus is not to become rich or famous, although that might happen anyway. It is not a motivator. The motivators for these people are answers to deep questions and the feeling of making a contribution to the world.

Activity: Adults living as adolescents can be highly respected members of society performing well in any variety of jobs. However, their interests often take them into the arts and the human service fields where they can feel they are making a contribution to others. They are highly experimental and adventurous, often leading lives that seem on the edge or even risky. They are experimental with cooking and sex, and they question the traditional ways of approaching the world. They explore different religions and philosophies and are at times at odds with their cultures because of this. They can be found carrying placards and demonstrating for and against causes that arouse emotions, such as war and the proliferation of nuclear weapons.

Values: Adult teenagers often value alone time in which they can recover from the stresses of a difficult world. They value art, philosophy, freedom of expression, and the freedom to explore life without censure by others. They value new ideas and solutions, and they like to be with other people who want to grow and develop themselves. These people greatly value personal responsibility in changing the world. Their values include ecology and the rights of animals.

In the spiritual realm, adult adolescents often seek religions that have a social conscience or offer the opportunity to be silent and meditate. They seek answers in religion and are demanding of church leaders that they practice what they preach. Often they are agnostics because they don't understand why a god would create suffering.

Adult teenagers are more comfortable with death than adults fixated at younger ages, but they are often afraid they will die before they figure everything out or make their contribution. They often struggle with not liking parts of their bodies, and it is not unusual for them to reject themselves physically. However, they usually are more accepting as they get older.

Relationships: Adults fixated as adolescents usually maintain good eye contact if they are not plagued by emotional disturbances or serious self-deprecation. As mentioned already, their relationships are intense, deep, and can be enduring over a long period of time. They understand other people's problems but confuse the issues by overidentifying with them and projecting their own problems onto them.

Adult adolescents are attracted to animals because they can identify with them emotionally. They often care for strays and collect pets. They are upset by desecration of the land and feel more comfortable in nature than in a big crowd.

Examples: Reformers; therapists; people who are emotionally disturbed; teachers; seekers; eccentrics; people who dabble in world religions; people into alternative lifestyles; people interested in metaphysics, astrology, channeling, and so on; animal rights demonstrators; antiwar marchers; civil-rights workers; human rights activists; composers, artists, and musicians with a social message; liberals. Specific examples are: Beethoven, Bill and Hillary Clinton, Bob Dylan, Ernest Hemingway, Karl Marx, Timothy Leary, Shirley MacLaine, Mozart, and Gloria Steinem.

Examples of countries with a noticeable percentage of adult adolescents in their populations: Italy, Canada, Russia, Poland, England, Scandinavia, parts of the United States such as the Northwest and Southwest. These folks represent about one-third of the world's population. They do like to gravitate to communities and organizations where they can find others who understand them.

Stage Five: Adult

Adults are not fixated at any earlier level if they are acting like adults. Therefore, there is only one list of characteristics for adults. Many characteristics of adolescents are the same as those for adults. The difference is that adults have emotional detachment while adolescents do not. Adult have the perspective that comes with experience, while adolescents are still fresh out of the mold. Adolescents suffer more because they make more mistakes, and they are more attached to the outcome.

Age: Twenty to seventy-five. (Often thirty-five to seventy-five since adolescence is frequently prolonged to age thirty-five.)

An examination of human development shows that age thirty-five is a pivotal point in many people's lives. This is the time when people give up trying to please their parents and society and focus on their own personal goals. The transition is often accompanied by an abrupt change of career, a divorce, a remarriage, or a move from one geographic location to another. Many older people feel that they did not begin to live until this age.

Viewpoint: "Me" and "you" and "we are both part of something greater." The adult view of the world is: "I recognize that we are both human beings and that you have a right to be the way you are. I just ask that you allow me to be the way I am. So, live and let live." The emphasis is on "being" over "doing." Quality is better than quantity. The adult views life as a local passion play: "Life goes on, so emphasize the good and don't get too disappointed if things don't go your way. There is always something to learn from every situation. Instead of resisting life, find a way to adapt to it and take the suffering out. I cannot harm you without somehow harming myself." Adults can see the big picture.

Ability: Adults are fast learners and know how to adapt their learning from one situation to another fairly easily. They have learned how to learn, and therefore how to solve problems quickly. They are highly capable people who have experience and wisdom and do not get caught up in petty obstacles if they can at all help it. They often rely on their own creativity and liberally adapt the rule books to meet different situations. They believe in the spirit of the law rather than the letter of it. They may consult cookbooks but prefer to create their own dishes, relying on experience and creativity.

Thought and Emotion: Adults have succeeded in balancing their thoughts with their emotions and actions. All three work together; therefore, their approach is usually appropriate to a given situation. They are stable, in contrast to their adolescent counterparts. They are somewhat detached and do not over-identify with others' problems or the problems of the world. Instead of complaining, they quietly take the actions that will solve problems. They love discussion and philosophy but prefer to develop their own personal philosophy and understanding of the world. Their approach is usually direct, to the point, but diplomatic. They may be very intelligent, but they speak in simple terms that are easy to understand.

Emotionally, they can have their problems, of course. However, they are not afraid to ask for help when they feel they need it. They are aware that no person is an island and that successful living means cooperation with other human beings.

Focus: The focus of adults is pursuing personal evolution and contributing to the welfare of others by modeling adult behavior. Adults teach by example.

Adults may be rich or poor, famous or obscure, and socially powerful or quiet. If they have wealth, fame, or power, they handle it with grace and use it for the benefit of the less fortunate. They also know how to enjoy it themselves. Their inner moti-vators are spiritual expansion and understanding, making a contribution to the world, and enjoying the pleasures of family, friends, and work they love to do.

Adults see themselves as the main authority, and they look within for the answers to their questions. Rather than blame others when things go wrong, they accept responsibility and seek to correct the problems.

Activity: Adults are motivated to seek work that enriches and satisfies them regardless of the considerations of salary and fringe benefits. They prefer to set their own hours and work as independently as possible. They work so efficiently that they get more work done in a short time than a child-fixated adult. Adults know that they are sustained by the natural environment, and they spend as much time in nature as possible.

Adults seem to have natural talents in many areas and can usually figure out how to do things with a little practice. They are good at moving in and out of all social classes without necessarily identifying with any one class in particular. They are as at home with the poor as with the rich. They respect other cultures and customs and find them interesting and familiar (unless these cultures promote violence).

Adults like to play, relax, and be sensual. They can hang around like fat cats after a big meal. Therefore to some, they seem lazy or unmotivated because they are not always working. This is because adults value "being" over "doing." When they do work, they like to work hard, and they don't mind getting sweaty and dirty. Their surroundings can become messy and cluttered, but they know where everything is.

Values: Adults value substance over appearance. They prefer comfy, tattered sportscoats to brand-new, stiff suits. They don't care what other people think as long as they themselves are satisfied. They bend rules to fit different situations or to be as fair as possible. They enjoy their work, time off, nature, friendship, good food, good sex with intimacy and communication, free self-expression, independence, responsibility, contemplating the universe, dreams, and considering what happens after death. They are not afraid of death and are comfortable with the topic, even blunt about it at times. They see death as a rite of passage, a transition to a different state of existence.

Adults have strong spiritual lives but may not be religious. They don't necessarily find solace in a temple or church, but they do commune spiritually in the great outdoors. They are given to meditation and contemplation, and they do this informally and quite naturally. Adults enjoy their bodies no matter what they might look like and they are glad to have these bodies.

Relationships: Adults acting as adults feel related to all people, animals, plants, and the planet itself, with all its forms. This is because adults feel that everything is part of a greater whole. This philosophy engenders a basic feeling of respect for all life and a live-and-let-live frame of reference.

The relationships of adults are intimate and caring, and they can be long lasting. They do not include the soap-opera dramas of adolescents, however. When adults part ways, they do not come to blows. There is mutual consent and a respect for differences. While children demand that everyone be like themselves, adults welcome differences in people and even enjoy them.

Sometimes adult adolescents or children may feel that adults acting as adults are uncaring because they are somewhat detached. An adolescent in the throes of a romantic breakup gets angry when a parent wisely says, "You will survive this. You are still young." Adults have a philosophical attitude about relationships. They are acutely aware of the impermanence of life and are prepared for sudden changes caused by death or relocation. Adults grieve and then get on with the business of living. They maintain solid and enduring eye contact without a trace of fear.

Examples: Some alternative healers; eccentrics; philosophers; spiritual teachers; many ordinary people living ordinary lives pursuing spiritual growth; nature lovers; caretakers and healers of animals; people with the ability to communicate with plants; a few world leaders with vision and an ability to transcend local politics; some ecologists with action plans and visions; artists; composers; musicians and writers who produce works of timeless beauty, Mark Twain, John Muir, and Walt Whitman, to name a few.

Examples of countries with a noticeable percentage of adults in their populations: Iceland, Switzerland, Finland, Holland, Sweden, Denmark, pockets in Russia and the United States. Often, adult-oriented countries attempt to maintain neutrality in times of conflict. Adults are scattered about in the populations of all countries. They most likely number less than one-tenth of the world's population at this time. They cluster together in some communities here and there.

Stage Six: Elder

Age: This is quite arbitrary. Some people never become elders and some people do so at a very young age. These people have no noticeable dragons to contend with. They are too busy making a contribution.

Viewpoint: "We." "When I see you I see me." No more personal agenda. "I don't care anymore what happens to myself—not because I don't love myself, but because I no longer have any fear. When I serve my brother or sister, I serve myself."

Ability: Elders have experience, skills, and talents. There is no effort to their work. They are quietly powerful and effective, and have the ability to communicate with anyone. They have a unique calming effect on others and their presence can disarm tense situations. They have natural authority, and people listen to them with respect. They can move mountains if necessary to accomplish their goals. Their goals are always altruistic. They are not plagued by dragons.

Thought and Emotion: All levels of mental functioning are available to elders. They maintain a balance of emotions, rationality, and action. However, they also have a mystical sixth sense that allows them to know things that are unexplainable. They sense the future and display strong intuition. They know all about people even though they have never met them before. They display wisdom and are only interested in the truth.

Focus: The focus of elders is the greater good of humankind. They know themselves well but are not focused on themselves at all. Motivators for them are the ending of human suffering and the increase of spiritual development. They are kind but firm. They are serene and tranquil.

Activity: Usually philanthropy and teaching. They can do any work, however.

Values: Elders value the freedom and happiness of new generations. They work toward peace on Earth and value hard work and the enjoyment of beauty. Money, fame, fortune, and power have no luster for them. These offer no motivation whatsoever. Spiritual awareness is their main motivator; however, this has little to do with religion. These people are regarded as mystics and healers.

Relationships: Elders are less focused on personal relationships and more focused on their relationships with everyone. The man or woman dying on the street is their brother or sister. An orphaned child is their daughter or son. They are less dedicated to a significant other; rather, they are dedicated to humanity. Animals are their brothers and sisters, and they have a special way of talking with animals and knowing what they want. The tree is their cousin, the cloud their grandmother. The outdoors is their home. They feel safe anywhere. They have few preferences for one thing or the other. They maintain strong, unwavering, kind eye contact.

Examples: Gandhi, Mother Teresa, Saint Francis of Assisi, Rumi, Gurdjieff, Seneca, Chief Seattle, many mystics and wise people.

Currently, there are no countries with a significant population of elders. However, there are communities where they can be found. They are probably less than one-thousandth of one percent of the total population.

Stage Seven: Master

Age: Totally arbitrary. These people seem to have great age. They exhibit no dragons.

Viewpoint: "I." Masters perceive no dualities. There is no "me" and "you." All is one. Things are perfect the way they are. They simply want others to remember their true natures—that they are also one with all. They have no personal agenda or issues.

Ability: Masters have supernatural abilities. They are able to perform miracles. They can suspend the laws of the physical universe at will.

Thought and Emotion: Masters are totally telepathic. They know the future. They are able to read minds, and they exude love for all. They have no fear.

Focus: Enlightenment

Activity: Teaching, healing, role modeling, being. They answer questions and speak in parables. They may do any kind of work early in life.

Values: Peace, harmony, love, balance, ecstasy, oneness, kindness, compassion, strength. No physical object is a motivator.

Relationships: "All is related." Masters experience everything as self. They are not in relationship because they experience no duality. Just "I."

Examples: Jesus Christ, Buddha, Krishna, Lao Tzu, avatars.

There are no countries with populations exhibiting these traits. The presence of masters is scattered throughout history in various parts of the world.

The Seven Dragons and the Stages of Maturation

The above descriptions of each stage of maturation are very generalized. In the case of the adult, the description represents the ideal. If you have reached the adult stage in your maturation, it is possible for you to slide, on occasion, to any of the stages you have already passed through. If you are rejected by a lover, you might temporarily slide into feeling like an adolescent and believe yourself to be terribly misunderstood and unfairly treated. However, as an adult, you will snap out of this soon enough. Or, if you are cut off by another driver on the freeway, you may temporarily regress to the toddler level of response. You may want to get back at the other driver. That is because you have been a toddler and you know how it feels to be one. However, you probably will not remain in this stage for more than a few minutes.

If you have fixated at the adolescent level, you can also slide to all the stages you have been through. However, since you have not progressed to the adult level, you will not move there until you actually go through that step in development.

Likewise, if you are fixated at the child level, you can slide to toddler and infant stages on occasion, but it is unlikely you will behave as an adolescent or an adult in most situations.

Fixation at the toddler level gives you the option of sliding to the infant stage only.

How do you release a fixation on a younger stage and move on to older levels of maturation? That is a massive topic to say the least. Transforming your dragons has much to do with maturation. Yet, not everyone is interested or motivated to mature. There are many people perfectly content to continue to operate at the level at which they are fixated. This has to do with culture, opportunity, fear level, belief systems and evolution. Hindus, Tibetan Buddhists, Taoists, early Christians, those who study the Cabbalah, and many world-renowned philosophers say maturation reflects the age of the soul in a reincarnation sense. This is the way I see it as well.

There is a kind of paradox in this matter of fixation. The older your level of maturation, the more you are motivated to slay your dragons and move on to adulthood. The younger your maturation level, the more your dragons dominate you and the less interested you are in slaying them. The reason for this is obvious. A certain level of maturity is necessary to be able to look at yourself and notice that you have a dragon that needs slaying. Usually it is not until the end of childhood and the beginning of adolescence that this insight becomes available. This type of energy dynamic is exemplified in the old saying, "It takes money to make money." This seems unfair, but it happens to be true. Fairness is not the issue.

Something else to consider is the fact that you may exhibit different levels of maturity in different parts of your life. For example, you may be quite an adult in your relationships with men, but when it comes to women, especially women in authority, you may act like an adolescent. You may be fixated as a child in your business operations but as a toddler when it comes to dealing with your spouse or children.

The various possibilities are endless in the population at large, yet it is possible to make a map of your own levels of maturity with a little thought. Simply take a sheet of paper and make headings across the top. These headings may include business, romance, men, women, Mom, Dad, strangers, and any others that come to your mind. After contemplation, write down the fixation level that you see in yourself in relation to each heading. After you understand the dragons, you can also list the dragons that affect each area of your life. Then you will know what work and healing need to be done.

By learning about the fixations at the different stages of maturation, you can understand how the dragons operate at each stage. You can see that the greed dragon is particularly active in those stuck at the child stage, while the self-deprecation dragon is prevalent in those stuck at the adolescent stage. Nevertheless, it is possible to see every dragon in early stage of maturation, including the adult level.

There is an important rule of thumb with respect to dragons and maturation. The younger the fixation level, the more the dragons run wild and the more the activities of the dragons are acted out in the world. The older the fixation level, the more the dragon's activities are subtle. Rather than running amok, the dragons are sneaky. In adult adolescents and adults, it is common for dragons to hide and to affect the people intrapsychically. Their dragons are not acted out toward other people so much as they torture the people who harbor them.

For example, greedy people fixated at the child stage may amass fortunes by stealing and pirating away the wealth of others. They may make no attempt to stop themselves, and may perhaps even be proud of their behavior. Lacking insight, they are unaware that their behavior does not achieve what would actually satisfy them: love. However, these same people fixated at the adolescent stage may struggle internally with their great hunger and constantly try to control this aspect of themselves. The result would be fewer victims in the world but greater suffering for the individuals. They would know at some level that their hunger is forever—elusive love.

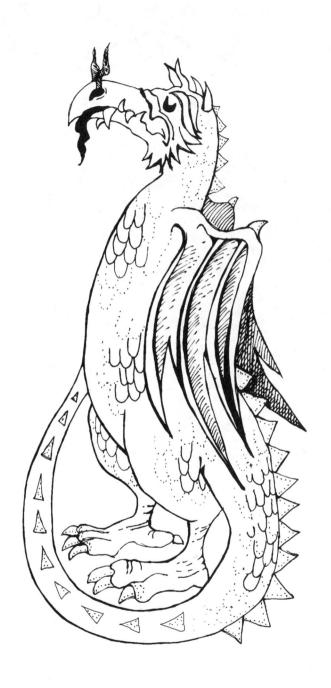

Chapter Three

THE
ARROGANCE
DRAGON

Positive Pole—Pride
Negative Pole—Vanity

External manifestation

Narcissistic; conceited; filled with braggadocio or machismo; smug; boastful; egotistical; supercilious; complacent; self-important; vainglorious; big-headed; inflated; (archaic: the sin of being prideful).

Internal manifestation

Self-conscious; shy; embarrassed; uncomfortable.

Examples of situations and conditions that can feed the arrogance dragon

Latin cultures with their notions of machismo; white culture with its notions of racial superiority; Japanese culture with its notion of superiority in the workplace; any culture with its notion of superiority; Hollywood egos; big money and high class; executive or first class on airlines; elite clubs; traditional butlers; limousines; high-status cars including muscle cars and low riders; purebred dogs and horses; name dropping; high fash-

ion; posh stores; the class system; private clubs; gated communities; fad items; titles; ancestral blueblood lines or family names.

People associated with these groups or situations do not
always exhibit the arrogance dragon. These are simply situations
that tend to promote the arrogance dragon's activities and make
it easier for this parasite to get a foothold in the personality.

Physical appearance and presentation

People affected by the arrogance dragon may appear cool,
distant, and perfect. Their noses and chins may be slightly ele-
vated, and they may seem hard to reach—with all their i's dot-
ted and t's crossed. Their chests may betray shallow breathing.
There is a tendency to hold in their bellies, producing tight
diaphragms. Their eyes look down their noses and their voices
have some disdain in them, sounding bored or above it all. On
the other hand, these people may appear rather shy, with eyes
averted, looking as if they want to disappear.

Notice how you feel when you step inside a posh club.
Usually, no matter who you are, you feel that you are being
looked over and that you had better look good. This is a mini
experience of the arrogance dragon. If you want to try this dragon on for size in an exaggerated way, stand on your tiptoes, suck
in your belly, raise your chin and nose a bit, get a cool or distant
look in your eyes, and feel insecure. Now try to breathe. Would
it be easy to make genuine intimate contact with other human
beings from this posture? Keep in mind that this is an exaggera-
tion and that these characteristics exist only at a subtle level in
most people. They tend to come out more when people are in
stress rather than when they are relaxed.

The Development of the Arrogance Dragon

The children learn to hide

Children are not born with a need to appear other than
they are. Infants and very small children are naturally them-

selves and do not have a false personality or front that they fab-
ricate for other people. If their noses are snotty or their clothes
are soiled, they wear these things like a badge proclaiming to
the world exactly what they are. They have not developed the
mental sophistication that it takes to hide their feelings.
Typically, false fronts do not appear until children have attained
the age of reason at around seven years old. With the development of abstract thought, children initiate the ability to appear
one way while feeling another. This is a more sophisticated and
abstract process.

To some extent, all human beings develop this ability. It
allows people to play poker or other games in which they must
fake out other people in order to win. This ability also allows
entertainers and actors to convincingly play roles for brief periods of time. People might find it necessary to hide their feelings
in emergency situations or wartime, when it could endanger
their own lives or the lives of others to reveal the truth. This
ability to hide the inner feelings is a necessary skill that humans
learn for their own or others' survival. It is a talent or capability
that is meant to be used for specific, appropriate situations.
However, this skill can easily be developed into a defense mechanism to protect older children from unpleasant feelings of
shame and guilt.

The children face criticism

The beginnings of the arrogance process may occur very
early in children's lives, long before they are capable of protect-
ing themselves emotionally. The earliest source of this dragon
can be the moment when children sense that somehow they
have displeased their parents by being nuisances, by being born
the wrong sex, or by somehow being born imperfect. This is
especially true if the children have a sibling whom they perceive
as being more loved than they are.

If a child is a girl, she may sense that her brother is more
loved and that if only she had been born a boy she would be

loved, too. She may feel that she is a disappointment to her parents by virtue of having been born a girl. Or, she may sense that she was an accident and that her parents did not intend to have a second or third child. She may feel that her timing was wrong or that she is just not acceptable. If the parents exacerbate this through messages of displeasure or criticism, the seeds are sown for the dragon of arrogance to take over.

In the development of the arrogance dragon, children feel partially criticized, not completely rejected. The parents may be loving, but with conditions. If the children feel completely rejected, the dragon of self-destruction enters instead, and that is another story.

In almost all cases of arrogance, there are critical parents, guardians, or older siblings. In many cases critical parents compare children unfavorably to siblings or other children. These parents or guardians may say, "Why can't you be more like your brother or sister? Why can't you be more like the neighbors' children?" Often, children are compared to images or ideal children who do not actually exist outside the fantasies of the parents. The children can never measure up to these idealized images and become vulnerable to the encroachment of the dragon. This is especially true if the parents regard the children as reflections of themselves.

Sometimes the critical ones are older siblings who never fail to remind the children how imperfect they are or in what bad taste it was for them to be born. Sibling rivalry of this sort is quite common, but it becomes a real problem when parents fail to intervene to bolster the younger children's confidence. If the parents are negligent or always at work, the small children may struggle under the oppressive older siblings.

Conditional love

The main characteristic in the development of the arrogant dragon is conditional love. "I love you, but can't you be smarter, quieter, cleaner, more attractive, good, charming", and so on. "I love you, but I love your brother or sister just a bit more." "I love you somewhat, but there are some things about you I just can't love." "I love you if you do everything I say."

In their earliest years, small children cannot protect themselves from this kind of comparison or criticism. Often, children are shamed by being told not to cry like babies or to shape up. Children are honest and they simply cry out of hurt. Sometimes ignorant parents believe that criticism toughens children and prepares them for adulthood.

If parents or guardians are basically loving during the period of infancy and early childhood, and the criticism begins later, children will be more mildly affected by the dragon of arrogance. If children sense from the very beginning of life that they are unacceptable in certain ways, the dragon will have a much stronger grip upon them in later life.

When these children grow and develop some sophistication, the dragon, also gradually growing inside, makes its first ominous appearance.

Miguel's Tale: A Story of Arrogance

Miguel's childhood years were spent in a lower middle-class neighborhood of east Los Angeles. His father was a butcher, a curt and blunt sort of man who valued hard work and, although a good provider, was not affectionate with his family. His mother worked at a dry cleaner's. With her additional duties as a housewife she was frequently exhausted and short tempered. Miguel's two older brothers were athletic and good looking. They gained recognition at school for their exploits with the girls and their expertise in sports. This reputation pleased both their father and mother and fulfilled the Latin expectation of male machismo.

Miguel, on the other hand, was slightly built, quiet, and not at all athletic. He was sensitive and enjoyed music, reading, and especially drawing. In fact, his sketches of cartoon characters indicated considerable talent. However, he was mercilessly put down by his brothers for what they considered feminine qualities, and his talent did not win him the respect of his father. His mother, while admiring his brothers, sought to protect him when she could. This increased his brothers' judgments of him as a mama's boy and a wimp. He felt ashamed and became self-conscious. His mother worried about his shyness.

Miguel's mother began to give him double messages. On the one hand, she was effusive about how wonderful his brothers were. On the other hand, she let Miguel know that she had a special relationship with him because he was like her in so many ways. This caused confusion for Miguel. Was he worthless because he couldn't be like his brothers? Or was he extra special because he was his mother's secret favorite?

The result was inevitable. The dragon of arrogance began to sniff around Miguel, finding a suitable home in him. The dragon whispered in his ear, seducing him and becoming his secret ally.

The dragon said to Miguel, "Yes, you are special, very special—better than your brothers, better than other people. They will find out someday, and they will be sorry they teased you. Mama secretly loves you better than anyone."

At the same time, the dragon encouraged Miguel to withdraw from other people, to create distance and be aloof.

By the time Miguel was a teenager, he walked with a distinctly 'cool' gait. He held his chin slightly up and looked ever so slightly down his nose at the world. Some girls began to notice him because he seemed so cool and unreachable. They thought he was something special. Gradually, however, as they tried to get to know him, they decided he was arrogant and cold, so they rejected him. This wounded him deeply, but he could never let on that he was hurt. He became further isolated.

Miguel became more and more desperate for attention and recognition. He worked hard to buy and remodel a car that was the envy of the other boys. He drove it by his brothers' friends to gain their acceptance, but he did not stop to talk with them. He dressed in stylish clothes and affected the mannerisms of someone with great sophistication. He learned to smoke with an aloof air and attracted a small band of insecure boys who thought he was truly Mr. Cool. But he was not relieved of loneliness because he could never let them know how vulnerable he felt.

Eventually, Miguel was driven to more desperate measures to impress his mother and to prove that he was as good as his brothers. The dragon suggested that he get hold of a handgun and let others know that he had moved up to a new level of impressiveness.

The next step in the dragon's escalation was an attempt by Miguel to rob a liquor store. With the other boys watching from a distance, he pulled his gun on the clerk and demanded money. However, the liquor store happened to be under surveillance because it was a frequent target. Miguel was immediately apprehended.

This action set the stage for the dragon's ultimate victory. Miguel was humiliated in front of his friends, not for getting caught but for crying when he was arrested. In juvenile hall, his facade completely fell apart. He could not effectively maintain his cool, aloof attitude. He became a frightened, isolated boy who experienced deep shame. All his plans to be special and superior collapsed in one humiliating heap. The dragon laughed long and loud at the fix Miguel was in. This was great fun for the dragon of arrogance.

Fortunately, however, this was not the end of Miguel's story. When the dragon belly-laughed over its delicious game, it became slightly vulnerable. A window of opportunity opened to beat the dragon back, perhaps even slay it while it was laughing. Transformation became possible.

An experienced probation officer took a particular interest in Miguel. Bill, the probation officer, seeing through Miguel's facade, determined that he could be reached because he was not so far along into criminal activity that he was a lost cause.

From looking at Miguel's artistic handwriting, doodles, and constant sketching, Bill could see that Miguel had artistic talent that was not actualized. When he suggested this to Miguel, he was met by Miguel's detached and disdainful demeanor. Bill persisted and, by taking special interest in Miguel, began to wear down his aloofness and defensive stance. Gradually Miguel began to open up with Bill and allow his feelings out. He admitted his loneliness, his frustration with striving for his brothers' respect, and his distance from his father.

Bill encouraged Miguel to develop his artistic talent and arranged for him to enter a local contest in cartooning. Miguel was so hungry for male validation that he responded to Bill without too much further resistance. He still wanted to be special, and Bill, because of his experience, used this desire to make progress with him. Thus came the first reversal in the dragon's fortunes. The dragon was forced to retreat to lick its wounds and gather its forces. Miguel was not yet ready to explore his ambivalence toward his mother, and that is where the dragon made its home.

Some years later, Miguel, while in art school, met Cassandra and fell in love with her. Cassandra adored Miguel and would do almost anything for him. After a brief, intense romance, they married and began struggling to make ends meet on her limited salary as a part-time medical clerk and his freelance art work. Before long, Cassandra, fearful and frustrated with their limited funds, began to compare Miguel with more financially successful husbands who had careers in business. Miguel became hypercritical of her cooking, style of dressing, and general behavior. Their relationship degenerated into endless quarrels and hurt feelings. Losing his confidence, Miguel became afraid to assert himself as an artist. He responded to Cassandra by becoming cold and distant and withdrawing his affection from her. When she began to have an affair with an aggressive salesman, a familiar pattern manifested. Miguel fell apart and became seriously depressed. He could no longer create as an artist.

Miguel lost his special relationship with Cassandra when he became threatened by her critical judgments and her comparisons of him with more successful men. Instead of trying to work things out, he withdrew and responded with the hypercritical activity of the arrogance dragon. The dragon had been biding its time, waiting for an opportunity to take control of him again. Nesting in his unexamined, ambivalent relationship with his mother, the dragon grabbed the opportunity of a replay in that arena.

This story has two possible endings. In one, Miguel loses his relationship with Cassandra and embarks on a series of unfortunate relationships that replay the same humiliating process over and over again. Miguel becomes a man who brings out the worst in the women he meets. First he impresses them; then he fails to deliver somehow. They lose their esteem for him, he becomes critical and withdraws, and they leave him after getting involved with someone else. Depression and humiliation follow for Miguel. In this scenario, the dragon wins and becomes stronger with every episode.

The second scenario involves a different set of results. Miguel and Cassandra see a perceptive (adult) marriage counselor who helps them sort out their feelings. Miguel begins to see how he is replaying his relationship with his mother with Cassandra. He wants to be special to her but fears he is actually a disappointment and not valued. He sees how he responds with critical nitpicking in order to protect himself. He notices how he withdraws and allows the dragon to complete its destruction of his relationship. Miguel gradually learns to let go of his need to be the favorite. Rather than judge his wife in revenge and become aloof, he learns to listen to Cassandra's fears. Together they make constructive plans to improve their lot. He builds his confidence in himself as a successful artist and, rather than withdrawing, seeks out opportunities to be productive. The arrogance dragon is rooted out of its comfortable nest and must search for a new home.

The Seven Steps of Development
of the Arrogance Dragon

The development of the arrogance dragon occurs in seven distinct steps. Behaviors that are exhibited later in life are based on each step.

Step one: The children learn to turn against themselves.

Step two: The children try to be perfect people who are not themselves.

Step three: The children learn to hide their flaws and pretend to be invulnerable.

Step four: The children learn to scrutinize others for clues about being acceptable.

Step five: The children learn to scrutinize and police themselves.

Step six: The children identify with their aggressors and judge themselves.

Step seven: The children learn to turn the tables by trying to be better than others.

Step one: The children learn to turn against themselves.

The children experience the critical atmosphere of their homes and feel compared to high standards or to older successful siblings. Feeling the conditional nature of love, the children begin to turn against themselves. The fetal dragon inside them says, in the form of their thoughts, "I don't want to be a little creep that all of them don't like. I'll be like the person they want to see. Then I'll be loved. I am not OK the way I am. I'll have to hide who I really am."
Belief and decision: "I am not OK."

Step two: The children try to be perfect people who are not themselves.

The children learn to act like others. Their thinking may go like this: "I am going to try to be different from the way I am.

I am going to strive to be perfect so that they won't have any-thing to criticize anymore. I will be perfect. I will excel. When they hurt me by being critical, I'll pretend it doesn't bother me. I'll pretend to be above it. I'm not that person anyway. Actually, I'm secretly special. Underneath the criticism, they love me best because I'm so perfect after all."

Belief and decision: "I'm perfect and therefore I'm special."

Step three: The children learn to hide their flaws and pretend to be invulnerable.

Every effort goes into invulnerability. Aloofness and dis-tance develop. The children figure that if people don't get too close, they will never see the flaws or fears. The children think, "I am tired of being hurt. I am not going to show them any flaws or any limitations whatsoever. They will never see my flaws again."

Belief and decision: "I can successfully hide my feelings from others."

Step four: The children learn to scrutinize others for clues about being acceptable.

The children learn to look for clues about how to be. They become hyperalert and constantly scan their environment to see what will or will not impress others. The children say to them-selves, "I am going to examine others very closely and try to find out what they value. Then I am going to try to be that way." The dragon takes its first steps toward running the chil-dren's behavior.

Belief and decision: "I must try to find out what others want from me. I must look to others for clues."

Step five: The children learn to scrutinize and police themselves.

The dragon inside the children thinks, "They are always on my case. They are always watching me. In order to win their approval, I will have to monitor myself very closely. I'll need to be one step ahead of them and notice my mistakes first. I'll watch closely to see if I am about to say, do, or be anything that might bring scorn upon me. I'll always be watching myself."

The children always feel under scrutiny and this makes them overly self-conscious. Added to this feeling of being scrutinized by others is their own intense self-scrutiny. They feel they are being watched from all sides, inside and out. (Under extreme stress, this process results in the condition known as paranoia.) The feeling of being under the gun becomes intolerable, and the children long to hide from all the watching. They become shy. They learn to hate being noticed or watched. They feel shame. They become embarrassed at the drop of a hat.

Later in life these people can feel embarrassed by almost anything that draws attention to them. They automatically think that everyone is watching them wherever they go. This gives them a false sense of importance. They become very shy but appear to others to be aloof, snobbish, distant, self-important, and hard to know.

If they are ignored by others, these people feel devastated, because they get their importance from being watched. So they do things to attract attention to themselves and then pretend not to notice. They may wear diamonds, dress in the best of clothes, drive flashy cars, and then pretend that no one is watching them. They may accentuate their good looks, only to be aloof when people approach them. This earns them the bad reputation of being cold hearted ice queens or teasers. Thus they bring upon themselves what they are most trying to get away from: judgment and criticism.

The paradox these people struggle with is that they secretly want to be noticed and loved. They fear they will be noticed and judged negatively, or even worse, dismissed as unimportant. They live under the constant tension of wanting to avoid notice, yet wanting to be noticed. Either way, they suffer and die the thousand deaths of a coward.

This process is clearly apparent in the early teenage years when adolescents do not want to be seen with their parents under any circumstances. Teenagers suffer acute embarrassment because they are sure everyone is noticing them. As you probably know, all teenagers cycle through this, but most grow out of it. The ones who do not are the ones with the arrogance dragon controlling them.

Belief and decision: "I must monitor myself constantly."

Step Six: The children identify with their aggressors and judge themselves.

The next step in the development of this dragon is self-criticism. The dragon inside says, "If I notice myself about to do anything that I'll be criticized for, I'll quickly criticize myself unmercifully so that I'll shape up and then they can't criticize me. I'll shame myself, and by doing so, spare myself the more awful, public shame. To others, I'll appear perfect. I'll deal with myself harshly."

The children take over the task of criticizing themselves. This is known as identifying with the aggressor. It is a good defense strategy in hopeless situations.

Belief and decision: "I must be harshly critical with myself. I'll see through the critical eyes of others."

Step Seven: The children learn to turn the tables by trying to be better than others.

The dragon inside whispers: "I secretly doubt my worth because I get so much negative feedback from those I need love from. They send me messages that I should be different. I have worked and worked to be different and I have succeeded. I have become a very good critic myself. I am so good at it, I can now criticize others and find them wanting.

"I am very successful and have managed to do quite well for myself. In fact, I'm pretty great, and they aren't as good as I am. I'm better. They just don't know it yet, but they'll see. One day I will be honored and respected and they will be nothing. They will be sorry they ever judged me negatively. They will feel like fools. They will try to act like they know me so they can brag to their friends that they know a famous person, but I'll walk by them as if they don't exist. That will teach them."

The dragon in older children makes the complete distortion. It says, "I am now better than you who judged me. I am better than anyone who might judge me. I now judge you negatively. Ha! Ha! Ha!"

Belief and decision: "I must criticize others before they criticize me. I have a right to because I am better than they are."

The Arrogance Dragon's Big Lie

The problem with people afflicted by the arrogance dragon is that, deep down, they do not really believe the dragon when it says they are better than others. They want desperately to believe the words of the dragon, but during moments of clarity, they know the dragon is lying. Inside themselves, they still feel unsure. At times, they even feel a loss of identity. They know they are participating in a big sham, a lie, and they always worry that their act is not good enough. They fear someone will see through their charade and see that they are really miserable snails, slugs, lowly worms with no value at all. At least worms are something, however. These people's worst fear is that they will be ignored entirely. The greater their fear of being found out, the more energy they put into perfecting their charade, and the lonelier they become. The arrogance dragon wins.

The Great Dragon Exchange: From Great to Worthless

The more the arrogance dragon tries to build up their facade, the more these people fear being found out. This fear causes them to be acutely aware that, in reality, they are the opposite of wonderful and great. Their charade of perfection works until an event occurs that pierces or punctures their balloon of pretense. Typically, this involves a rejection in romance, being overlooked for a promotion, a failure to get a job after interviewing for it, or being passed over for an award or honor.

The result is a precipitous plunge from the arrogance dragon to the self-deprecation dragon. The people slide into horrific self-loathing and feelings of worthlessness.

Arrogant people often swing between the two dragons— "I'm worthless. No, I'm great, No, worthless. No, great"—until in desperation and exhaustion they tell the truth: "What the hell am I, anyway?" They realize, "I don't know my value." In this realization lies the beginning of healing, the potential for slaying the dragon.

The Wonderful Dragon: Wanting to be Special

Because people who have the arrogance dragon inside of them have lived under the shadow of better-loved siblings or images, they have a great desire to be the special loved ones. They want to be the favorites, the golden apples, the teacher's pets. The internal dialogue around the development of this aspect of the dragon goes something like this:

"I fear I am not special. I will work hard to project the image of the person my parents would like me to be. I will produce. I will tailor myself to their wishes. I will make myself special.

"I have succeeded at being what they want so well that now they love me more than anyone. Even though they don't show it, I know they must love me more because I am now the best."

This inner dialogue is, of course, a radical case of self-deception, yet the desire is a powerful one. As these children grow up, the campaign to be the special loved person often grows stronger and stronger. Mothers, fathers, and guardians are replaced by teachers, coaches, spouses, bosses, or therapists. Much of the campaign to be special takes place on the fantasy level.

The shy children in school, afraid of being ignored by their teachers, fantasize that they are the most brilliant students in class. They may also fantasize that they will go on to prestigious universities where they will garner top honors. Based on these fantasies, they begin to believe that their teachers consider them special because they are going to be great someday. This same strategy may be played out with athletic coaches and other authority figures. When, due to limited contact, the teachers or coaches forget the students' names, the students' fantasies are severely threatened, at times plunging them into despair. The reality is often that the students are shy, perhaps average students who do not stand out in class.

Another strategy is more active. Because arrogant people are shy, they do not feel they can compete with their more vocal extroverted peers. They figure they will have to make up the difference through hard work. Their strategy is, "If I work ten times as hard as everyone else, then they will notice me and love me." These children identify with their achievements and performances rather than their true selves. Many dutiful employees apply this strategy to gain the notice of their bosses, only to eventually meet with painful realizations. It is often the more charming, less hard-working people who are selected for promotion. The shy people realize that they cannot substitute hard work for personality and expect to be loved for it. The world is a harsh teacher in this respect.

Sometimes the strategy applies to possessions rather than hard work. The arrogance dragon urges shy people to acquire attractive possessions to make them more desirable. The dragon inside says, "If I just have that new hot-looking car, then I'll be noticed and loved. If I live in the right part of town or am seen in the right restaurants, then I'll be considered part of the 'in' crowd. I'll be noticed and valued for sure then." There can be several results with this strategy. One is that these people may work very hard to acquire all the expensive possessions they need to be desirable, only to find that they sit alone and lonely in their fine new homes. This is a double-edged sword. On the one hand, they feel isolated and sad, but on the other hand they feel safe being alone. There is no external criticism coming from a television set—unless, of course, paranoia sets in.

Often, people who are overcome by the arrogance dragon meet up with other arrogant types who are busy avoiding intimacy yet looking for someone to hold them in the highest esteem. In relationships, these people are oriented toward appearances only. Although each has the other's company, each of them feels undervalued and not seen by the other. The result is lack of intimacy and mutual loneliness. Each feels emotionally bankrupt and wants the other to make him or her feel special. These relationships cannot last. Yet the double-edged sword holds true here as well. By selecting someone else who is not intimate, the arrogant person, though lonely, is safe from vulnerability.

The arrogance dragon, wanting to be special, can employ another strategy to keep the deception going. People under its influence can say to themselves in relationships, "If only these people really knew me, they would love me." This actually may be true. But then the lie comes: "If only they knew how great I really am, they would love me more than anyone else." In this fashion, the arrogant people learn to control their self-esteem by keeping up a fantasy that is almost fail-safe: "If they knew me, they would know I'm the greatest. But I won't let them know me. I'm in charge of that."

Over the years, this strategy can become very strong and lead to other related fantasies. For example, arrogant people often avoid activities that require performance. They might say, "Well, if I took the college entrance exam I would probably do so well that I would get a scholarship. But I can't be bothered." Or they might say, "If I really tried, I could win over that attractive woman, but I'm too busy. I'll let the other guy have her." This can lead to a withdrawal from many of life's opportunities and to more isolation. It is almost a blueprint for failure.

Stages of Maturity and the Arrogance Dragon

The arrogance dragon plays itself out differently at each stage of maturity.

Infant stage: biggest gorilla
Toddler stage: petty bureaucrat
Child stage: high status
Adolescent stage: shy
Adult stage: philosophical arrogance

Since elders and masters are without dragons, they are not discussed here.

Arrogance at the infant stage

At this level, the arrogance dragon does not have any sophistication to work with. There are no elaborate strategies or fantasies. There is no internal considering. The arrogance is played out in the most blatant, raw forms. This is the level of the biggest gorilla. Infantile arrogance says, "You deserve to die because I'm stronger." Adult infants boast in a primitive, transparent fashion that has a kind of stereotypical pattern. These people huff and puff and present the movie version of the quintessential bad guys who deserve to be blown to bits by the end of the movie. They have no scruples, arrogantly carve people up, and sneer and dispatch people without a trace of compassion.

Arrogance at the toddler stage

At the toddler level, there is little sophistication. Again, the arrogance dragon works with fairly primitive structures in the personality. Adults behaving as toddlers want to focus on the rules and regulations in life. These are the arrogant bureaucrats who preside over the local government offices, making you wait for hours until they give you the privilege of their brief attention. They usually look over your head as if you were nothing. They are the border guards who look disdainfully at your passport or legal papers and hold you up just to display their own importance.

Adult toddlers are not comfortable with people of different types. They are the petty people who treat you with contempt because you are a foreigner or are of the wrong ethnic group. They are the people who say with derision, "I can't tell them apart—all Chinese look alike to me." They are the gang members who beat a foreigner to show solidarity with their gangs. They are the local policemen who enjoy intimidating the poor while accepting bribes from cronies for illegal activities.

This is arrogance in the world of toddlers, petty and small, loud and basic, without rationale or any internal consideration.

Arrogance at the child stage

At this level, the arrogance dragon begins to take on a different appearance. In fact, appearance is what the latency age is all about. Adult children affected by this dragon wear diamonds, pearls, and expensive watches. They drive Rolls Royces and put on airs. They are flashy and they try to demonstrate that they are better than their peers. They elbow to be seen with the best of society for the sake of appearance.

Yet, there is also a new level of sophistication. Adult children with this dragon exhibit the quiet arrogance of the highest members of society who do not stoop to flash their wealth. With the arrogance of old wealth, they marry off their children to the best matches, keeping the wealth in their families and shutting out those less fortunate souls who happen to be of the wrong color or class. This is sophisticated arrogance, with the uplifted eyebrow and half-hidden disdain. This is the arrogance of people who put on the appearance of being concerned about the masses while privately working to create greater distance from them. This is the level of masquerade. They tell other people what they want to hear, then proceed with their original plans to make a killing at the expense of these people.

These adult children have the arrogance of those with reputations to uphold: the scientists, doctors, lawyers, and academics who want so badly to reach the top that they publicly scorn the theories and abilities of their competitors in order to enhance their own standing.

Arrogance at the adolescent stage

At this level, the arrogance dragon takes an entirely new twist because it can use a much higher level of sophistication for its machinations. The arrogance frequently goes underground and takes the form of apparent shyness and discomfort with others. Adults at the adolescent level are aware of shame, a feeling that the younger levels are only dimly aware of. Adolescent adults feel shame acutely, and when controlled by the arrogance dragon, they will do almost anything to hide it.

They are the people who avoid social situations out of discomfort. They experience terrible cowardice about calling up potential dates. They cry themselves to sleep at night out of frustration and loneliness, but don't want anyone to see them. Within these people, the dragon contrives numerous fantasies and deceptions that protect them from uncomfortable situations, only to sink them deeper into loneliness.

Arrogance at the adult stage

At this stage the arrogance dragon may go underground entirely. Other people may not be able to see any vanity in these people whatsoever. Others who meet them might wonder what could possibly be arrogant about them since they do not act aloof or invulnerable. The arrogance may be hidden so well within them that they themselves do not see it. Unlike adolescents who are acutely aware of their shyness and shame, adults may not be plagued by these feelings. These individuals may go out of their way to show how open and vulnerable they are with other people. They say, "See, I have nothing to hide. I am just my humble self." However, inside this charade the dragon is lurking, grinning slyly. These people have cleverly devised ways to appear vulnerable and open to the extent that they seem totally available to others. But those who truly know them discover that they are somehow remote and walled off at a deeper level.

There is a secret critical nature in these adults. They judge others very quietly and internally without revealing to others these less than perfect thoughts. The critical side of them is mostly turned toward themselves so that they are split into two selves. One self arrogantly and harshly criticizes the other self. To make this even more complex, that harsh self often harangues the other side about being arrogant. The inner conversation might go something like this: "Why didn't you say hello to those people at the other table. You've met them before. Do you think you're better or something? What's the matter with you anyway? Why can't you take a few more social risks? I'll be watching you. I don't want you to do that again, even if that person is sort of a creep anyway." This internal dialogue is never heard by anyone else or even guessed at, yet it is a habitual fixture in the reality of arrogant adults.

How the Arrogance Dragon Will Get You in the End: Public Humiliation

The arrogance dragon has a special surprise for you. This dragon has great fun arranging situations in which you will be publicly humiliated. It knows that you will do anything to avoid embarrassment or humiliation, so nothing is more fun for this dragon, than to arrange for you to lose your toupee in public. The greater your arrogance, the greater will be your public humiliation.

You will trip and fall on your face as you go on stage to receive the great award. You will call the attractive man or woman by the wrong name at the crucial moment. Just when you thought the boss was going to give you a bonus for being so outstanding, you are called in to the office and told your work is substandard. As you are running for public office on a platform

of moral decency, your secret adultery is discovered and plastered across the tabloids. Your children find your pornography
after you have warned them of the evils of indecency. Another
woman wears the same designer dress that you thought would
wow the crowds.

You are compromised, humiliated, and shamed more than
any other person. Why? Because the dragon is having fun at
your expense. If you remain under the dragon's claw, you can
expect public humiliation. There is only one solution, and that
is to transform the dragon. Then a curious thing will happen.
You will no longer find yourself in shaming situations.

How the Arrogance Dragon Affects Your Life

The impact of the arrogance dragon on your health

The arrogance dragon impacts your health in a variety of
ways. First of all, it inflates your assessment of your own tough-
ness. You go out into the freezing rain without your jacket to
impress your friends about how resilient you are. You get sick.
You go to work anyway to show that a little sickness doesn't get
you down. You are tough, of course. You get sicker, perhaps
come down with pneumonia. The dragon laughs at you, at your
own expense.

You regularly overestimate your abilities and refuse to accept
the limitations of your body. Your body gets tired and needs rest
but you don't want to admit to others that you are tired so you
keep on going. You suffer an accident or become ill because you
are trying to impress others and are not listening to your body.
This can be the case when you have a few drinks but don't want
to admit that you are too drunk to drive.

Isolation, loneliness, shyness, and keeping up a facade are
quite stressful on the human body. The stress that comes from
your unhappiness lowers your resistance and weakens your
immune system. You then become more vulnerable to many
physical illnesses.

The impact of the arrogance dragon on your creativity

The arrogance dragon binds up so much of your energy in judging and appearance that it seriously curtails your creative expression. Creativity requires freedom of expression and spontaneity, both of which the dragon of arrogance prevents. To be truly creative, you must be a risk taker. Your creativity pushes you into new and previously unknown territory. In this unknown territory, you may make errors, or in your initial steps you may fumble around. This could be embarrassing to you.

Arrogance says, "Better not try anything new at all; only do what you have already perfected and know how to appear good at. Stay with the tried and true. Don't go into that unknown restaurant or hotel because you don't know the process there and you may seem to not know what you are doing. Don't go to places where you don't know the people because you will appear shy and that would be humiliating. Don't try that foreign language because you may say a word incorrectly and someone will point it out."

Gradually your world becomes smaller and smaller as you eliminate the possibilities for embarrassment. The dragon squashes your creative expression. You end up in a tiny little world that is hopelessly boring and isolated but safe from embarrassment.

The impact of the arrogance dragon on your presence

The arrogance dragon pushes you to survey the environment for potentially embarrassing situations. Much of your attention is focused on the near future so that you can anticipate and avoid any uncomfortable events. You don't want to be caught with the wrong apparrel at a social event, and you don't want to get caught not remembering someone's name at a meeting or party. You definitely watch out for bad breath and body odor and one hundred other deadly possibilities.

You worry about upcoming events you cannot avoid that could pose problems. At the same time, you remember previous

humiliating events—like the time you were trying to be so perfect and you walked into the closet instead of letting yourself
out the front door. All this takes so much attention that there is
little energy left for being present. When you are not present
with people, they lose interest in you quickly. You are bound to
be ignored when your attention is so taken up with the past and
future and everything you are worried about. This, of course,
brings about your worst fears: being ignored or being judged negatively.

As you drive this dragon out of your life, all of this reverses.
You become more present with people and they feel good about
you. You feel more powerful and are able to take risks. Many of
the risks you take pay off and your life will become more interesting, more colorful, and more alive.

The impact of the arrogance dragon on your relationships

The arrogance dragon affects your relationships by creating
distance and isolation. This dragon keeps intimacy at bay by
insisting on aloofness and criticalness—both enemies of close,
trusting, human contact. Appearance of competence is everything to the arrogance dragon. Vulnerable communication is
very threatening and usually avoided.

Arrogance intrudes into the sexual arena by emphasizing
performance over communication. You may avoid sex altogether rather than risk the dangers of nakedness in bed. You may
show all the signs of being sexually active by dressing provocatively and talking seductively, yet when it comes to the moment
of truth, you either back out or become walled off. Even if sexual activity results, your partner may feel somehow distanced,
kept out, or at worst reduced to an object.

If you are a man, sexual intercourse may be the coup de
grace when, with such emphasis on performance, you cannot
hold an erection. Your poor penis shrivels with all the self-consciousness and attention on it. When it senses danger, it refuses
to play. The arrogance dragon has great fun with this because

the greater the humiliation, the more victorious the dragon. Getting the attention off yourself is the secret to healthy erections, but this ruins the dragon's fun.

The impact of the arrogance dragon on your spiritual life

Many religions and spiritual paths point to the sin of pride as an obstacle to heaven, enlightenment, or ultimate liberation. Obviously, if you are self-absorbed it is difficult to focus on objectives that demand that you look at a much larger context. Your energy is taken up in defense maneuvers and protections for your fragile ego, and not much is left over for your search for meaning and spiritual growth.

The arrogance dragon has many methods for using spiritual interests to manipulate its own ends. Since most spiritual paths refer to a god or higher power, arrogance projects judgment and criticalness onto that power. The higher power becomes the critical parent whom it is important to defend against, please, or prove wrong. You must appear perfect even in the eyes of God, or God's representatives in the form of the local temple or church.

Better yet, you may in fact become one of these local representatives in order to hide even more completely. The arrogance dragon may shove you into the clergy or onto a spiritual path— not for enlightenment but for additional vanity. This is what is referred to as spiritual materialism. By practicing all the most difficult exercises and ascetic practices, you can prove that you are the best practitioner around.

Even better is the strategy of becoming a guru or cult leader for others. This way, you get the attention away from yourself and onto the sins of the followers. You become inaccessible to all but a select few. That is a great way to hide. However, the arrogance dragon likes to create public humiliation. Sooner or later this strategy backfires, and a big public scandal shames you. The dragon has its fun with you.

At times, the arrogance dragon takes on a different strategy to inflate your persona or surface personality. You become intellectually aloof from all spiritual "tripe" and the emotional weakness that you perceive in those with a spiritual interest. You turn into an arrogant skeptic who scathingly attacks spirituality or categorically dismisses this area of interest. You become above it all and aloof from any sort of need for a spiritual life. This offers you a temporary protection from the fear of the unknown or the mystery. When you adopt this strategy, you curiously make a god out of science and become devoted to the ritual and ceremony embodied therein. The dragon laughs uproariously at such hypocrisy and foolishness.

How to Slay the Arrogance Dragon

This is the important part: how to slay the dragon and live in freedom and happiness. Don't be surprised if you start to get sleepy at this point, or even put the book down and get interested in something else. Why? Because the arrogance dragon has a vested interest in remaining alive. The dragon is not going to roll over and die without a fight. It resorts to all sorts of ploys to distract you and lead you away from the trail. One of its favorite antics is to discourage you from paying attention to it or from doing anything to wipe it out. It makes you sleepy; makes you interested in something else; makes you feel depressed or discouraged; makes you afraid that you are wasting your time; makes you believe that you can't live without it; makes you rationalize and believe that it actually has some good traits and that it would be better to keep it. The dragon's arsenal of tricks is awesome, and it takes more than a little discipline to fight them. However, keep in mind that no matter how puny you feel in face of the dragon, you have resources that the dragon does not have. As in all the fairy tales, there are secret weapons that allow you to slay this dragon that appears to be much bigger and stronger than you are.

At this point, your path is blocked by the dragon at the narrowest spot between the canyon walls: there is no scaling the cliffs; no side path; no turning back; no tunneling underneath;

no way to jump over or avoid the dragon. The only way to transform the dragon is to face it down. That is secret number one.

Affirmations to Beat the Arrogance Dragon

> I am amazed at how accepting I have become of both myself and other people.
> I am equal to, not better or worse than, other people.
> I have become confident in my ability to let others see all of me, warts and all.
> I make friends easily.
> Others experience me as warm and open.
> I am proud of my accomplishments. I need not advertise my successes. They are seen by others naturally.
> I am happy to see how tolerant I have become of criticism. I learn from it.

Seven Weapons to Slay the Arrogance Dragon

> **Weapon one:** Realize that you are not the dragon.
> **Weapon two:** Admit that you are isolated.
> **Weapon three:** Show vulnerability.
> **Weapon four:** Pay attention to others.
> **Weapon five:** Let yourself be.
> **Weapon six:** Release judgment of yourself and others.
> **Weapon seven:** Be equal to others.

Weapon one: Realize that you are not the dragon.

The dragon is not who you are; it never was, and it never actually will be. It is a parasite that has been living with you. If you maintain this perspective, it helps you create some distance from the dragon—a distance you need in order to see it objectively. The key is to find that you can survive without the dragon.

Who is the you that is not judgmental, shy, isolated, or inflated? You have moments when none of these words apply to you. You are free and feel remarkably good. This is usually with close friends whom you completely trust. This is your essence-self expressing itself. All the pain and suffering is not necessary for you to be you. The true you is the person who is free of judgment.

Weapon two: Admit that you are isolated.

By its very definition, the arrogance dragon does not want you to admit that you are miserably lonely. This is just too humiliating to let anybody know. You have to appear as if everything is OK and that you don't really need anybody. However, this strategy only perpetuates your isolation. The only way out is the hard way: tell the truth. Getting some distance from the dragon can help you do this.

The truth might sound something like this: "The arrogance dragon has been making me lonely, isolated, and unhappy. I'm tired of being so separate. I want to get back to the self that is connected with others and feels OK about just being me. All this other paraphernalia I've been using to get attention—cars, clothes, haircuts, name dropping, and bragging—is failing to get me what I really want."

A part of recognizing loneliness is acknowledging the isolation of the small child within. This small child has sealed itself off from further pain and lives in a kind of limbo state outside of time. This lost child holds much life energy that is unavailable for everyday projects and relationships. The amount of energy held by this lost child may vary from person to person, yet the consequences of its isolation are always the same: diminished energy in the present; a sense of loss; depression; despair; and a feeling that a part of yourself is missing. This lost part of yourself wishes to be reclaimed, and it can be regained through a variety of powerful techniques. The services of a competent therapist or counselor can be invaluable here. Hypnosis, visualization, shamanic journeying, and journal work can bring this part of yourself back to the fold.

Weapon three: Show vulnerability.

Be refreshingly imperfect. This is the decision to say, "Yes, world, my zipper is down, and I'm OK, because I am not my zipper." However, admitting your imperfection has to be done gradually—at a pace that you can handle. One of the arrogance dragon's greatest tricks is to undermine your best efforts to transform it.

> Marty decided to work on his vulnerability and forced himself to go to Alcoholics Anonymous, a group dedicated to healing through public revelation. While there, he forced himself to spill his guts in front of many strangers. He felt a rush of shame and humiliation and decided never to go back again. Every time he thought of the experience, he cringed with embarrassment and rejected any experience that might be similar. The arrogance dragon won by getting him to ignore his natural pace, pushing him into a revealing, unsafe, public confession.

Revealing your imperfections is a process that needs to be very gradual. There was nothing wrong with Marty going to an AA meeting. The problem was that he pushed himself too fast to reveal his imperfections in front of everyone. He needed to attend a couple of meetings as an observer first. Then he could have introduced himself and said a word or two before fully opening up. Gradually, as he felt trust, he could have opened up more and more.

To beat the arrogance dragon, start with a trusted friend, relative, or therapist and become just a little more open with that person. Take a few risks and feel the sense of release it gives you. If you feel too much shame, you are going too fast. The experience has to feel good to you. The secret is that the dragon does not want you to feel good. So feeling a good release is an indication that you are transforming the dragon. The dragon will try to make you skeptical of these good feelings. The truth is that the good feeling of release comes from your true self and nowhere else.

When you discover that you survive the little revelations about yourself, you can graduate to larger and larger ones. These revelations will feel quite frightening to you, but other people will regard them as normal.

> Kathy was attracted to someone but was too frightened to ever mention it. She feared that revelation of her attraction might lead to rejection or vulnerability to criticism. Instead, she acted like she was not interested at all. She was engaged in a big charade. However, she decided to slay her dragon and took a risk that was very big for her. She told the person that she found him handsome. He responded warmly, as if what she said was not the revelation of the year but just a nice thing to say. Later, he told her that he had been aware that she was attracted to him all along but that he had not had the courage to respond. Kathy discovered that her efforts to hide her feelings had been ineffective.

The truth is that feelings of attraction are almost impossible to hide. The human body instinctively emits and picks up pheromones that tell the whole story. There is no hiding.

As you go through the experience of revealing yourself, you learn with some chagrin that you have not been so good at hiding your vulnerability after all. Often, people have seen right through your aloofness and have been remarkably kind to you anyway. You gradually learn that the world is not nearly as critical as you yourself have been. You learn that you can survive an opening up of the armor with which you surround yourself.

Weapon four: Pay attention to others.

If you are under the influence of the arrogance dragon, you tend to scrutinize others to check for clues about what they want from you. You are sensitive to the slightest criticisms or appearances of judgment. You assume that everyone in the world is judging you and has a way they want you to be. You think they want you to be perfect.

The truth is that people are mostly occupied with their own concerns and are not spending all of their energy noticing you. The revelation of this truth is bitter fruit because it means that you are not so darned important after all. However, it can also be a relief to you. Not everyone is your mother or older sister making your life miserable for your first twenty years. Not everyone is devoting their life to making you miserable.

Once you realize this, you can take an interest in people yourself. You can notice interesting things about them and ask them about themselves instead of waiting for them to come to you. You can recognize that they are vulnerable human beings, too. They may need a word of support or recognition from you so that they can relax and blossom. When you address a group of people, you can know that they have come to gain something for themselves, hoping you will deliver it to them. They are more interested in your information than in your slightly crooked nose or unmanageable hair. You can look to see how you can be of service to other people. You can pay attention and recognize them as fellow human beings who want your love and support no matter how gritty their facades. You can begin to love them, and you will be much less concerned with whether they are judging you or not.

Weapon five: Let yourself be.

This is easier said than done. As mentioned earlier, one of the most effective ways to accept yourself is to recognize your inner child. The hurt child inside has been beleaguered for a long time. This child has withdrawn, believing that it is unlovable and that the world is a frightening, cruel place. The inner child needs kindness and compassion shown it. That child needs recognition. Chances are that your inner child no longer trusts you because of the activities of the dragon.

A first effective step in learning to accept yourself is to find a therapist who functions at the adult stage in the world. This adult will have the capacity to nurture the child in you to the point that you can take over. During the course of this process, the arrogance dragon will do battle with the therapist as well as with your true self. If the therapist is strong, she or he will not succumb to the dragon's ploys. These ploys are what the therapist would call "resistance to change" or "resistance within the therapy process." Wanting to be your therapist's favorite or special client is all the work of the dragon. Being furious with the therapist for making you face your inflation and deflation swings is also the work of the dragon.

Weapon six: Release judgment of yourself and others.

It is very important that you not be harshly critical of yourself for the resistance you feel, the upsets you go through, and the confusion you face. Find a sense of humor. Realize that the suffering you feel is a result of the arrogance dragon's behavior. Notice it, then let yourself be. You can say, "Ah yes, I see the dragon has been having fun with me again. Well, it may have won the skirmish but it will not win the war. I am not the dragon."

As you gradually open up to others and look to see how you can serve them better, you will automatically release judgment of yourself. As you judge yourself less, you will also judge others less. The less you judge others, the more people will like you and give you positive feedback. You will get what you wanted all along: you will be liked for who you are. You will not be compared, and if you are compared you will care much less. You will be more secure about yourself and feel much greater confidence. You will be able to join the real world.

Weapon seven: Be equal to others.

As you look for the commonalities you share with others, you will learn respect. You have spent your life wanting respect and wanting to be valued for your performance and your productivity. However, this respect is not forthcoming until you respect others for who and what they are. Respecting others does not mean a diminishment of yourself. When you respect others, you earn their respect of you. When you respect yourself, it then becomes easier to respect others.

Learning equality can be a long, hard road. It means letting go of wanting to be special, letting go of wanting to be better than others, letting go of self-inflation and self-aggrandizing, letting go of machismo, letting go of bragging, letting go of name dropping, and letting go of all the petty little ways you bolster your sagging ego. However, it also means letting go of withdrawal, aloofness, distance, hiding, coolness, shyness, and all the ways you hide from being seen. It is not a crime to be shy or fearful of being seen. However, it is unfortunate to let these things rule your behavior.

Seven Exercises to Transform the Arrogance Dragon

Exercise one: Speak in public.
Exercise two: Take three social risks a day.
Exercise three: Get counseling.
Exercise four: Forgive the people who judged you.
Exercise five: Make a fool of yourself on purpose.
Exercise six: Review your embarrassments.
Exercise seven: Develop your weak side.

Exercise one: Speak in public.

People who suffer from subjugation by the dragon of arrogance are often terrified of public speaking because they are frightened of being seen. Therefore, it is a good idea to meet this fear head-on by enrolling in a public speaking course or by seeking opportunities to speak in public. This brings you face to face with your fears so that you can see them. Meet the dragon. Remember to start small in a safe environment. You can work up to larger, more risky groups.

> When I was a boy, I was so shy that I would hide in the bathroom when guests came to the house. In the Boy Scouts, I was encouraged to work toward a public speaking merit badge by entering a contest given by the Toast-

masters Club of America. No one forced me to do this, yet I considered it a major challenge. I somehow knew it was good for me. I went on to place third in a competition that involved speaking to a large audience. I was very nervous, but I survived and was helped by the experience. Now I speak regularly to large audiences, and although I still get nervous, I do an excellent job of it without dying from embarrassment.

Exercise two: Take three social risks a day.

You can start with one risk, if that feels safer: smile at someone; say hello to a clerk at the checkout counter of the supermarket; notice someone's earrings or tie; stoop to saying something trite or common—you do not have to say something earthshaking. Be an everyday, ordinary person who reaches out toward other people.

Exercise three: Get counseling.

As mentioned earlier, find a good counselor, preferably an adult acting as an adult, who can support and assist you in overcoming your shyness and self-centeredness to become an ordinary human being. Group work is especially recommended because it involves sharing with other people. You will not be able to hide.

Exercise four: Forgive the people who judged you.

Forgiveness is possible only after you become fairly neutral about your judges. The way you become neutral about those who have oppressed you is to first tell the truth about them. This involves tears, upset, getting furious at what they did to you, seeing that they did these things to you because they too were stuck, and finally forgiving them. Bear in mind that you can accomplish much of this without dealing directly with these bewildered people. You can accomplish this by proxy—that is, in your journal, in the form of letters that you burn, in your therapist's office, or in meditation that involves visualization. On some occasions, direct communication with those you need to forgive is necessary.

Exercise five: Make a fool of yourself on purpose.

Seek out opportunities to be uncool.

I had a therapist once who encouraged me to sing a song from a musical in front of a group. I was paired with a shy woman who sang the female part. We did a good job and had to survive a big applause. I lived.

There are many opportunities to be outrageous or act like a child. Costume parties provide a good opportunity. Allow yourself to be silly or ridiculous. Remember to go at your own speed because the dragon will grab any opportunity in which you are humiliated. Go slowly. Start with a silly hat or mustache. You can graduate to the whole costume in time.

Exercise six: Review your embarrassments.

Instead of trying to suppress embarrassments, review all the most embarrassing moments of your life. This is not to torture yourself but to face the dragon head-on. Go over the embarrassing moments detail by detail. What exactly is the shame involved in each memory? See that your inner child was scared to death about not surviving the event. Go back, in your mind's eye, and support that scared person (yourself) who is feeling so shamed. Find something amusing about the event if you can. When you can laugh, you have begun the healing process.

Exercise seven: Develop your weak side.

If you are possessed by the arrogance dragon, the chances are, if you are a highly mental person, that you are arrogantly intellectual. You think you are the smartest person around. For you, emotional people appear to be irrational and hysterical. Athletic types are dumb jocks.

If you are an emotional person, you may arrogantly think that feeling is the best way to respond. You may put other people down for being more intellectual or athletic.

If you are kinesthetic, you may pride yourself on your great coordination and skill as an athlete. You might judge mental types to be eggheads or nerds. For you, emotional types are hysterical.

A sure cure for any of this judgment is to put yourself in situations where you are forced to use the quality that you are weakest in: intellect, emotions, or athletics. You will learn humility in a hurry. However, watch out for the tendency to dive into total humiliation. That will just set you back. By slowly practicing a foreign talent, you will have the opportunity to see how the dragon inside of you operates.

> Ted was an arrogant, brainy type who was also quite good at sports. I encouraged him to enroll in an art class that required the exercise of his emotions. I also encouraged him to be willing to be the slow learner in the class. We both noticed the arrogance dragon going into overdrive trying to get him out of there and back to the safety of his intellect. The dragon gave him many good reasons to quit. It told him he was too smart to be wasting his time with these artsy types. He found himself judging everyone in the class, including the teacher. This alternated with his hating himself for being so slow and untalented. By sticking with this class, he was able to see the full repertoire of the arrogance dragon that infiltrated every part of his life. Later he was to say that this was the most enlightening experience he ever had. He was forced to confront his judgments of others as well as his own harsh criticism of himself. When he got past all this energy leakage, he actually began to enjoy his primitive efforts to apply color to canvas.

Conclusion

When the arrogance dragon takes possession of the personality, it introduces suffering and pain. With honesty, discipline, and focus of intention, you can oust the dragon and emerge an experienced, transformed knight—a person capable of loving yourself and others. You can be someone who has compassion for others caught in the same difficult trap, and you are uniquely able to offer assistance to those for whom the dragon still roars.

You need not buy into the games played by their dragons. Behind their aloof, arrogant, superior personae lie lonely and frightened individuals who are in terrible doubt about their value as human beings. You can help remind them of their true natures as noble and valuable people who are no better and no worse than others on the hero's journey.

Chapter Four

THE SELF-DEPRECATION DRAGON

Positive Pole—Humility
Negative Pole—Abasement

External manifestation

Having drooping shoulders and a tendency to breathe shallowly; groveling; deflated; mortified; humiliated; meek; servile; lonely; resigned; prostrated; disgraced; shamed; dishonored; chagrined; despised; intimidated; apologetic; penitent.

Internal manifestation

Self-accusatory; self-condemning; self-reproaching; self-conscious; feeling like a worm; feeling undeserved; self-punishing; disheartened.

Examples of situations and conditions that promote the self-deprecation dragon

Slavery; immigration; minority group status; students placed in slow-learner tracks; many women in patriarchal societies; low-paid social servants; refugees; members of clergy in monastic settings; followers of punitive religions focused on sin and hell;

poverty; homelessness; countries long subject to totalitarian rule such as Poland, Slovakia, and Romania; people interested in subjects laughed at by the media; nerd status; wimp status; most high school students not in the "in" crowd; anyone out of favor with the powers that be.

Not all people associated with these groups or situations are controlled by the self-deprecation dragon. These settings and situations simply make ripe conditions for this dragon's takeover.

Physical appearance and presentation

Self-deprecators tend to have stooped shoulders, caved-in chests, or the appearance of bad posture. Their heads are held forward, their eyes are hesitant or downward cast, their gaits are shuffling, and their voices are muffled or whisper-light. They may chew their lips or fingernails, pull at their hair, or pick at their skin. These habits may become more apparent when they are under stress. They can display very defensive attitudes, but crumble easily. In most people, these characteristics may not even be visible at times.

If you want to duplicate the feeling of someone with this dragon, try the following: Curve your shoulders forward to protect your chest. Look downward and chew your lower lip. Hold your arms or hands tightly over your solar plexus or your genitals. Get a defensive feeling. How would you feel trying to make contact with other people from this position?

The Development of Self-Deprecation

Expectations

Self-deprecation begins in a fashion similar to arrogance, with a few basic differences. For the self-deprecation dragon to take hold, children must face the high expectations of parents or guardians which are clearly unattainable. These parents are often idealists who have high standards and make their love conditional to meeting these high expectations. They expect their children to attain the highest marks in school, achieve the greatest results on the sport field, or play the piano like virtuosos at young ages. Often, these parents were themselves high achievers or even child prodigies, and they expect the same of their children. In some situations, the parents adhere to the rigid standards of their religions or cultural belief systems, and these children cannot possibly meet the standards set. It is almost impossible for children at age four to sit quietly without singing or giggling, or chatting at the dinner table. If these children are sent in disgrace from the table over and over, the stage is set for the self-deprecation dragon's entrance.

These children learn that no amount of striving will ever please their parents. These youngsters develop a dread of failing to pass the endless tests and measures of their adequacy. The result is constant apology. They begin to cringe and adopt an automatic penitent attitude because they already know in advance that they are going to fail. The fear of failure and then the certainty of it creates its own self-fulfilling prophecy. As the children believe in and expect failure, so they set up the experience of failure. Then they have the slight integrity-saving knowledge that they were right all along: "I knew I couldn't do it. At least I was right. I won't bother to try again." After thousands of such incidents, the dragon has nested securely within these children.

Learning to apologize

Children under the influence of the self-deprecation dragon develop the habit of qualifying everything they say or do with apologies or warnings about their incompetence. For example, when confronted with doing something new like riding a bicycle, these children might say something like, "I'm a real klutz; I'll probably fall on my face; here goes nothing." When forced to ask a question, they are likely to look at their feet and mumble, "Excuse me, I know I probably don't know what I'm talking

about, but could I ask you a question?" Often, these children are
so concerned with the demands being placed on them that they
cover their mouths with their hands, making what they say
impossible to understand. It is as if they are saying, "I know
what I have to say is unimportant and you will probably criticize
me for it anyway, so it's better if you don't hear it."

Learning to be small

These children adopt an orientation of smallness, as if they
are trying to hide from the world. Their heads are bowed and
their shoulders are wrapped forward and down as if they are trying to cover up their vulnerable hearts. Sometimes they tuck
their heads between their raised shoulders, almost like turtles
hiding their heads from possible attack. Steps forward are hesitant, and their arms and hands are used to cover up the vulnerable fronts of their bodies. A typical stance for them is to cross
one arm over the solar plexus and hold the other arm vertically
over the chest, hand on the chin or mouth. Often these children hold a hand over the throat to protect that area.

With the attempt to become small and the fear of being
attacked, there is a tendency for these children to reduce their
breathing to a shallow level. It is as if they are hiding from the
enemy behind bushes, so they hardly breathe to avoid detection.
When they are in this state all the time, their circulation is
impaired, their extremities get cold, and they look pale and
unhealthy. With restricted air intake, the oxygen to their brains
is reduced and they do not access memory or think well. This
adds to the impression that they are not very smart.

These children grow up into adults impaired by the dragon
of self-deprecation. They are timid about asserting themselves or
attempting new tasks, so they miss out on many life experiences.
When this condition is severe, they may avoid dating completely and live a solitary life of loneliness because they consider
themselves too ugly or too inadequate to attract anyone. They
fail to realize that it is not physical features that are attractive or
unattractive, but vitality level and energy.

Caroline's Story: A Tale of Self-Deprecation

Caroline was born the sixth of seven children in a large Catholic family. Although her parents were working-class Irish, they placed heavy demands on all the children to succeed in school and proceed into professional life. Caroline was neither the brightest nor the prettiest of her siblings, and although she achieved B's in school, she was overshadowed by the achievements of her older sister. She could sense the lack of enthusiasm that greeted her report cards and minor achievements in school. It was as if she constantly lived in the shadow of the sophistication of her siblings. The stage was set for the self-deprecation dragon to take over her personality.

Although Caroline was not beaten or mistreated physically, she was mostly ignored or given cursory attention. To make matters worse, Caroline attended a parochial school where she was taught that she was responsible for Jesus' suffering on the cross and that she was born with original sin. She took this to heart and despised herself for being such a terrible person. She felt that she did not have the right to feel good about herself in any way. In fact, she adopted the practice of doing penance daily for her sins. By bits and pieces, Caroline felt her self-esteem being chipped away until little was left.

After graduating from her all-girls Catholic high school, she was the only one in her family to enter junior college before attending the local university, a far cry from Harvard, where two of her brothers attended on scholarship. In addition, throughout her high school and early college years, Caroline felt too ugly and fat to date any boys, even though she was average looking and only mildly heavy.

By the time Caroline graduated from college, she had gained considerably more weight and adopted an apologetic demeanor. Her voice was so soft that people often asked her to repeat what she said. When introduced to people, she usually held her arms across her solar plexus as if hugging herself. Her posture was poor, and she almost never exercised.

Caroline had adopted the identity of an inadequate personality. She had long before given up attempting to compete with her siblings and had accepted the role of low achiever in the family. She actually began to fear success because it brought her only trifling interest from her family, which was more painful than not succeeding at all.

In school, Caroline had demonstrated promise working with children and the mentally handicapped. She was encouraged by a school counselor to attend graduate school in social work, advice that she followed to earn her master's degree in that field. She was able to find work in a local hospital under a domineering boss who made her life miserable and used her as a scapegoat. Caroline disliked the treatment but felt that she deserved it and seldom complained.

During this time, she met and married an engineer who was devoted to his work but who knew little about intimacy and was quite emotionally immature. Caroline's married life was lonely until two children were born, to whom she devoted herself entirely. All was well until the children grew old enough to perceive her low self-esteem and began to use it against her. The children became disrespectful and sided with their father against her regularly. Caroline felt helpless against this onslaught and often cried herself to sleep at night. The dragon of self-deprecation was firmly in control of Caroline's life.

When Caroline was thirty-three-years old, a crisis drove her into psychotherapy. Her two high-achieving brothers, one a successful businessman and the other a lawyer, were killed in a plane crash on their way to complete a major real estate acquisition. Caroline was thrown into major grief and confusion. She felt that she should have been the one to die in the crash, not these men with such promise. On the other hand, she felt worried that, rather than grieving for her brothers, she actually felt that they deserved what they got. This made her feel so uncomfortable that she actually thought of killing herself. She did not try, however, because she was certain that she would bungle the job.

Thus began for Caroline a major breakthrough that proved to be a terrible setback for the dragon. Over a period of two years, Caroline worked hard on her self-esteem in counseling. At times her sense of personal failure was so profound that I, her therapist, driven to the wall with her discouragement, felt like giving up, too. Nevertheless, we both persisted, and Caroline began to recognize the rage within her at the lack of attention and faith of her family. She saw that the family had a script for her entitled, "reject" or "she who will bungle everything she does." Even worse, she saw that she had bought into this script and was faithfully playing it out. Her rage swung precipitously from members of her family to herself. Her terrible guilt at feeling so angry often played right into the dragon's claws. The dragon enjoyed her guilt and actively promoted her mood swings.

Caroline continued to battle and eventually accepted responsibility for her decisions in life. Between bouts of rage and grief for her lost years, Caroline began to emerge as a real person with wishes and wants of her own. Naturally, this put a strain on her unsatisfactory marriage, and it came near to dissolution. Eventually her husband entered into counseling, and the rocky marriage began to improve as he learned to tolerate intimacy and she learned to speak up. Caroline began to assert herself with her children, who at first resisted but eventually responded favorably to her new strength. She began to dress in a more attractive style, had her hair done, and took herself to Hawaii, the first vacation she had had in years. She quit her position at the hospital, interviewed for a much better position, and got it.

Eventually Caroline was able to grieve for her lost brothers, but not until the rage was out. Dealing with her family was not easy because the family was still invested in her old identity, the "reject." The dragon tried hard to regain a foothold in this territory, but because Caroline was a fighter, it was not successful. There were rough times of misunderstandings and hurt feelings, but eventually Caroline achieved an improved relationship with her father and a more tolerable one with her mother. The main success was a newfound friendship with her older sister, a relationship that had not been good in the past.

Caroline finds that the work of fighting the dragon has not ended. She occasionally finds herself apologizing before saying something and has to remind herself to get exercise. She often needs support and encouragement to buy herself something nice and to be kind to herself. But the long battle actually broke the dragon's back, and although the dragon still tries to bite, Caroline has the upper hand.

The Seven Steps of Development for the Self-Deprecation Dragon

The dragon of self-deprecation finds a foothold in the personality and comes to live there in seven steps. These steps do not always develop linearly, but rather in bits and pieces, here and there.

Step one: The children learn that love in the home is conditional.

Step two: The children fear being inadequate.

Step three: The children learn to apologize for everything.

Step four: The children learn to make themselves small.

Step five: The children learn that they can be right about being losers.

Step six: The children learn to criticize themselves.

Step seven: The children learn to avoid success at all costs.

Step one: The children learn that love in the home is conditional.

The children are faced with parental expectations that are too high.

Belief and decision: "I'm not loved for who I am."

This atmosphere of conditional love is similar to the atmosphere in the homes of children who develop the arrogance dragon. The children feel that somehow they are not valuable enough in and of themselves, and that there are hoops to jump through to gain acceptance and love.

Step two: The children fear being inadequate.

Somehow these children cannot discover how to please their parents. They don't know how to fix the problem of "underachieving," and the fear builds that they will never meet the requirements for love.

Belief and decision: "I'm inadequate."

In this step, the difference between the development of the arrogance dragon and the self-deprecation dragon begins to emerge. Children developing the arrogance dragon learn strategies to hide their feelings of inadequacy and to present a false front. Children developing a nest for the self-deprecation dragon take a different tack: rather than trying to please by succeeding, they tend to give up. They identify with being inadequate.

Step three: The children apologize for everything.

Children under the influence of the self-deprecation dragon develop a system of apologizing to warn others and ward off their high expectations. They learn to survive by wiping out any anticipation that they might perform well, and they try to eliminate others' disappointment before it can get started. They tell self-deprecatory jokes, point to their limitations first, and qualify everything they say.

These children experience a feeling of inadequacy and, rather than hide it, they learn to advertise it. They dramatize their inadequacy and later in life show up with dirty hair, slumped shoulders, downcast eyes, and a shuffling gait. They actually indulge the self-deprecation dragon. Anyone who has tried to convince people with serious self-deprecation that they are worthwhile human beings can testify to how tenaciously these people cling to their identities as self-trashers.

I once tried to cure a child of ten of the habit of saying "I'm sorry" literally hundreds of times a day. This was a very difficult task, and the only thing that finally worked was a reward system

that promised her movies and other treats for "sorry"-free minutes, hours, and then days. Just removing the "sorry" habit
helped a great deal, but there was more work to do to improve
her self-esteem.

Belief and decision: "Always apologize before doing or saying
anything."

Step four: The children learn to make themselves small.

To avoid negative attention or criticism, these children
physically and psychically pull in their energy. They learn to
breathe shallowly as if they are avoiding detection by hiding.
Their heads shrink down toward their shoulders, their eyes look
down, and their shoulders curve over and downward. They
often fold their arms across their solar plexuses in a protective
gesture. Their voices get small and they learn to slip silently
into or out of rooms without being noticed. They learn to
become invisible.

This is the step responsible for the physical manifestations
of the self-deprecation dragon. Not only do these people learn
to cringe and mumble but they also develop strategies to hide
behind other people in photographs and at social events. They
hide so well that others cannot even remember if they were at
parties or meetings.

Belief and decision: "If I'm small, nobody will expect anything
from me."

Step five: The children learn that they can be right about being losers.

These children learn that they can cling to a small sense of
self-esteem by at least being right about themselves as losers.
The idea as they see it is to be inadequate before someone else
accuses them of it. In fact, they come to the conclusion, "I
won't even try to win. I'll predict that I'll lose or that I can't do
it ahead of time." That way, the children can at least say, "I
knew it all along."

This is a deadly step because the children get rewarded

internally by the dragon for being losers. The self-deprecation dragon settles in for a prolonged stay. The dragon can now give the children good reasons for not giving up their losers' attitudes. This begins a downward, negative spiral because the children actually search for ways to hide, to be mediocre, and to veer away from leadership.

Belief and decision: "I can't do it, and I'll predict that ahead of time. At least I can be right about that."

Step six: The children learn to criticize themselves.

For children affected by the self-deprecation dragon, self-talk becomes a constant put-down: "Stupid, stupid, stupid. Can't I do anything right? I should never have been born. I'm such an idiot."

The children's identity forms around the concept of being inadequate. Once this occurs, the children no longer need their parents or guardians to disapprove of them. They can now carry the whole operation within themselves wherever they go. They have their own private little put-down machine. They can be around the most loving people in the world but it will not necessarily cause them to stop the self-criticism. The self-deprecation dragon is firmly in place.

Belief and decision: "If I can't beat them, I'll join them at being critical. I despise me, too."

Step seven: The children learn to avoid success at all costs.

Success means raising other people's expectations and then being sure to fail them the next time. If these children succeed, they will have to go through the discomfort of feeling inadequate again because they cannot keep up the success. They decide it is best not to start.

This is the famous fear-of-success syndrome so common in the population at large. These children fear that one success will cause their parents to expect ever more difficult tasks at which they will surely fail. So their reasoning goes, "Why walk into a lion's mouth and feel like a failure for sure tomorrow? I'd better

get the whole thing out of the way now. I'll dash the expectations before they ruin me. At least this way I'll have some control over the whole situation."
Belief and decision: "Don't succeed."

The Self-Deprecation Dragon's Big Lie

The self-deprecation dragon wants people to believe that
they are actually winning by perpetuating their inadequate personas. The dragon tells them that the more they apologize and
cringe the better off they will be. It exhorts them to avoid pain
and to seek solace in hibernation and disappearance. Of course,
unless they are prisoners of war, such a strategy is disastrous in
the long run because it perpetuates itself. The people end up ful-
filling the expectations of inadequacy over and over again until
the main consequence is depression. Those who possess this
unpleasant dragon live their lives in either mild or severe
depression because they feel so hopeless and defeated. Instead of
winning through self-deprecation, the reality is that the whole
experience is a net loss. The truth is that there are no saving
graces to this dragon, and the affected people always know this
at a deep level.

The depression that accompanies this dragon is insidious
because it can hide for long periods of time. The affected people
can lead fairly ordinary lives with only modest manifestations of
self-deprecation. However, when the structures that prop up
their self-esteem fail, depression can suddenly rear its gloomy
head. This often happens to people who retire and lose the
sense of adequacy that their jobs gave them. The same may be
true for parents whose children leave home or for people who
are recently widowed or divorced. What was once a light modesty becomes a full-blown case of dragon-fed self-deprecation.

The Great Dragon Exchange: Sliding from Self-Deprecation to Arrogance

Inside every self-deprecator is an arrogant voice that feels it has the right to comment negatively about everything the personality does. This voice comes unbidden—at any time of day or night, in any social situation. This voice is the alter ego of the self-deprecation dragon, the arrogance dragon. The arrogance dragon has a chapter devoted exclusively to it, something it finds disagreeable, because all dragons like to hide in their lairs most of the time.

Because the self-deprecation dragon shares certain developmental features with the arrogance dragon, there are characteristics common to people with both of these dragons. For example, both sets of people share the feature of self-consciousness because both feel from a young age that they are being scrutinized, watched, and compared by their elders. Later in life, this turns into a kind of exaggerated sense of self-importance, as if everyone were interested in judging them. Self-deprecators have this arrogance hidden underneath layers of unnecessary humility. In addition, the dragon of self-deprecation often makes people bigoted, prejudiced, racist, sexist, and ageist.

Twenty-year-old Jonathon, a college student, was my client for a two-year period. His self-deprecation was blatant and relentless, and the going was very difficult for both of us. The first months in therapy were spent bolstering his badly eroded self-esteem. Later came the tricky, deeper work of helping him see that his inner judge had an exceptionally arrogant attitude. He was so used to identifying with his inadequacy that it was hard for him to see how successful and supercilious his inner critic was. This inner critic sounded somewhat like his older sister and his mother, who were rather arrogant, yet he carried them around with him everywhere he went. The problem was that he did not want to take responsibility for feeding this voice every day. When he finally saw that his part in the inner dialogue included both sides, he was shocked. He began to see other indirect ways that arrogance showed up in him. When he saw someone else with more inadequacy than he saw in himself, he would become ruthlessly critical of them. He had to admit that his bigotry toward fat women and minority groups was a sign of his inner arrogance. True healing of his self-esteem began at this point in therapy.

Amazing Inadequacy: The Sly Dragon of Self-Deprecation

Self-deprecators can get into competitions over who is more inadequate. Therefore, they secretly pride themselves on their less-than-important status. In historic China, the self-deprecation dragon infiltrated the deepest fabric of society and culture. Visitors to the emperor competed to see who could bow the lowest and hurl the most lowly insults at themselves in the emperor's presence. After prostrating themselves on the floor several times, the visitors might say, "Please excuse this lowly worm of a person who is no more than the dung of an ass, and permit this idiot to ask a foolish question of his most royal highness."

With the advent of Christianity, the self-deprecation dragon saw an opportunity to imbed itself into the spiritual practices of that religion. The dragon twisted the teachings of Jesus over the years, and people were taught to doubt themselves and feel badly about their very existence. Church dogma taught that people were born sinful and, without cleansing by the church, they could never be saved. People were encouraged to recount their sins, often confessing their inadequacies in public in order to gain greater merit in the eyes of the community, the church, or God.

People came to equate salvation with self-deprecation, and generations of humans were imprinted with low self-worth from early childhood. The result was a strange, upside-down philosophy. Only by feeling worthless as human beings, and totally inadequate next to God's perfection, could people expect to be loved by God. Only a sly dragon could come up with such an amazing untruth and get away with it.

The self-deprecation dragon was hard at work in other arenas as well. In some parts of the world, where people were believed to be born sinful, children came to be seen as animals, not yet quite human beings. In eighteenth- and nineteenth-century England, this philosophy was carried to the extreme. Children were abused physically, sexually, and in almost every way imaginable. This treatment ensured deep feelings of inadequacy in those adults who survived childhood. Many of these children became self-destructive, and the self-deprecation dragon was having a heyday.

Stages of Maturity and the Self-Deprecation Dragon

Infant stage: cringing savage
Toddler stage: pawn
Child stage: phobic about age and appearance
Adolescent stage: social misfit; misunderstood
Adult stage: low confidence

Self-deprecation at the infant stage

Self-deprecation is the most blatant at the infant stage because there is no insight and no sophistication at this level of development. Infant self-deprecation shows up in crude forms such as shabby appearance, dirty clothes, unwashed hair, downcast eyes, inaudible expression, and a slow shuffle. Adults manifesting at the infant stage are not noble indigenous natives but cringing savages with no self-esteem. They are the slaves who feel worthless and are willing to do anything to demonstrate their inadequacy. They are the natives who readily overthrow their own rich culture to grovel at the feet of invaders for a few trinkets. They are the people who take up with drug addicts because they feel they have no other worth.

Self-deprecation at the toddler stage

Adults acting as toddlers demonstrate their inadequacy in mundane and petty ways. They seek out religions that exhort them to grovel, and they do so without question. They readily follow the orders of authorities like physicians, gurus, local bosses, ministers, and political officials because they feel they know little compared to these honored, credentialed people. They readily accept human indignities and social inequity because these are, after all, "what they deserve." When asked if they feel it is unfair that the nobility has all the money and privilege and they have nothing, they simply shrug and say, "That is how it should be."

The self-deprecation dragon can take on other forms at the toddler level as well. These adult toddlers are the natives whose self-worth is so low that they readily join the invaders and oppress their own people for a little reward. They are the welfare recipients who make no effort to become self-sufficient, or the overworked housewives who accept their drunk husbands' beatings because they feel they deserve nothing better. They are the women who know their place and accept low pay because, after all, "men are superior," in their belief system. The main quality in this kind of self-deprecation is a lack of questioning—an agreement that abuse and low station in life are acceptable because they are deserved.

Self-deprecation at the child stage

The self-deprecation dragon does not have a strong clawhold in people fixated at the child stage because typically they are much more oriented toward the arrogance dragon. Nevertheless, adult children affected by this dragon are, for example, the starlets who allow their bodies to be shamelessly exploited for a movie contract opportunity. They are the self-loathing business executives who drink away discomfort at the end of each day. They are the deeply depressed athletes who fail to win a medal at the Olympics, or the self-flagellating stockbrokers who lose badly in the market.

Self-derogatory jokes, and references to baldness, weight, short stature, breast size, penis size, and beaked noses all demonstrate the presence of the self-deprecation dragon in adults fixated at the child level. Self-deprecation reflects the concern about demonstrating competence in a wildly competitive culture in which very few can shine as stars in the public eye. Without the self-deprecation dragon there would be no market for deodorants, breath fresheners, room sprays, breast implants, plastic surgery, expensive coffins, hair dyes, and dozens of products advertised to make people feel more acceptable in a culture demanding perfection.

One of the most significant manifestations of the self-deprecation dragon in this group of people is their preoccupation with aging and their fear of death. Since, to the child death is unthinkable and also scary, these adult children do anything to ward off the slightest sign of age. They feel very badly about wrinkles and skin blotches and graying hair. They can be heard to lament, "I'm too old to find a man now; no one will look my way." This fear of inadequacy that comes with age can be so strong that these people refuse to look in mirrors any more. The main manifestations of the self-deprecation dragon in adult children are concerns about not winning or a loss of the ability to compete.

Self-deprecation at the adolescent stage

The self-deprecation dragon is rampant at the adolescent stage. This is the level at which the dragon revels because it has so much opportunity to take over. Adolescents are between children and adults and are therefore in a highly vulnerable place when it comes to self-esteem. Adolescents know enough to know that they don't know what they are doing much of the time. Many of their experiments with dating and interfacing with the adult world go awry, and they are by definition unsure of themselves. Add to this acne and awkward bodies with raging hormones and the stage is set. Adults fixated as adolescents are extremely vulnerable to this dragon because they live their lives as if they were adolescents.

These folks often feel misunderstood by their families of origin for good reason: their parents may be fixated at earlier levels yet. How can a father fixated at the toddler stage understand his son fixated at the adolescent stage? So these people grow up feeling like there is something wrong with their feelings and questions. They identify with the unfairly treated members of society and suffer the self-deprecation that they see there. Sometimes they suffer much more than the people who actually exist at those levels.

These adult adolescents often accept poor pay for social service work, or they just can't seem to find a way to make money that makes them feel good. They feel inadequate because they see everyone else in their undergraduate peer group making a killing while they, with their master's degrees, are underemployed or unemployed. They rush around seeking answers to the meaning of life and often spend their hard-earned money on gurus, psychiatrists, and self-styled teachers who know less than they do. They simply do not feel they know anything valid.

One of the ways that the self-deprecation dragon manipulates adult adolescents is by causing them to doubt their sanity. Some of these highly intelligent, capable people allow themselves to be drugged and hospitalized because they feel so powerless and incompetent.

Self-deprecation at the adult stage

Adults function at more sophisticated levels. Therefore, the self-deprecation dragon has to grow more subtle to survive within their more discerning personalities. Self-deprecation at this stage does not take the form of the blatant outcast with unwashed hair, ragged clothes, and urine-soaked pants. Rather, it is quiet and masks itself as simple humility with the occasional self-deprecatory remark. Nonetheless, it is insidious because it quietly causes people to breathe less deeply, effectively diminishing their opportunity to feel heightened feelings and even ecstasy.

Quiet self-deprecation subtly reduces the opportunities for these highly capable people to participate at an effective level in the world. It diminishes their contribution to society. It undermines their self-confidence and causes them to allow other less-capable people to step into positions of authority. Many of these adults, lacking confidence, do not believe they are capable of leadership or speaking out. Feeling inarticulate or stupid, they allow loud, egotistical types fixated at the child level to dictate the rules. Then they beat themselves up quietly for being such cowards as to allow these follies. This is actually the chief scenario in the world today. Many of those with the most developed value systems lack the confidence to take up the responsibility of leadership. In this way, the self-deprecation dragon keeps the world subjugated and anchored to a more primitive consciousness.

How the Self-Deprecation Dragon Affects Your Life

The impact of the self-deprecation dragon on health

Self-deprecation reduces the deep, even breathing so vital to sustaining a healthy body. With diminished oxygen, cells literally starve and die, depleting the immune system and paving the way for infection and disease. Low self-esteem is the cause of more illness and hospitalization than any other source. Aside from exposure to toxic materials and grief over loss, battered self-esteem is perhaps the leading cause of cancer formation.

Most physicians would agree that feeling good about yourself is vital to rapid healing and remaining healthy. Self-deprecation reduces your will to live, saps your vitality, and robs your life of meaning, making you much more vulnerable to illness and even death.

Perhaps most significantly, self-deprecation causes you to neglect the care and hygiene of your own body. Your attitude may be, "Why take care of this piece of crap?" You may eat poorly, drink too much, neglect the care of your teeth, and neglect medical treatment in time to avoid catastrophic illness. Feelings of self-hatred and loathing tend to result in brittle hair, picked-at skin, rotten teeth, bent posture, and dull vacant eyes. The self-deprecation dragon is just as hard on the human body as are the dragons of greed and self-destruction.

The impact of the self-deprecation dragon on creativity

Tremendous creative energy is squandered during bouts of depression and self-loathing. To accomplish anything in life, even to make a simple breakfast, requires the expression of your creative energy. Even trashing yourself is a creative act, albeit a destructive one, not unlike cancer.

On the other hand, creativity flows into constructive patterns with the building of confidence. This is not because there is more creativity, but because the form it takes is pleasure-producing and satisfying when the self-deprecation dragon is erased. The self-deprecation dragon feeds off your creative energy and uses it for its own nefarious purposes. The question is, who is benefiting from the creativity, the dragon or you? With the dragon in charge, you become the victim of the dragon's manipulations.

Imagine an actor or actress who is about to play the role of someone who is a loser in life, someone who feels grossly inadequate. The actor must memorize the script, get into the character, and rehearse regularly in order to portray the loser character in a convincing fashion. Playing the loser is just as challenging as playing any other character in the story, perhaps even harder. When you struggle with self-deprecation, it is no different than that actor. The challenge is the same and the creative energy expended is the same. To be a nonconfident, inadequate person is a hard act to carry off. To maintain a loser's identity is an Academy Award-winning proposition.

The impact of the self-deprecation dragon on your presence

As with the arrogance dragon, the self-deprecation dragon drives you out of the present moment and displaces your life energy into the past and future. When you feel badly about yourself, you spend much time remembering former failures and prior fears. This leads to an avoidance of present experiences. Faced with a spontaneous choice or circumstance, you retreat into the past and have no energy left for responding to the present event.

Likewise, when the self-deprecation dragon rears its ugly head, you anticipate the pain of future failure and promptly give up on your present circumstances. This future orientation also robs you of the power inherent in responding in the present moment.

When you are busy with apologies and plagued with self-doubt, there is literally no one home to experience the event. When you are complimented, you may respond mechanically, automatically rejecting the compliment without any thought on the matter. Your eyes may glaze over and you may literally not hear the compliment. You have shielded yourself from the experience so well that the person administering the compliment feels abandoned and not heard.

I have worked with many people in group therapy settings on this very phenomenon. People receiving compliments are asked to repeat what they heard. Nine times out of ten, they cannot repeat the compliments accurately, if at all. The compliments are given again and the people are again asked to repeat them. Amazing to other members of the group who heard the compliments clearly, the people receiving the compliments are still not able to repeat them accurately. Sometimes the compliments have to be repeated many times before people get them. When they do get them, they almost always experience fear rather than pleasure—almost as if, just by listening, they are doing something they will get in trouble for. They are waiting for the other shoe to drop.

On the other hand, the people giving the compliments report how exhausting it is to try to get the messages across. They feel unheard and unseen until the other people finally acknowledge the compliments. This is an exercise in being present for experiences, and having the courage to stay there.

The impact of the self-deprecation dragon on relationships

The self-deprecation dragon is devastating on relationships. Self-esteem is the glue that holds relationships together, and without it relationships are profoundly hard to develop and harder yet to keep. Because this dragon destroys confidence, if you are dominated by it you are often passive, afraid to make any decision or take any action that could succeed. Your actions are frequently half-hearted or you do not carry through. If you suffer from passivity in relationships, you most likely carry the self-deprecation dragon. Because this dragon blocks inspiration, you lack the inspiration to live up to your potential in relationships. The self-deprecation dragon prevents many relationships from ever getting started in the first place.

John feels totally inadequate to call Sue. He feels he may never call Sue, and there will be no relationship. However, when he does have the courage to call her, he still has to cope with his fear of inadequacy and his expectation that he is going to botch the relationship anyway.

When John and Sue do get together, at first Sue finds John's self-deprecation kind of sweet and disarming. She seems to feel closer to him because he is unlike the other men she has known who have been arrogant and self-serving. However, after a while the charm of his feelings of inadequacy begins to wear out. Sue attempts to bolster his confidence by encouraging him to try new things and take advantage of opportunities. She supports him in his relationship with her by giving him constant encouragement and trying to make it easier for him to take charge of the relationship. Several years down the road, the relationship looks very different indeed. Sue is sick and tired of bolstering John's confidence and finds that no matter what she says or does, she has no impact on John's self-esteem. She has lost respect for him and is tired of bearing the responsibility for the relationship. She wants some relief and equality for a change, desiring an equal rather than a child. Sue decides to leave John, who uses her abandonment as proof that he is totally inadequate.

Following are some other examples of the ways the self-deprecation dragon interferes with relationships: A young man feels inadequate to stand up to his tyrannical father; he caves into his father's demands that he go into business instead of becoming a minister. A woman fails to report a man who has raped her because she feels too inadequate; she somehow feels that she must have deserved it, even though she did nothing to encourage it. A student fails to tell anyone that bullies are destroying his homework and threatening him after school. A young woman marries a confident-appearing man for security instead of following a career in medicine for which she has much talent, but no confidence.

The impact of the self-deprecation dragon on your spiritual life

Whatever your religion or spiritual practice, the self-deprecation dragon uses it to try to destroy you. This may sound dramatic, but it is simply true. Because spiritual orientation is so personal and emotional in nature, it is a perfect playground for this sneaky dragon. Whether you consider God to be the Great Spirit, Atman, Allah, God the Father, Jesus Christ, the Holy Spirit, Yahweh, nature, the tao, the gods, or the Goddess, you feel inadequate in relationship to your spiritual entity if you listen to the self-deprecation dragon. The dragon makes you feel that you are not worth saving, not worth attention, not acceptable, not worthy, a failure. You then readily adopt an identity as a hopelessly inadequate sinner or incompetent who will fail in your spiritual quest. If you believe in reincarnation, you may feel that you will never get out of the circle of lives you are in and will probably fail to graduate. You may even believe you are headed for being an insect in your next life because you are failing so abysmally in this one.

The outcome of all this is deadly because it can cause you to give up on yourself and settle for hell, oblivion, insecthood, or whatever you believe. This spiral has been historically called "despair," and leads to terrible suffering. Luckily, the mystic sects of most religions correctly see despair as a difficult but passable step in the spiritual path. That is, they acknowledge that the dragon can be defeated.

Almost all religions suggest that if you ask for help spiritually, you will receive it in one form or another. However, if you feel totally worthless, you are unlikely to even ask for help. In this way, the self-deprecation dragon maintains control and creates the illusion that it is the master.

To make matters more complicated, the dragon often adopts the colors and forms of religious beliefs and camouflages itself within them. For Christians, the self-deprecation dragon may masquerade as humility or meekness. It may warn of the dangers of vanity or selfishness. For Buddhists and ascetics, it may warn of the dangers of ego and exhort you to move away from your natural talents or abilities. The dragon, appearing to work in the service of spirituality, undermines, confuses, and wreaks havoc on aspirants. Only the wise searcher understands when a given action is truly a deterrent on the spiritual path and when it is an asset. That is why advanced spiritual teachers are so hard to understand. They speak in paradoxes.

How to Slay the Self-Deprecation Dragon

No dragon likes to be seen, and all seven dragons resist efforts to root them out of their comfortable nests. The self-deprecation dragon is no exception, and it will try to go underground when you face it down. This dragon looks like it has no power and it does not make a splashy appearance. Yet it is insidious and lurks in dark corners and unobstrusive doorways of your psyche. Nevertheless, this dragon can be brought into the light and transformed.

There is no way to overcome the debilitating effects of the dragon without calling its name and meeting it head on, in that narrow section of your path between the canyon walls. When you call the dragon's name, you can do so with courage, knowing you are about to engage in battle with the most worthy opponent you have ever known.

Affirmations to Beat the Self-Deprecation Dragon

I am amazed at the success I experience in everything I do.

I experience great confidence in my ability to handle all the challenges with which life presents me.

I find it easy to receive compliments and praise.

I know that people like me and want to spend time with me.

When I fail, I learn something valuable about how to succeed.

I am adequate to meet any experience in life.

I am a lovable person, and I know I make an important contribution to the world.

Seven Weapons to Slay the Self-Deprecation Dragon

Weapon one: Recognize that you are not the self-deprecation dragon.

Weapon two: Acknowledge that you are afraid of being inadequate.

Weapon three: Be willing to be successful.

Weapon four: Ruthlessly eliminate apologies.

Weapon five: Expand yourself at every opportunity.

Weapon six: Validate yourself at all times.

Weapon seven: Give up the reward of being right about being a failure.

**Weapon one: Recognize that you are not
the self-deprecation dragon.**

This dragon is a parasite living on your sacred life energy, depleting it day by day. You can live without this dragon, but it cannot continue to live without you. That should tell you who is truly in charge here. You can live happily without the dragon and retain your identity, but you will have to give up the questionable entertainment it affords you.

Weapon two: Acknowledge that you are afraid of being inadequate.

Recognize your belief in your own inadequacy. Admit that your fear of inadequacy has caused you to underperform and to avoid situations in which you could excel.

There is a lost child left in limbo many years ago within yourself. This child holds a great deal of your energy. Because of the fear of not being able to perform, this child split off and went into hiding outside of time. To this inner child, no time has actually passed. The conditions that caused the fear feel present and real. This part of yourself must be contacted, retrieved, and rejoined for healing to occur. As long as your lost child remains apart, the dragon has power over you. Believe it or not, the dragon is terrified of the liberation of that child.

Weapon three: Be willing to be successful.

Being successful, of course, requires taking risks. Risk-taking strikes fear in the heart of the self-deprecation dragon because it senses that risks will lead to its death knell, and it is quite right about this. The self-deprecation dragon flourishes by keeping the status quo. It wants you to keep out of sight, not try anything new, definitely succeed at nothing but failure, and apologize heavily for your existence. If you struggle with self-deprecation, a mild success is a big risk. The dragon, of course, uses the strategy of getting you to take risks that are too big, making sure you fail so you will give up and not try again to succeed. So take little risks, not big ones, at first.

Weapon four: Ruthlessly eliminate apologies.

Stop apologizing and eliminate constant qualifiers from your vocabulary and conversation. When you are afflicted with this dragon, apologies become habitual and obsessive. Therefore, you may have to undergo some kind of self-imposed behavior-modification program to help you break the habit. Hypnosis is also a useful tool for this. Of course, just eliminating self-apologies will not raise your self-esteem to astronomical heights but certainly it will raise it from rock bottom. One method for eradicating this habit is to keep track of how many times you actually apologize. Keep a notebook with you and mark every time you hear yourself say something that sounds like an apology.

Just becoming conscious of the apology problem will begin the process of healing. However, you must beware of the dragon's strategy for defeating you at this game. Chances are, as you notice the number of times you apologize and how hard it is for you to stop, you will feel terribly inadequate and trash yourself for being so inadequate as to be unable to stop apologizing. This, of course, will defeat you. The dragon will win by turning your anger against yourself. It is important for you to be patient with yourself and validate yourself for being willing to face this menace. The anger needs to be turned outward at the dragon, not inward toward yourself.

Weapon five: Expand yourself at every opportunity.

It is important that you breathe more deeply and more often than you are used to. Aerobics are a help, yoga and deep-tissue massage can assist enormously. Watch out for the self-deprecation dragon's trick of causing you an injury when you try any of these techniques.

If you have endured twenty-five years of shallow breathing, you may need some outside help getting your body to tolerate deeper breaths. Your ribs may have become immobilized by muscles that have rigidified. They can be loosened with deep-tissue massage. When you breathe more deeply, you will feel more, and if you have been under the influence of the self-deprecation dragon for years, you will most likely feel fear and then sadness. Facing your fear by feeling it is your only hope of success at defeating this dragon.

There are numerous ways to expand yourself in addition to deepening your breathing. Stretching your entire body is excellent if you are a self-deprecator. Public speaking, that kiss of death, is also highly recommended, as well as all manner of public activity that can bring you recognition and validation.

Remember that the dragon, not wanting to die, will fight you every step of the way. The dragon does not want you to expand. It will throw fear into your face, and if that fails to daunt you, the dragon will try to convince you that expanding will hurt you. It may even try the ploy of warning you that if you expand you are flirting with the sin of pride. "After all," the dragon says, "Who do you think you are anyway, trying to be better than you are, a lowly sinful worm?" Or, it says, "Thinking of yourself too highly is selfish and therefore sinful. Besides, you are just being like one of those selfish yuppies of the *me* generation, overconcerned with yourself." Perhaps you've heard these ploys or you have your own versions. Erase them!

Weapon six: Validate yourself at all times.

Validate yourself! Break the habit of putting yourself down. If you monitor yourself, you will find a quiet voice within you that carries out a monologue of criticism. This voice has comments about everything you do. It is amazingly opinionated and seems to feel that it has the right to comment about everything and anything you think, do, or feel (notice the hidden arrogance of this voice). This voice must be ignored and eventually silenced because it is the voice of the dragon. To accomplish this, you must adopt countermeasures that poke and prod the dragon.

Consider that, despite endless research in Western psychology demonstrating without question that animals and people respond to love and praise more than to punishment, you persist in criticizing yourself mercilessly in the vague hope that it will somehow make you a better person. This is poison. You can see its negative effect on pets and small children who wilt under attacks of criticism or disapproval. A good rule of thumb is to treat yourself at least as well as you treat your favorite pet.

Chances are that you are one of many people who generally lives your life in a way that does not harm other people by maiming or killing them. In fact, if the rest of the world lived their lives as you do, there would be a great reduction in carnage, rape, murder, and destruction of all kinds. That actually makes you a role model for many people of the world. Let yourself feel good about that. As an adult in a kindergarten, you are a role model for children no matter how inadequate you feel. Be aware of this position of responsibility. It is not always what you do in the world that counts, it is how you are that makes a difference.

Weapon seven: Give up the reward of being right about being a failure.

Have the courage to be wrong about being a failure. Allow yourself to succeed and to tolerate that success. Begin to form an identity around being adequate.

Be willing to be equal to others. The arrogance dragon thrives on having you think you are better than others. The self-deprecation dragon thrives on having you feel you are less than everyone else. Healing involves inflating you to your proper level, not cutting you down to size. An underinflated tire is a hazard in an automobile because it produces instability in a team of four tires. Just as an underinflated tire can throw the entire car out of balance, so can a person with the self-deprecation dragon derail the cooperative efforts of people working together as a team. Self-deprecation can drain the energy of others who are trying to work cooperatively, and sink an entire project. Many a talented athlete has choked with doubt in crucial moments of a championship game, causing the coach to put in a less-talented substitute as replacement and the game was lost. What is needed is equal value in members of a team. You need to see that you are no less valuable and no more valuable than the other players.

Seven Exercises to Transform the Self-Deprecation Dragon

> **Exercise one:** Open dialogue with your inner critic.
> **Exercise two:** List your successes daily.
> **Exercise three:** Record and listen to the validation of your loved ones.
> **Exercise four:** Develop a relationship with yourself in the mirror.
> **Exercise five:** Accept compliments with grace.
> **Exercise six:** Take risks daily.
> **Exercise seven:** Take action and make decisions.

Exercise one: Open dialogue with your inner critic.

Learn to talk back to the negative voice of the critic inside you. Open a dialogue instead of just listening to the voice. Allow yourself to feel irritation at the voice putting you down, instead of being intimidated by it. Question the voice with a philosophical approach. Ask yourself, "Who am I when the voice is not there?"

One excellent way to proceed is through journal work or the use of a notebook. Allow yourself to write down all the things that the negative voice wants to say. Don't hold back. Let it totally do its trashing; let it dump. It is better not to resist, but to allow the voice to speak in the second person. That is, instead of writing, "I am a jerk," write "You are a jerk." Then reply as if you are talking to a blustering but frightened bully. A good reply to the voice of the bully is, "So what?"

Exercise two: List your successes daily.

Before going to sleep at night, make a list of at least three and preferably seven things that you did particularly well that day, no matter how bad the day seemed to be.

You will have a tendency to automatically review what you did badly that day. This is an old habit perpetrated by the dragon. With an act of will, turn your attention away from this habit and proceed with the exercise of focusing on what you accomplished that day. At first this will take great effort and may even seem impossible to do. After a period of discipline, it will come easier. Persevere. Eventually you will become good at it.

Exercise three: Record and listen to the validation of your loved ones.

This process takes great courage. First, make a list of several friends or relatives who you know love you and care for you. Then, give them a blank cassette tape and ask them to record why they care for you. Pass the tape around to all the people on your list. When they have finished recording, listen to the entire tape, if you dare. When you can listen to the tape without cringing, crying, or squirming, you have made progress in ridding yourself of the dragon. Of course, the dragon will try to have you lose the tape, break the recorder, or participate in various other sabotage techniques. Allow nothing to stop you. You can substitute a notebook for the tape, and this will accomplish similar results. It will, however, spare you the torture of listening to the actual voices of the people who love you.

> I suggested to Melissa, a client of mine, that she try the tape exercise. After struggling for a week to make her list, she was ready to approach the first person on her list, her sister-in-law. She took another week to work up the courage to approach her, and this was only after I told her to tell her sister-in-law that this was a homework assignment from her therapist. After the tape was completed with testimonies from several people on her list, we listened to the tape together. She sobbed and sobbed before we got through the first message. Afterward, I asked her what the message had said. She was unable to remember very much of it, so we listened to it again and there were more tears. Eventually she was able to hear accurately

what was on the tape without the trauma. This represented a major breakthrough in Melissa's therapy. She felt and
expressed the pain of her inadequacy and discovered that
not only could she survive it but that she no longer identified with it. The fear of inadequacy began to feel alien to
her.

**Exercise four: Develop a relationship with yourself in the
mirror.**

Take courage and look at yourself in the mirror with your
clothes on. Eventually, work up to looking at yourself without
your clothes on. Make eye contact with yourself. Naturally, at
first you will cringe and squirm and feel that this is absolute torture. Stick with it. Ask yourself, "What right do I have to judge
this body, this person?" The person in the mirror is like a plant.
She or he needs water and sunlight and nourishment, not a
steady diet of garbage. Ask the person in the mirror for forgiveness for all the years of abuse. Cry with that person. Chances are
that the aspects you see in the mirror that you hate are actually
those characteristics that remind you of your parents or difficult
siblings. You are probably angry with them for demanding so
much from you and giving so little in return. Give yourself permission to be angry but do not turn it toward yourself. First
comes anger, then comes sadness, finally comes release and forgiveness. Skipping one of these steps does not work.

I have used this technique with many clients with a good
deal of success. Sometimes it takes a long time for them to take
that first look in the mirror without wanting to smash it or run
from it. I encourage these people to take courage and relax with
the viewing. I encourage eye contact in the mirror, and we talk
as the clients look. Often they report how frightening it is to
have two people looking at them in the room, themselves and
me, the therapist. We discuss their judgments and critiques of
their mirror images and then we embark on guided conversations with these images. Sometimes I interview the people in
the mirror and ask them how they feel about what they are

being told. The possibilities are endless for this kind of creative mirror work. Approach this exercise gradually, beginning with periods of short duration and working up to longer ones.

Exercise five: Accept compliments with grace.

Denying nice things said about you, not listening, and spacing out when you are being acknowledged, are all the work of the self-deprecation dragon. This dragon is dedicated to preserving the status quo by keeping you in a state of avoidance. Paying attention and being present for compliments from others is deadly to the dragon.

Learning to accept compliments from yourself is even more difficult at times. You have learned to disavow anything that comes from yourself; therefore, your self-compliments have no value in your eyes. Turning this process around is like climbing Mount Everest, but it can be done and needs to be done.

I often have clients make lists of affirmations that they tape record and listen to, especially before going to bed. If their own voices have no credibility with them, we use my voice for awhile.

Exercise six: Take risks daily.

Since the self-deprecation dragon is a skinny dragon that reduces your profile in the world, you need to counteract this tendency by raising your profile. This means trying things that you have never done before such as dancing, interviewing for jobs, or trying your hand at skating or skiing or bowling or anything different. Activities that make you breathe hard are particularly useful because the self-deprecation dragon thrives on making your breathing shallow. Public speaking will certainly cause you to take bigger breaths than usual. The more experiences of a noncompetitive nature you give yourself, the greater your arsenal against the dragon. Avoid intense competition or activities that force you to compare yourself with others.

This exercise is a bit risky in the sense that the dragon can take over easily and turn the results into a disaster. One client took a risk and asked out a very attractive female. He was

rebuffed. This tempted him to reaffirm his inadequacy. After dis-
cussing the event thoroughly, the client realized that, by the
way he went about asking for the date, he actually arranged
for a rejection. This was a difficult but necessary admission
to make.

Exercise seven: Take action and make decisions.

Because self-deprecation tends to make you passive, your
ability to make decisions and take action has become weakened.
Therefore, use every opportunity to take responsibility and
make decisions. Then take action based on those decisions. If
your choice is to attend a graduate program, then your action is
to call or write for applications and fill them out on time. It
is amazing how many people get as far as filling everything out
on applications and then fail to mail them. The action step is
critical.

If you are struggling with this dragon, the telephone represents a major obstacle. Answering machines are intimidating,
and an actual voice answering the phone is even more scary.
There is a tendency to bungle calls by apologizing heavily and
then mumbling messages that are unclear, bringing up impatience in the other parties. This, of course, is the nightmare scenario of self-deprecation.

Your tendency is to avoid the phone, a decision that makes
success very difficult in today's world. The antidote is to attack
the dragon head-on by using the phone frequently. Make a certain number of calls at one time to overcome your dread of the
phone. Also, you can start by imagining the worst that could
happen. Your imagination is usually much worse than actual
events. After grappling with your nightmare fantasies, life is a
relief.

Conclusion

The self-deprecation dragon is so popular that it exists almost everywhere, from the slums of Calcutta to the White House in Washington, DC. As with all the dragons, you can transform its undermining character into a source of power and confidence. However, if you think that your self-deprecating style is actually humility or if you see it as saintly, you are blind to its corrosive effects on the human spirit. There is nothing good about it. True humility does not self-trash but rather honors the human spirit. Truly humble people do not lack confidence. They can be bears when they see fit.

Take every opportunity to clear this debilitating dragon from your life. Then you are in a position to make a contribution to the world in its time of great need.

Chapter Five

THE IMPATIENCE DRAGON

Positive Pole—Daring
Negative Pole—Intolerance

External manifestation

Excitable; brusque; cursory; snappish; short-tempered; short-fused; intolerant; abrupt; rash; hasty; reckless; rude.

Internal manifestion

Nervous; anxious; jittery; agitated; impulsive; fretful; antsy; eager; chafing; impetuous; heedless.

Examples of situations and conditions that support the impatience dragon's activities

Modern Western culture and rush mentality such as in Japan, France, and the United States; Wall Street; warfare; CNN, network news, and MTV; television in general, sales; working fathers and mothers; big-city living; pay-first gas stations; New York City; waiting in line for anything; professional athletics; traffic jams or heavy traffic; IRS audits and preparing taxes by deadlines; deadlines in general; amphetamines; coffee and caffeine; road work; the Academy Awards; all competition.

Physical appearance and presentation

People with the impatience dragon can appear many different ways because this dragon has no uniform physical characteristics. Generally, the impatience dragon makes persons look like they are preceding their bodies. Their heads are forward, their eyes are snappish, and they look as if they are already where they are headed. Their movements are abrupt and without grace. They may exhibit secondary movements such as pacing, drumming their fingers, kicking their ankles, rubbing their noses with the backs of their hands or fingers, ripping or chewing their fingernails, or scratching various body parts. There may be violent blowups or abrupt rude gestures or comments. These characteristics are not exhibited all the time but mostly show up during times of stress. In severe cases they may be chronic.

Not everyone who appears restless is impatient. Some people are simply more active and have a greater kinesthetic response to their environments. They also may pace, kick their feet or, in general, find it hard to sit still. They are not in the same kind of distress as impatient people.

To get a feel for the impatience dragon, strongly anticipate a future event that you cannot do anything about right now, such as getting to an important appointment when you are stuck in heavy traffic. Try to project yourself ahead of the traffic to see what is causing the delay. Move your head forward and strain your eyes. Do not accept your situation but resist it. Imagine trying to relate to another person this way. Can you be intimate?

The Development of the Impatience Dragon

The rushed environment

The development of the impatience dragon is a gradual process that is inculcated during many incidents from early childhood to young adulthood. There are several paths of development that stimulate a takeover by this dragon. Having parents or role models controlled by the impatience dragon is one royal road to impatience. If children are constantly rushed here and there and their family process is based on a fear of the lack of time, the children can easily adopt this same fear. Family and culture can communicate to children that time is a commodity like an apple pie. Because time is considered limited, it can be used up just like a pie is consumed. When all the slices are handed out, there is none left, and the family considers this a catastrophe. The family acts as if there is no time to lose, so everything is a rush.

Very small children are not future oriented but are totally in the present. Rushing, to small children of age three, makes no sense whatsoever. That is because these children have not developed abstract thought like adults or older children, and time is an abstraction. Abstract thought does not occur until age seven. However, small children are capable of responding emotionally to the activities going on in their families. Very young children pick up the fear that something is bad or wrong and that everybody is rushing to escape it as if it were a monster. This is the first step in the development of impatience.

As these children grow and reach their seventh year, the concept of time believed in by family and culture becomes clear. The children now understand what everybody was so worried about. They see that there is this thing called time, and it is in limited supply. They know they must never allow it to run out or very bad things will happen.

This scenario is only one version or understanding of time, and there are other points of view. Some forms of impatience arise out of quite different circumstances.

Future orientation

By the age of seven, children affected by the impatience dragon have developed a strong sense of goal orientation. They see that there are situations in the future that can be arrived at with work in the present. If they go to school and get good grades, they will go to college someday. If they practice the piano, they will be able to play an entire piece some day. And so on. This is part of normal human development. What is not normal is the sense that time is so limited that it is necessary to rush through these activities for the sole purpose of getting there—wherever "there" is. The result is that all enjoyment of the present moment is lost in favor of anticipating the future event. Of course, when the future event is arrived at, it is immediately replaced by an event even farther in the future, and on and on. Thus, the goal is not enjoyed either, and therefore life is not enjoyable. The pleasure of savoring the moment is replaced by the discomfort of anticipating the future. The glass is then half empty, not half full.

Deprivation

There is another process that creates a fertile environment for the dragon of impatience. This process often coincides with the family's tendency to rush, but can develop independently also. It ends in the same result: fear of loss of time. In this scenario, children are prohibited from taking part in many of the family activities for a variety of reasons. They may be disabled or ill and spend much time in hospitals while the rest of the family is busy with more desirable activities. The parents may restrict the activities of the children and never let them participate in family gatherings or events, constantly telling them that they are too young or too much trouble to be included.

In the case of older children, the family or culture may be so conservative that the children's activities are severely restricted. For example, their families might be members of rigidly orthodox religions that prohibit many activities such as dancing, dating, or entertainment of any kind. The children see that other children are participating in activities that they themselves are not able to do. This is evident in children of restricted cultures who see their counterparts in more liberal or wealthy countries doing more than they are able to do. This builds up to a sense of having lost time and missed out on life experiences in the early years. The fear, of course, is "What if I die before I get to do all of these things, too?" Thus the fear of death can be quite strong in impatient people.

People can allow the impatience dragon to take over their lives even if their families have not been particularly impatient. In fact, sometimes the opposite is the case. The rest of their families may move quite slowly or be content with a quiet, rural style of life. Their very slowness causes the impatient young people to crawl the walls with desire for action.

Mohammed's Story: A Tale of Impatience

Mohammed was born in a rural village in the Middle East. His father was a local physician and his mother cared for the rather large family of eight children. Because his father was an intellectual, Mohammed grew up with interesting reading material depicting life all over the world. The house was littered with *National Geographic* and other popular magazines from the United States and Europe. Although Mohammed's imagination was stimulated by the availability of this information, in reality limited finances and the large family prevented any travel or participation in life as depicted in developed countries. In addition, the strict religion of his culture frowned on the interesting, even decadent lifestyles of people abroad. Coupled with this scenario, Mohammed's mother was a rather impatient woman who frequently lost her temper with her many children. She felt resentment toward her husband, who had the liberty to leave the house for an interesting job in the world outside.

As Mohammed grew older, he began to feel, like his mother, that he was not really living. He sensed that he was missing out on the life he could be having elsewhere. He grew irritable and intolerant, demonstrating frequent bursts of temper when he felt thwarted. As an older child and adolescent, he became known in his family for his abrupt movements and accident proneness. He was always hurting himself by trying to cut corners and going too fast. Stimulated by reading and exposure to cultures abroad, Mohammed developed a burning passion to leave the Middle East and live his life in the United States. Because he was very bright, he excelled in school and, through connections, won a scholarship to the University of California in Berkeley. This represented his dream come true.

Upon arrival in the United States, Mohammed could hardly contain himself. The impatience dragon that had been festering inside him completely took control of his life. Due to his former restricted life, Mohammed now chased women relentlessly. Although he quickly gained experience with women, he found that he was not enjoying himself at all. And even though he was quite attractive, he eventually earned such a bad reputation that women would specifically shun him or go out of their way to avoid him.

Mohammed pursued a degree in business administration, but he was impatient to create his own business and become prosperous. While in school, he traded in used records, tapes, and CD's and soon had a thriving business on the side. Mohammed's life seemed like a video on fast forward. His fingers were always drumming, he was experiencing major success, he felt driven, isolated, and deeply unhappy. His attempts to deal with his unhappiness only led him deeper and deeper into the maw of the impatience dragon because he thought that by moving faster he would outrun his suffering.

Shortly after graduation, Mohammed met Sally, an American woman from a wealthy family whom he was attracted to because of her relaxed attitude about life and her contentment with simple pleasures. Of course, her attraction for him stemmed in part from his own need to develop similar qualities in himself. Subconsciously he believed that her wealthy background could help him recover the lost time from his youth.

Sally was attracted to Mohammed for his brilliance and his "go get it done" attitude, something that was also characteristic of her father, whom she resented but depended on. However, she was not quite aware of the extent of Mohammed's impatience. Mohammed actually slowed down during their courtship and honeymoon phase and experienced blissful moments of relaxation. The impatience dragon was at bay for the time being, which made for a romantic and wonderful interlude. The two of them spent much time together and communicated with each other at a level that Mohammed had never experienced before. Sally saw him as ambitious like her father, but unlike him in that Mohammed seemed relaxed. After a brief courtship, they married. However, like so many attractions of a similar nature, the marriage began to have problems. After the honeymoon period, the impatience dragon roared back with a vengeance.

Mohammed slowly returned to his habitual rushed pace and constant planning. Eventually, he was hardly present in the marriage anymore, and the relaxed times and communication ceased. He began to pick at Sally's slower pace and find fault with her in many small ways. He resumed his impatient intolerance. Sally saw more and more of the father she didn't like, and less of the man she thought she married. Both Mohammed and she were miserable with the relationship. The inevitable result was separation and deep disappointment.

In his desperation over the failure of his relationship and setbacks in his business affairs, Mohammed began to seek answers in unconventional places. Being Middle Eastern, he was not comfortable seeing a Western therapist. Through a friend, he heard about a spiritual teacher who taught meditation, yoga, and other Eastern methods of approaching problems. He began to attend lectures and then retreats given by this teacher, and he met with positive results in his life. He learned to slow down his thoughts through meditation and relax his body through the practice of yoga. He began to understand that the torture he had been going through was of his own making.

He learned that his fear of missing out in life caused him to rush about, missing life all the more. By slowing down, he was happier, and paradoxically he accomplished more than ever.

Although it was too late to save his relationship with Sally, Mohammed learned to approach other relationships quite differently, with much better results. His new spiritual practices taught him to be more present and attentive, and he learned how to listen better. The dragon of impatience suffered a major defeat.

The Seven Steps of Development for the Impatience Dragon

There are seven steps in children's development that lead to enslavement by the impatience dragon. Because the development of impatience can occur several different ways, these steps are an outline only, and all of them may or may not be a part of a given impatient person's development.

Step one: The children are rushed.
Step two: The children associate fear with rushing.
Step three: The children learn that time is limited.
Step four: The children associate goals with a limited time frame.
Step five: The children learn that time can be lost.
Step six: The children feel trapped by time.
Step seven: The children learn that the present is not important.

Step one: The children are rushed.

Children affected by the impatience dragon are not protected from it. They accompany their parents on hurried errands, and there is an atmosphere of worry about deadlines.

Janet's mother, Helen, was a demon on the road. Whenever she sat in the driver's seat of her car, Janet would cringe. Off they would go, with Helen tailgating every car on the road. All stop signs and signals were cursed viciously, and slow drivers got blasts from the horn, accompanied by Helen's rude comments. Traffic jams saw Helen fuming, and driving in parking lots was hair-raising as she outmaneuvered other cars for parking spaces. Janet knew better than to ever try to talk to her mother during these wild drives. She was terrified the whole time. Later, when Janet was grown and driving on her own, she discovered herself rushing strangely, even on leisurely drives.

Messages about hurry and hustle abound in the Western world. From the earliest ages, children are subjected to radio and television announcements exhorting them; "Don't miss the sale" and "Rush on down to Acme Dealership." Rapid music and fast-talking announcers sound the emergency of hurrying to get deals. Parents bustle children off to school, drop them at day care, and gulp coffee on the way to work each day. Horns honk, cars speed, and people rush everywhere. What else can these children learn but that the world is a place where people speed around? Therefore, it is difficult to find human beings in the modern world who do not have some element of impatience programmed into them. The impatience dragon has grown powerful in the electronic twentieth century with its "I hate to wait" mentality.

Belief and decision: "Rushing is how to be in the world."

Step two: The children associate fear with rushing.

Very young children do not know about time other than the present moment, but they can clearly identify the emotion, fear, related to impatient activity. The decision to be impatient takes place prior to age seven. It is actually more of an association than an active decision, but it can be discovered in the subconscious as if it were a decision. The association may take place as early as fetal life, where the fetus experiences its mother's adrenaline and identifies with her experiences of fear that come in bursts of activity.

Belief and decision: "Rushing must be important to my survival."

Step three: The children learn that time is limited.

These children learn to define time according to their cultures, believing that it goes too quickly or too slowly. They learn to tell time. Clocks are everywhere, especially the ones with the big black hands prominently displayed in the classrooms. Bells ring in schools to mark the end of one time and the beginning of a new time. When the bells ring at the end of lunch hour, there is a great rush to get back into the classrooms before getting tardy slips. This prepares these children for later discipline around getting to work on time and keeping track of the vast array of activities associated with specific times. Arriving late, of course, means braving disapproving stares and turned heads as well as professors looking at their watches with frowns.

Time on the clock seems to relentlessly run on, and it passes certain marks stating that specific lengths of time have run out. This apparently happens too quickly for these children. They get so used to rushing to beat time that when there is too much time, it seems to go horribly slowly. Thus, the impatient children are tortured by having to wait.

Belief and decision: "Time is something that there is too little or too much of."

Step four: The children associate goals with a limited time frame.

Impatient children develop the concept of goal-setting but associate the fear of lack of time to goals. They learn that setting goals is important in life in order to accomplish tasks. However, this goal-setting naturally becomes associated with the notions of their cultures and families about the shortage of time to accomplish those goals.

This awareness pushes these children to think of the future all the time. If time is in short supply, then they must rush to get as much done in that time as possible. Consequently, these children grow into people who try to cram too many events into available time. The result is that they become known for running late and missing appointments. They cannot be counted on because they make too many events their priority.

The concern about the shortage of time makes goals more important than they are. It is as if impatient people are playing a game in which time must be beat. The game involves running to a post and back before an hourglass runs out. Suddenly, something unimportant becomes very important: beating the hourglass. The fear of lack of time introduces distortion into life, and reaching the goal becomes overly important.

Belief and decision: "I must rush to complete my goals. If I don't rush, I'll never complete my goals."

Step Five: The children learn that time can be lost.

The process of haste has other negative side effects. When people rush, they tend to become sloppy in their execution of tasks. The result is many mistakes and even accidents. Of course, mistakes and accidents take up time, and according to impatient people, time is lost.

Thus the dragon creates these people's worst fear—the loss of time. When time is apparently lost this way, these people feel terrible, as if somehow they had lost a game for good. This becomes a chronic feeling, creating much suffering.

Harold did not know it, but he was completely controlled by the impatience dragon. As a violinist, he demonstrated exceptional talent, but his music teacher was tearing her hair out. She saw that Harold had great natural ability, but along with it terrible impatience. Harold did not seem to have the patience to practice and be with his instrument. When he tried to tune the violin, his impatience would take over, and in his hurry he would unbalance the entire set of strings. Then he would have to take extra time to completely retune the instrument. Half of his lesson time would be used up in this fashion.

The music teacher began to dread the lessons, as did Harold. Eventually, Harold gave up music entirely, motivated by his own feelings of acute failure and the disappointment of many people. The dragon had won.

Belief and decision: "I can lose time and it is forever lost. If time is lost, I am lost."

Step six: The children feel trapped by time.

Impatient children learn to feel that they are prisoners of time and that time is an obstacle outside of themselves. Time feels like a box or a trap in which they are imprisoned. These children begin to whine and complain that there is simply not enough time to do everything. They say, "If only I had enough time, I could get the job done. But since I don't have the time, I have no other alternatives." The children learn to blame time for their problems and to not take responsibility for their situations. This sounds very much like the martyrdom dragon because these two dragons are quite related.

Feeling trapped by time makes time into the boss. Instead of being masters of time, impatient people find themselves at the mercy of it. This is a strange twist of events.

Belief and decision: "I am the victim of time, particularly the lack of time. I am its prisoner."

Step seven: The children learn that the present is not important.

Impatient children are not taught to enjoy the processes of life experiences but rather to wish for them to be over with. The present is thus ignored or neglected in the rush to reach the future. Present activities are regarded as nuisances and therefore rejected. For impatient adults, most waking hours are consumed by anticipating, worrying, planning, scheming, and dreading. There is a tendency to drive across town and be so engrossed in planning that they do not remember how they got there. There is absolutely no memory of driving. This same process occurs around meals that are consumed but not remembered because there was no one present to enjoy them. Food is wolfed down without chewing; desserts are inhaled, not savored; drinks are gulped, not sipped.

With this step, enslavement is complete and the impatience dragon has attained complete control. If nothing occurs to interrupt its romp through these people's lives, there will be much suffering and vast confusion about the nature of time. The power will be in the dragon's claws and the people will feel powerless. There is a way out, of course, just as there is a way to defeat all the dragons.

Belief and decision: "The present is not important. Get rid of it."

The Impatient Dragon's Big Lie

The impatience dragon leads people to believe that if they go faster they can get to their goals quicker, thus being able to accomplish more goals in the time allotted. However they rush, only to be slowed down by mistakes, accidents, and errors. The truth is that moving more slowly is more efficient and therefore more productive. This is what the archetypal story of the tortoise and the hare is all about. Slow and steady wins the race.

Inside, when people are rushing, they secretly suspect that they are not going to make it to their destinations. In fact, they are affirming this all the time. When impatient people are rushing to the airport, under their breath they can often be heard to say, 'I'm not going to make it. I'm not going to make it.'" Their hearts are pounding as if they are already experiencing the consequences of not making it. If they had the confidence that they were going to make it, they would be calm. So, as usual, the dragon tells lies. Lie number one for the impatient dragon is, "It is better to hurry." Lie number two is, "Time is limited and it's going to run out on you." Lie number three is, "You are a victim of time."

The truth is actually the opposite. It is much better to take time to do things. There is plenty of time in the universe; in fact, that is all there is. In truth, time cannot run out. As Einstein discovered, time is relative, stretchable, condensable, and moldable. As is yet to be discovered by science, but as known by philosophers and spiritual teachers, time is influenced by the human mind. Time is a tool to be used by human beings and other creatures of the planet. In fact, humans are time travelers constantly surfing the wave of the present as time supports them. Just as surfers master waves, humans are meant to be the masters of time and not its slaves. The reason for this is simple: time is not a living thing but a construct, having no power of its own. So much for the dragon's ideas.

The Great Dragon Exchange

As expressed in step six, the impatience dragon turns into the martyrdom dragon as if by magic. That is because both dragons are based on a fear of being victimized by something. These two dragons can drift back and forth into each other and change their faces at will. Waiting impatiently in traffic or in lines can easily slide into victimization or martyrdom with the words, "Why do I always get in the longest line? This is always happening to me." When impatient actions lead to injuries such as twisted ankles or sliced fingers, martyrdom can easily take over with comments such as "Poor me" and "I was trying so hard, and look what happened to me; it's no use." At first, people feel trapped by time, then they feel trapped by their injuries. This switching back and forth of dragons keeps people nicely confused for long periods of time and allows the dragons to hide much more efficiently.

The Upside-Down Impatience Dragon

A fear of too much time is actually a fear of too little time. Imagine stopping in a foreign country en route to your ultimate destination. You discover that you need a visa to visit the country you are headed for. Immediately, you feel great consternation that it will take three whole days to obtain. "Three whole days in this god-forsaken place until I can get my visa," you complain. Why is this a problem? Because you don't like where you are, and you feel you are missing out on being where you are going. So your fear of too much time in one place is actually a fear of too little time somewhere else. Only a dragon could think of such a silly thing, and yet, how painful it can be.

For impatient people, time either drags or races, without much sensation in between. When they want time to fly because they are impatient to go home at the end of a long afternoon, time drags on endlessly. The clock hardly moves. When there is a deadline and much work to do to meet it, time flies around the clock like a demon. Yet no matter which end the dragon is playing, the bottom line is that impatient people are harnessed to time like a mule to a wagon. This is not liberation but slavery, and it is slavery to something that is as elusive as the wind.

Stages of Maturity and the Impatience Dragon

Infant stage: ruthless gratification
Toddler stage: bigoted irritability
Child stage: fast-track haste
Adolescent stage: intolerance at self and system
Adult stage: visionary impatience

Impatience at the infant stage

At the infant level of maturity, the hallmark of the impatience dragon is the need for immediate gratification at the most primitive level. This is the thief who, impatiently wanting to get to his next burglary, knocks the old woman down because she is too slow at handing over her purse. This is the trigger-happy soldier who, not wanting to wait for the carnage to begin, fires his rifle into the crowd without waiting for orders. His act initiates a massacre because it is seen as a signal to begin. This is the slave driver who, not wanting to wait for the fallen slave to get up under the heavy load, whips him to death in frustration. This is also the rapist who cannot wait to form a relationship but grabs a woman as an object to satisfy a sexual urge driven by impatience.

At the infant level, all acts of impatience and its offspring, intolerance, are related to treating people as objects for immediate gratification. The impatience is directed outwardly at all times.

Impatience at the toddler stage

At the toddler level, people cluster together for safety in their own communities, sharing the same beliefs and customs while resisting others outside their group. The impatience dragon shows up as intolerance for people with different skin colors or beliefs. There is a tendency to rush through a trial of a black man to obtain a guilty verdict, or to impatiently crack down on a protest or rally with batons and tear gas even if the meeting is peaceful. The toddler never questions authority, so the impatience is not directed toward those higher in the pecking order but only toward those perceived to be at a lower level.

Since the toddler stage is quite unsophisticated, there is no self-reflection. Impatience is directed outwardly with much blaming in the process. The impatience is not directed toward self. Picture a piano teacher who quickly loses patience with her students and hits their hands with a ruler when they don't place their fingers on the keys correctly. There is a tendency for the impatience to come out regarding doing things right or correctly. The expression of the impatience is often some kind of violent reaction, like a toddler having a tantrum.

Impatience at the child stage

The impatience dragon at the child level continues to be directed outwardly toward others, and especially toward the environment. Impatience practically runs the child level of Western culture, with its fast pace and vicious capitalistic competition. This is the corporate takeover artist with blood pressure through the ceiling, rushing to complete the deal before the competition can score a win. It is the impatience of Wall Street in all its glory as stockholders buy and sell impatiently at the wrong times to record losses. It is the world of news and journalism, with people rushing to get stories to the press before sunup even if it means getting partial stories or facts that are all wrong. Impatient adult children are professionals on the fast track everywhere, putting profits and status ahead of service, and giving patients and clients short shrift as they juggle more business than they can handle. The child stage in general is the rush for profit and the catastrophic destruction of jobs and lives in the wake of a few individuals impatient to become top baboon.

At the child stage of maturity, the impatience dragon ruins lives by making sure there is no time for spouses, children, parents, friends, or even self. Life becomes a frenzy of striving for success, and the quality of life suffers a terrific loss.

Impatience at the adolescent stage

At the adolescent stage, the impatience dragon changes strategies radically. Because adolescents are capable of self-reflection, the intolerance and impatience of this dragon become heavily directed at themselves. Much of these impatient people's pain is inflicted upon themselves rather than upon others. Adult adolescents attack themselves by becoming intolerant of their own personal slowness and clumsiness. Their minds are continually running a commentary such as, "What's the matter with me? I'm just too slow. Why can't I be a little quicker and get the jump for a change?" This may sound like self-deprecation, but it actually is not. These people are not feeling inadequate; they are feeling angry at themselves for losing time.

Impatient adults acting at the adolescent stage may be seen by others as quite patient. As teachers or parents they may exhibit exceptional patience with their charges on most occasions. However, pushed to the extreme, intolerance will show. The impatience is continual in other areas of life such as operating machines, attending events, and general rushing of themselves. After showing patience with others, adult adolescents may go on to rail at their cars for not starting quickly enough, or they might disable their VCRs in their efforts to cram video tapes into them. Then they might even feel like smashing their own hands for breaking the VCRs, as if the problem were their hands' fault.

Because adolescents are idealistic and reform minded, they become impatient with the old ways, the old structures, and the traditional methods. They want change yesterday. Impatience burns like a fire in the belly of many reformists and revolutionaries. They can be so impatient with the powers that be that they do not want to wait for the time-consuming process of legislation and the slow wheels of bureaucracy to turn. They take to the streets in protest and are willing to break the law if it seems unjust to them. In the case of organized religious structures, they willingly risk excommunication and censure for their efforts to create change. The impatience almost always creates a backlash that results in repression or tragic violent oppression. The dragon enjoys the theater in such scenarios.

Impatience at the adult stage

At the adult stage, impatience comes and goes. As with the adolescent level, it is primarily directed toward situations rather than toward other people. Impatient adults often put the cart before the horse and get fouled up because they are not willing to wait for the order of events to unfold. They might buy things before they have deposited money into their accounts, causing their checks to bounce. The problem results not from a lack of money but from improper order and the impatience to get things.

Adults are often visionary and are able to see events as they would like them to be several years hence. Impatient adults don't want to wait for the intervening process to take place, so they sometimes jump the gun and act as if the future is now. For example, the impatient owners of businesses may accept orders for merchandise that are simply beyond their current capacities to deliver. This is because, in the owners' minds, their businesses have already grown big enough to handle the orders. Such impatience creates endless snafus for adults.

Adults can sometimes be impatient in their relationships, trying to hurry along processes that need to take more time. They may jump into marriages or partnerships before getting to know their partners well enough. They want relationships to be at step five, expansion, when they are actually at step two, developing trust.

The impatience dragon can create havoc for adults trying to relax, meditate, or contemplate. The dragon likes to get into the mind and start speeding up the thoughts so that relaxation becomes impossible. Nervousness sets in, and these people feel plagued by what seems like a mysterious energy that causes them to wander around the house or workplace in an unfocused, unproductive manner. They feel antsy, bite their nails, pace, pull their hair out, and engage in any number of anxious behaviors. These things are all related to a disturbance in their relationship with time.

How the Impatience Dragon Affects Your Life

The impact of the impatience dragon on your health

Impatience contributes significantly to increased stress on all organs of the body, especially the vascular system. Therefore, impatience is life threatening because it not only contributes to heart attacks but it accelerates the aging of your body. Impatience often inhibits the healing of illness due to other causes. You may not want to wait for complete healing; you leave your house or hospital too early, only to suffer a relapse because you are still weak and vulnerable. Impatience causes you to move abruptly, risking more serious injury, when you need to move slowly because of an illness or injury.

Most people who suffer from Epstein Barr Virus and Chronic Fatigue Syndrome are afflicted by the impatience dragon. Prior to their illness, they are usually people who stress their bodies with endless impatience and hurry. Meals are skipped, and junk food is wolfed down, all in the interest of saving time. After many years of this abuse, their immune systems break down, forcing them to shut down or to go more slowly. This is very painful for people who were so impatient before, yet they seldom recognize the source of their illness.

If you are under the influence of the impatience dragon, you may not enjoy your food because you gobble it down without tasting it. I know a man who finishes his entire plate before I can take three bites. Needless to say, this impatience affects your digestion and stresses your body. I know a woman who can chew her way through an ice cream cone in about four bites. Where is the enjoyment of licking through it?

Not only does the impatience dragon affect your internal physiology but it rather significantly contributes to accidents that in some cases can be critical or fatal. How many automobile accidents are a consequence of impatient motorists attempting to pass strings of cars on blind curves or swerving quickly to turn left before oncoming traffic arrives? Skiers on their way up to the mountains are perhaps the most impatient drivers on Earth, and the most dangerous. Not only does this impatience injure or end the life of the people afflicted by this dragon, but it maims and kills countless innocent bystanders and safe-driving motorists.

Countless other physical injuries, both industrial and recreational, are the result of impatient behavior. From the athlete who fails to warm up and pulls a muscle, to the machinist whose fingers are lost due to impatience while operating machinery, the impatience dragon creates havoc with health.

I was once hiking with a friend when we came to a treacherous ravine that we had to negotiate to get across. While others searched for a longer but safer route around, my impatient friend tried to get across by himself. While doing so, he slipped and crashed to the bottom. He tore ligaments in his shoulder and was disabled for many months. The injury resulted in surgery, hospitalization, and much pain, not to mention the tremendous expense incurred from one simple rash act of impatience. The dragon had a field day that afternoon. These are the situations it looks for.

Consider the various wars and battles throughout history initiated by impatient generals, assassins, kings, or queens. How many lives have been lost due to a single impatient act? Seen in this light, you can see how deadly the impatience dragon is. Far from being cute, it is a horror.

These are just a few of the myriad ways that impatience leads to illness, injury, and death for countless millions. You can come up with many of your own examples.

The impact of the impatience dragon on your creativity

The creative process is gradual for most people. Creativity involves gestating and building slowly, often with an explosion of expression in the end. If you are impatient, you may want to get to the explosion part without going through the slow evolution part. The results are usually poor. Art cannot be rushed; nor can the composition of music or the writing of books. That is why people who create for short commercial deadlines often produce works of inferior quality compared with those who let the process dictate the evolution of the work. I have personally experienced writing a book in only two months time, but only after a much longer period of letting it build within me.

Plastic surgery or dentistry can be creative work, but can you imagine going under the knife of an impatient doctor? A doctor told me the story of an actual case in which impatience played a major disconcerting role. An impatient doctor removed all of a patient's teeth because he incorrectly assumed the teeth were causing another painful condition in the body. He did not want to wait for the lab tests. When the lab tests came in, they showed that the patient's teeth had nothing to do with the condition in question.

Creative people are visionary and can see an idea in their

mind's eye, already completed. If you are impatient, you may never get around to making the idea real and physical. You may start a project, only to leave it unfinished to go on to another project, and yet another. You may leave a string of unfinished projects behind you. Patient creative artists take the time to bring their visions into fruition, and in doing so they make great contributions to the joy and pleasure of humanity. Can you imagine an impatient Michelangelo or Beethoven? There would be no results.

The impact of the impatience dragon on your presence

No two things could be more related than patience and presence. When you have presence, your focus is on your immediate location. You are able to be with people here and now. When you are in a rush or busily rehearsing for the future, you do not have presence, nor are you present. Impatience robs you of presence with others and at the same time eliminates your ability to be in present time. Many spiritual traditions refer to the present as the point of power. From the present the past can be healed, and from the present the future can be shaped; from the present anything can be done. The impatience dragon makes it impossible to be present and therefore robs you of the power to make changes. The debilitating effects of the impatience dragon on presence is obvious.

The impact of the impatience dragon on your relationships

Impatience causes intolerance, and intolerance directed at other people ruins relationships quickly. Finishing people's sentences for them, constantly interrupting them before they have finished speaking, or rushing in late and leaving early are all ways of irritating and alienating others to the point that they do not want anything to do with you.

> A young woman came to me for therapy, and although she was very attractive, she complained that men seemed to leave her over and over again before she could get a relationship going with them. It was quite apparent from the

beginning that she was being run by the impatience dragon because she interrupted me often and did not wait for
my responses before plunging ahead with her next thought
or question. I found that after a short time with her in the
office, I felt irritable—like I wanted to get away from her
myself. I discussed this with her and wondered if she had
noticed her severe impatience. She thought a bit and
agrèed that it was quite a problem for her but said that she
had simply not seen how it had infiltrated all her relationships. She talked about how she did not want to wait for
men to call her, so she would call them right away after a
date. She thought that she was simply being a liberated
female, and she judged men for not being able to handle
that. She was blind to the fact that her impatience made
the men feel pressured and forced against a wall. As she
reflected on this, she was able to see that in reality she had
trouble with both men and women because of her impatience.

I got the woman's permission to stop her every time she
interrupted, did not listen, or was otherwise acting impatient. At first it was very slow going because I had to stop
her all the time. She thought that the content of what she
had to say was more important than her process and felt
that I was wasting her valuable time by stopping her. On
the other hand, luckily, she was able to laugh about this
and see the incredible influence of the impatience dragon
within her. She was helped by seeing that this impatience
was not truly sourced in herself but was more of a parasite
that she could rid herself of. Because she was motivated,
she was able to make significant progress in slowing down
after a few sessions. Needless to say, her relationships
began to improve. Later, I got her permission to start the
sessions with five minutes of silent meditation, a challenge
that she gradually warmed to. When I forgot, she would
remind me because she grew to like it.

This woman's experience is a very typical scenario for a person with impatience. If you are impatient, your tendency is to blame others for going away when your impatience is actually driving them away.

Impatience is the source of endless problems around sexuality because the truth is that impatience and sex are like oil and water. They simply do not mix. In a man, impatience with sexual attraction causes inappropriate advances or clumsy, ineffective attempts to contact a partner. Once in bed, the man rushes through the act like he is on his way to a fire. The effect is "slam-bam-thank you-ma'am" (or "man," as the case may be). Impatience in a woman tends to turn her partners off. Impatience does not promote intimacy.

Once the contact has been made, impatience in men can have another, more devastating effect: premature ejaculation. I have found that most men who suffer from this social embarrassment on a chronic basis are quite simply run by the dragon of impatience. Usually they suffer from premature everything in their lives. Therapy starts there.

On the other hand, an impatient woman often blocks the intimacy a partner is trying to establish with her by rushing toward climax, either her own or her partner's. After orgasm, the woman is out of bed and already on to her next activity while her partner is busy trying to figure out what happened. In these cases, the dragon of impatience is in charge.

The impact of the impatience dragon on your spiritual life

Like impatience and sex, impatience and spirituality do not mix. Can you imagine impatiently praying or meditating? No great spiritual teacher I know of has urged people to speed up their lives, rush about, and ignore the present. Rather, spiritual teachers send a consistent message to humanity about slowing down, paying attention, being aware, and making changes from the point of the present moment.

On the other hand, because the impatient dragon likes to infiltrate wherever it can, it has succeeded in distorting these teachings to reflect the opposite viewpoint. Millions of people have been led to believe that they should ignore the present, avoid life, and impatiently wait for future salvation. Some people have even rushed into death, to get there sooner.

In therapy, I have heard many people say, "I hope this is my last life, because I can't wait for this to be over." Others have been so in a hurry to be enlightened that they have proclaimed it a little bit early. Many cult leaders, spiritual leaders, false masters, and instant shamans have proclaimed their enlightenment and said, "Follow me," only to be later discovered in the compromising, unenlightened embarrassment of theft, violence, sexual abuse, and the like.

As an instructor in the John F. Kennedy University Transpersonal Counseling Program, I came across some students who, in their impatience to be more spiritually developed, had decided that they were no longer impacted by the more base emotions of anger, grief, envy, and jealousy. A few of them floated around like angelic beings, holier than thou, ready to save the world. Because the graduate program included a kind of group therapy as a mandatory class, these types would participate by saying that they had already transcended to higher levels and that they had little left to work on in themselves.

Within a very short time, it became obvious to everyone what a lie that was because the anger and grief would come pouring out of these people in buckets. They had been rushing their so-called evolution and had tried to cut corners on the emotional clearing needed for transformation. There are no shortcuts to emotional development and resulting spiritual growth. These folks either decided that they were too advanced for such base work and left, or they decided to return to the present facts and do the basic homework like everyone else.

How to Transform the Impatience Dragon

When you see what a scourge the impatience dragon really is, you may be motivated to oust it from your life forever. Following are the weapons and special tricks to fight this quick-moving dragon. However, be careful, because you might feel impatient to get the battle over with. This would mean, of course, that the dragon has already won.

Fighting impatience is a kind of paradox because it requires practicing silence and moving slowly, the very things you have the most difficulty with if you are an impatient person. Remember that impatience is not really meant to win in the long run. The dragon is there as a challenge to make you stronger and wiser as you confront it and do battle with it. Also, doing battle does not mean resisting impatience or smashing it with an act of violence or force. If you use these tactics, the dragon will probably win, because it is better at this form of attack. You need to be cannier and smarter. Doing battle can mean many things. In many cases it means watching and knowing your enemy and finding humor about it just when it wants you to be angry and upset. The dragon can usually beat you if you respond with great anxiety.

Affirmations to Beat the Impatience Dragon

I have all the time I need to accomplish everything I want
    in life.
Time is my friend.
Just when I seem to need it the most, I find I have all the
    time I need.
I enjoy just being, without having to do anything.
The more relaxed my pace, the more I seem to accomplish.
When I slow down, I accomplish more.
Time is always on my side.
I am smooth and graceful in everything I do.
I have learned how to be here now.

Seven Weapons to Transform the Impatience Dragon

Weapon one: Waste time.
Weapon two: Learn silence.
Weapon three: Cut out intrusions.
Weapon four: Be graceful.
Weapon five: Develop rhythm.
Weapon six: Be mindful.
Weapon seven: Learn the true nature of time.

Weapon one: Waste time.

If there is one thing you can't stand as an impatient person, it is wasting time. You dread having time on your hands for any reason, so you tend to cram in extra activities to make sure none of your time is wasted. You make lists of things to do that are too long for the time allotted. You always run late because you are unrealistic about how long it takes to accomplish a task. On occasion, you may actually arrive early because you are so impatient to arrive. This is stressful, because then you have time on your hands. However, time to kill is actually an opportunity to fight the dragon on its own turf. Unstructured time can become your greatest ally because it allows you to see how you operate.

You may act as if time is your master. You can be a slave to the clock, the alarm, the wristwatch, and the beeper. You give your power away to a timepiece and become its slave. Only by turning this relationship around can you experience freedom from the typranny of time. If you cannot waste your own time, you do not own your own life. Time owns you. So, the first sign of self-mastery is learning how to take time and throw it away at will.

Not only is wasting time of value, but simply spending time that has not been planned is an excellent weapon against the impatience dragon. Spending unstructured time calls for spontaneity and being in the moment. It may be that something useful comes from this time, but that is not the goal. The goal is to be in the moment.

Weapon two: Learn silence.

If you are impatient, you may be addicted to noise and cacophony. You are so afraid of missing something that you tend to have the radio or television on while you are doing other things. You become attached to the constant driving force of big city noise and often contribute to the racket yourself. If the noise is not coming from the environment, then it is coming from inside your head. The impatience dragon contributes an endless mental dialogue whose content is mostly things to do, places to go, and people to meet. This mental din goes on from wake-up time to sleep time and sometimes carries right through to dreamland.

The antidote to all this is the impatient dragon's nemesis: silence. Silence is both a torture and a blessing to you because it is so hard to accomplish and so relieving at the same time. Silence slows you down, quiets your mind, and brings your focus acutely to the present. This orientation to the present moment creates a powerful challenge because it makes you more aware than ever of the fearful state of impatience. At the same time, it is a cure for the pain of your impatience. You may think that sitting quietly is just too painful. Yet, it is not the silence that is painful, but your awareness of the constant chatter. After a period of silence, this torment gradually recedes and is replaced by serenity and tranquillity. This is proof that silence of itself is a great pleasure.

Silence is a wonderful teacher because it instructs through experience. Silence teaches you about the chronic discomfort in which you live. Zooming along in a state of impatience, you are never in the present enough to feel how you truly feel. Your usual feeling may be fatigue, exhaustion, mental and physical tension, and a kind of wired-up state of dis-ease. By stopping all activity and sitting in silence, the physical discomfort becomes quite apparent. However, you may so dread this moment of truth that you prevent any such quiet moments from taking place. Your dragon-influenced philosophy is that it is better to be busy and deny pain than to be aware of pain and address its cause.

Silence is perhaps the most powerful weapon against the impatience dragon. Most amazing of all, silence is absolutely free.

Weapon three: Cut out intrusions.

As mentioned, the impatience dragon thrives on the loud intrusions of advertising, television, radio, and general noise. If you are impatient, you can hardly drive your car without turning on some music, news, or talk show program. On the surface, you can appear quite social, but on closer inspection, you are moving too fast for any real intimacy to develop. You place greater importance on intrusions than on personal experience. You are more likely to be captivated by the television or radio than by listening to your children, spouse, or friend trying to make contact. And the next event is always more important than the current one, so the future is always intruding as well.

It is a real threat to the dragon when you develop the habit of cutting out all intrusions. This is not easy, considering that if you have the impatience dragon you don't know what an unnecessary intrusion is. You need help from others to discern this. To begin with, turn off radios, televisions, and other sources of racket. Seek peaceful environments and help to create them.

Weapon four: Be graceful.

If you are under the influence of the impatience dragon, you have a tendency toward clumsiness and quick dangerous movements. This makes you quite deadly behind the wheel of a car, where you often engage in such sports as tailgating; passing on the shoulder or the right; speeding in fog, dust, and snow; and changing three lanes in one fell swoop. You are known for knocking over floor lamps, flower pots, vases, statues, drinks, and plates of food. You constantly knock the skin off your fingers, knuckles, and elbows, and bang your head, and suffer black-and-blue marks on all your extremities from crashing into tables, cupboards, and car doors and roofs.

Sandra was a classic case of impatience. Rushed, ahead of herself, and clumsy, she went through glasses and dishes so fast her husband replaced them all with plastic. When she prepared for a trip, she rushed about so much that, inevitably, important items like jackets, toothbrushes, and necessary papers were left behind. She was known for leaving the oven on, the windows open, and her keys in the door, requiring return trips to correct the problems. Her attempts at computer work were disastrous because she skipped important commands and rushed through without consulting the manual. Her frequent injuries had her partially bandaged up most of the time and sometimes caused the cancellation of entire family events. She could not hold a job for over three months. Sandra's children would just shake their heads and roll their eyes suggesting that Mom was a hopeless case. Sandra's husband was at his wit's end.

Eventually, Sandra's impatience on the road drove her to have a serious automobile accident that required hospitalization for several months. As she recovered, she worked with a physical therapist who taught her how to move slowly and gracefully. Anything else caused Sandra severe physical pain. By the time she returned home, she had made great progress in slowing down the dragon of impatience. Her family and friends noticed a major change in her personality. She had actually developed the ability to listen to others and to move with a modicum of gracefulness.

You do not need to battle the dragon the hard way. With discipline and attention, impatience can be erased little by little. You can learn appreciably from a course in gracefulness, balance, and polish. These endeavors force you to attend to your movements in the here and now and ensure that you will know where your body is and what it is doing. Can you imagine an impatient ballet dancer, gymnast, acrobat, or t'ai chi teacher? These activities are the very antithesis of impatience and are absolutely deadly for the dragon's survival.

Listening to others is an act of gracefulness as well as graciousness. Listening requires silence as well as the discipline of waiting for others to finish without interrupting or finishing sentences for them.

Weapon five: Develop rhythm.

If you are impatient, you are constantly out of rhythm with your environment, your body, and other people. The impatience dragon works actively to disrupt your sense of timing and rhythm by speeding up your tempo until chaos results. You can see this in children learning to play musical pieces or speaking lines in plays for the first time. The children are anxious and in such a hurry to get things over with that they speed up the tempo until they lose their train of thought. Then they have to start over again. This is the classic style of impatience, in which hurry results in a lack of overall movement. The children must be taught to relax into the natural tempo of the notes or words. Then they are able to move smoothly through their musical pieces or speeches.

All of life involves rhythm, from bodily functions to communication with others. When rhythm is disrupted, life goes wrong in every way. For example, bowel movements cannot be forced, and yet if you are afflicted with the impatience dragon you may try to speed them up, only to be cursed with hemorrhoids and pain. Natural rhythmic digestion follows eating slowly, yet if you are impatient you may down endless digestive aids to pay for eating fast food on the run. You may not notice the correlation between your impatience and your physical discomfort.

Good communication involves a rhythm of listening and speaking in turns, yet impatience turns communication topsy turvy so that neither you nor your partner finds the experience enlightening or enjoyable. Effective work, study, and play are all derived from the rhythm of synchronized effort and relaxation. Impatience often eliminates relaxation and play, upsetting the balance and leading to destabilization of projects and health. Rhythm is always at the heart of the natural world and all of life, and the impatience dragon always destroys rhythm. Consequently, the impatience dragon and the rhythm of life are mutually incompatible.

This is why illness is often so important to healing you if you are impatient. You are forced to lie still and notice the gradual rhythms of the day and the night: the bird songs of the morning, the traffic of the day, the crickets of the evening. It is not the illness itself that has value but the secondary effects of stillness, quiet, and slowing down.

The primary thing that fosters rhythm is relaxation. Relaxation promotes the healthy rhythm of the heartbeat. Fear disrupts it. Any movement in the direction of establishing a rhythm is diametrically opposed to the ambitions of the impatience dragon. Hence, the weapon of rhythm fights the dragon of fear.

Weapon six: Be mindful.

When you are impatient, you hurt yourself and create accidents because you are so far ahead of yourself that you are not paying attention to your immediate situation. You are not in present time and often are not present in your own body. This condition of not being present translates into "having no presence." Having no presence means having no power in the immediate situation to be effective and to make a positive difference.

Your weapon of choice is mindfulness: paying attention and being aware. "Noticing" has much to do with mindfulness. To notice where your body is, what your hands are doing, and what your mind is thinking are all practices in being mindful. This is not the same as being self-conscious, which suggests embarrassment and the shame of feeling judged. Mindfulness is simply noticing what is happening while you are doing it. When you are mindful, it becomes difficult to leave the burner on, run out of gas in your car, or smash into the furniture in your house.

Weapon seven: Learn the true nature of time.

Time cannot be touched, seen, tasted, smelled, or heard. If time has so little substance, how can it gain such control over your life? Perhaps the invention of the clock has created more problems than benefits for humankind because it makes time seem as if it is a thing to be carved into distinct units. However, as Einstein and other physicists have discovered, time is quite relative. Shamans have known all along that time is relative to human consciousness. Rather than being the fixed thing that people in Western culture have been led to believe, time is moldable, stretchable, contractible, and ephemeral. Time is not a pie that can be sliced into a fixed number of pieces as the clock would lead you to believe. Clocks in spacecraft going to the moon and on space shuttles actually move at a slower pace than their brethren on terra firma. When these same clocks return to Earth, they speed up again.

The closer something moves to the speed of light, the slower time appears to go until, theoretically speaking, it can actually reverse itself. That is why, in the context of impatience, the faster you go, the slower you go.

Think of time as a tool used to organize experiences into a historical context, knowing that history is a relative phenomenon. If time is a tool, and you are afflicted by the impatience dragon, you have turned this tool against yourself and now experience it as a harsh ruler that dictates the terms of each day. This has unfortunate consequences for your happiness.

Research into altered states has revealed that time is intimately associated with the human mind. It is influenced, stretched, and contracted by the human imagination. With insight into the true nature of time, you can notice the plasticity of it and begin to mold it at will. You will not be late, although you will contend with crowded freeways. You will sometimes experience magical alterations of time and do the impossible—such as cross town in ten minutes at rush hour without speeding or hurrying. As an enlightened human being, you can be the master of this tool called time, not the slave of it.

Seven Exercises to Transform the Impatience Dragon

Exercise one: Experience unstructured time.
Exercise two: Become silent.
Exercise three: Learn to cut out intrusions.
Exercise four: Develop gracefulness.
Exercise five: Develop rhythm.
Exercise six: Develop mindfulness.
Exercise seven: Play with time.

Exercise one: Experience unstructured time.

Make it a habit to include some unstructured time in your life every day and every week. Unstructured time means not knowing in advance what you are going to be doing during that time. The time frame can be as short as five minutes or as long as several hours. On occasion, it can be several days in length.

There is a tendency for the mere contemplation of unstructured time to bring up fear, and the response to that fear is usually planning. Notice your tendency to fill unstructured time by gathering entertainment items such as books, radios, notebooks, and so on. The point in spending unstructured time is to experience being, not doing.

There are a number of ways to approach your unstructured time. If you are at work, it may be best to leave your office or workplace for a short time because of the many distractions. The point is "to be" in a way that is not your ordinary routine. If you do not normally do so, perhaps you might write in a notebook. If you never sketch, then perhaps that is something you might do. The point is not necessarily to accomplish something but to simply be with yourself in a different way in which you are more present. Do not expect this experience to automatically be pleasant. It may be or it may not be. At first, it will probably be rather challenging. Later it may be richly rewarding.

You can:
go for a walk.
sit down on the grass or on a park bench.
meditate.
contemplate.
draw.
sing.

Notice when you begin to plan for the future or are occupied with worries about a future event. At first, you may associate unstructured time with wasted time. So, go ahead and waste your time. That is the only way you are going to eventually get in charge of it. The more successful you are at wasting designated time, the better.

A variation of this exercise is to do a personal vision quest out in the mountains or the desert. Pick an isolated quiet spot and remain there for twenty-four to forty-eight hours with nothing more than a sleeping bag and perhaps a notebook. The object is to pose a question, simply be, and listen to the messages of nature. I have increasingly found this to be an effective tool in erasing impatience.

Exercise two: Become silent.

The true challenge for you as an impatient person is to silence your mind. This, as most spiritual teachers warn, can be the greatest struggle of all. However, there are helpers that can make the job easier. You may want to begin by listening to a relaxation tape or quiet relaxing music. The sound of running water or gentle rain can be very effective. These are available in nature itself or on tape. Learning some basic techniques of self-hypnosis can also be a powerful way of inducing silence. For example, you can focus your eyes on a fixed spot across the room and begin to count your breaths slowly, counting backward from ten to one while suggesting to yourself that you are deeply relaxed.

You can also do the following exercise:
1. Sit in a chair or lie down on your back with your legs and arms uncrossed.
2. Focus your attention on the invisible force of gravity that keeps you planted on the chair or plastered to the floor.
3. Notice all the ways that gravity keeps all parts of your body and clothing nailed down on the ground.
4. Allow gravity to work its magic. Offer no resistance, and see how much you can cooperate with it.
5. As you do this, repeat to yourself slowly, "Let go, let go, let goooooo."

Being silent inside does not mean you have to close yourself in a totally quiet room. You can carry out any ordinary activity and even conduct business while having a silent, efficient mind. What you are working toward is silence while you are living an ordinary life; silence inside while listening or talking to someone; silence inside while driving; silence inside while making love.

Exercise three: Learn to cut out intrusions.

Shut off the radio in your car or elsewhere. Turn off your television set. Turn off your CD and tape players. Turn off the ringer on your phone and turn down the sound on your answering machine. Shut off your beeper. Shut off all the external noise you can. That leaves you with only the ongoing cacophony inside your own head.

Notice how easily distracted you are by thoughts about future events while your spouse, child, or friend is trying to talk to you. Notice the intolerance that pops up when you feel caught between listening to them and overhearing a news broadcast or commercial on television or radio. Restrict your newspaper reading to the bathroom or cancel your subscription entirely.

In lovemaking, notice the intrusions that enter your mind. Refocus on your partner. Notice your intolerance with details about your partner's performance. This means you have not relaxed enough. Practice making love without necessarily having orgasm as the goal. Leave plenty of time for lovemaking. Take your watch off.

Defy the impatience dragon by purposely not accomplishing some of your plans. Take charge.

Exercise four: Develop gracefulness.

Take ballet or dance lessons that involve discipline of movement and gracefulness. Enroll in a t'ai chi course or martial arts class that involves learning slow disciplined movements. Study the Japanese Tea Ceremony or flower arranging. This may sound corny to you, but there is a reason that these art forms have come into existence: to teach the very things that you need to learn—presence and grace.

Go to an art gallery and spend fifteen minutes to half an hour in front of a single painting or photograph that intrigues you. Ansel Adams, the great photographer, used to give his students a special exercise. He would tell them to go out and spend the day searching for possible photographs by looking through the camera viewfinder and framing pictures. However, he instructed them to take only one photograph. This was one photograph in one day, not twenty-four or thirty-six. Such an exercise teaches discipline and grace, both weapons against the impatience dragon. Ansel Adams knew that patience is the friend of art and beauty.

Exercise five: Develop rhythm.

There is rhythm in all aspects of life, from the patterns of day and night to the progression of seasons, from the rhythms of the body to the beat of rain falling. Although these cycles exist automatically, paying attention to them is the key if you are an impatient person. One basic exercise is to notice the natural rhythms in everything and to study them. Taking the time to notice how a flower opens gradually to first light and then closes with darkness is a powerful deterrent to impatience.

Learning to dance or skate, especially in partnership, is an excellent exercise to combat impatience because this art cannot be rushed even if it follows a rapid tempo. Singing, especially choral singing, and public speaking likewise teach the discipline of rhythm and synchronization.

Many sports teach rhythm, including tennis, golf, distance running and swimming, diving, marksmanship, and even bowling. Aficionados of these sports will tell you that perhaps the single most important factor in developing expertise is timing and rhythm. The impatient athlete is injury prone and seldom excels.

Breathing is perhaps the most basic rhythm you can work with. Impatient people tend to breathe erratically and out of sync. Watching your breath and gradually regulating it is an ancient technique that not only combats impatience but is a key to meditation and concentration.

The truth is that since rhythm exists everywhere, all of life can become an exercise in eliminating the impatience dragon. Pay attention to the rhythms of nature, the cadence of crickets, the buzz of bees, the chortle of a brook, the lengthening and shortening of shadows, the building of clouds, and the movements of the sun, moon, and stars.

Exercise six: Develop mindfulness.

The Sufi-trained psychiatrist Claudio Naranjo teaches an excellent but challenging method of producing mindfulness: Slowly remove the matches from a large box of matches one by one and count them; when they are all removed, gradually replace them, counting again. On the one hand, this may seem like a complete waste of time, a tortuous exercise in futility.

On the other hand, it is a powerful way to learn about paying attention.

The truth is, I found this exercise very challenging and difficult. I could not go very far without losing count because my mind wandered so easily. The experience made a strong impression on me, which I have never forgotten. I learned how little I actually paid attention to what I was doing.

A well-known communications exercise for mindfulness is the following: Person A tells person B something about herself or himself, preferably something with an emotional content. person B listens without interruption. After five minutes or less, Person B repeats back what he or she heard person A say. If person A is not completely satisfied that she or he was heard correctly, person A tells person B again. The exercise is repeated until person B gets it exactly right.

This exercise is an excellent family-therapy and marriage-counseling tool. It teaches listening skills as well as mindfulness, otherwise known as paying attention or staying awake. Marriages improve and families are happier when the members develop mindfulness.

There are hundreds of exercises in mindfulness, many developed by Zen Buddhists and practitioners of Vipassana and other forms of meditation. A technique in Vipassana meditation is to observe your thoughts as they drift by without getting caught up in them. The mystic Jorges Gurdjieff suggested categorizing your thoughts as they go by, titling each of them a "worry thought," "review-past thought," or a "problem-solving thought." The idea behind such exercises is not to become obsessive but to pay attention for even a few minutes to the endless parade of distractions. By being mindful of them, you reduce these distractions.

Exercise seven: Play with time.

Spend the day without your watch. If this seems too threatening on a work day, then arrange to do it on a weekend. If you are addicted to and highly dependent on your watch, you will find this exercise uncomfortable. After a time you, like many others, will find that time seems to regulate itself. There are high achievers and top executives who have learned to go, and prefer to go, without a watch. The day becomes more organic, more intuitive. Relying on a watch is like relying on eyeglasses. The more you rely on them, the weaker your senses get.

Notice the little coincidences in your life that occur around timing: when you reach for the phone to call someone, you pick up the phone only to find that person already on the line. You get clear across town in a matter of moments when at other times it takes you an hour. Sometimes every obstacle vanishes before you, and at other times obstacles appear from nowhere to obstruct you. Traffic is not always a factor. Your state of mind plays an important part.

On a recent trip to Chaco Canyon in New Mexico, my family and another family were traveling together in two cars. We all agreed to doff our watches for the weekend. Although we took off in different directions to see many different sights, we always ended up meeting each other at the necessary times for meals, even though no one knew what time it was, and the park stretches for miles in every direction. These occurrences are more likely to happen when you are relaxed. Notice them; prize them.

Play with time rather than struggling with it. When you play with something, you master it. That is why children spend so much of their time playing. There are many games you can play with time; the ones listed above are but a few.

Conclusion

The impatience dragon is erasable, but not unless you identify it as an obstacle in your path. Otherwise, you are stalemated and cannot proceed because, whether you admit it or deny it, the dragon continues to sit squarely in the middle of your trail.

Western culture promotes this dragon, and to fight it you must go against the cultural grain to a certain extent. You may have to change your lifestyle. And yes, in the course of that change, you may no longer be able to put up with certain work conditions. However, you will certainly live longer, and the change will ensure a happier prospect for your old age.

Chapter Six

THE
MARTYRDOM
DRAGON

Positive Pole—Selflessness
Negative Pole—Victimization

External manifestation

Whiny; complaining; resentful; spiteful; guilt-inducing; acting "woe is me"; blaming; sighing; acting exploited or taken advantage of; long suffering; crucified; sadistic; sacrificing; self-righteous; stricken.

Internal manifestation

Agonized; immolated; tormented; anguished; masochistic; trapped; persecuted; victimized; tortured.

Examples of situations, conditions, and people that can support the martyrdom dragon's activities

Displaced refugee camps; disenfranchised minority groups; monks; nuns; religious devotees who are taught that to suffer is to become free; religious refugees such as the historically persecuted Jews and Christians; residents of New York City and other inner cities; resentful mothers; neurotic sons of those mothers; people who live on floodplains or the banks of rivers that regularly flood; residents of trailer parks in tornado country; the homeless; sexual masochists; poverty; hunger; war; oppression.

Physical appearance and presentation

People affected by the martyrdom dragon look as if they have the world on their shoulders. They often appear to have humps on their backs. They tend to gain weight around the thighs and buttocks. They carry a stricken or pained look on their faces and have soulful, sad eyes that can turn spiteful. They tend to crumble when confronted, or cry instead of getting angry. Martyrs have a hard time saying "no" but can outlast everyone in the long run due to the tremendous perseverance of their identities as victims.

To get the feeling of this dragon's influence, produce a pained look on your face but carry a spiteful look in your eyes, as if the way you feel is someone else's fault. Hunch your shoulders up in back but not forward. Get the notion that you are carrying a heavy weight on your shoulders so that your movement is restricted. Feel trapped or oppressed, as if someone else is caus-ing you to be miserable. That is about as close as you can get to the flavor of martyrdom. What is your relationship to the world from this position? Is it fun?

The Development of the Martyrdom Dragon

"Good" behavior: the good children

The martyrdom dragon makes its appearance within the first three years of life. There are several ways it can develop, but the most common way results from having parents or guardians with a worldview that children must earn love with "good" behavior. This good behavior does not always translate into achievement or high marks in school, although it may. The specific "good behavior" required is often a mystery to these children.

The parents take the point of view that having children is a lot of work. They feel they must somehow be repaid for their nine months of pregnancy, the hard work of paying for the expenses of the children, and so on. These parents, while not necessarily abusive, may regularly withhold love and affection because the children have not somehow paid their debts by being "nice" to Mom and Dad. Not being "nice" can range from having colds and being up all night coughing to refusing to eat at convenient times to resisting bowel movements at the appropriate times. The children, early on, feel that they are not deserving of love for being who they are. There is always something elusive they must do to earn love. Since they either don't know what that is or they are not capable of meeting the requirements by virtue of their young age, they feel trapped and worthless.

For example, small children may have colds and cough all night. Their parents feel that they have worked very hard and deserve a good night's sleep. They irrationally believe that the children are punishing them by getting sick and that they are coughing on purpose. The parents feel enraged at the children and make it clear to them that they will get no affection because of their "bad" behavior. The children, who are ill, cannot stop coughing. They fear that they will be considered worthless unless they can stop. Since they cannot stop, they feel trapped and victimized. Enter the dragon.

The dragon whispers in their ears, "It's not fair. No matter what you do, you are worthless. You are truly trapped. Never forget it—but you can make them pay. You can make them feel guilty through your suffering. That's your reward. They will find out how badly they have treated you, but no matter what they do to try to make it up to you, they won't be able to. They will feel bad forever, and you will win."

Crushed assertiveness

Another path to martyrdom is overpowering parents and children's responses to their abusiveness. Small children are not equipped to respond maturely to adults' rage. They may quail and fall apart under angry onslaughts. When two-year-olds naturally assert their wills by refusing to cooperate, parents are sorely tested to respond in a manner that is both firm and kind. Many parents, in their exhaustion and frustration, respond with a crushing rage that demands the children submit to their wills. In the face of these perceived threats to their survival, the children learn to surrender categorically and no longer assert their wills. They become obedient but resentful, like beaten dogs. They get their revenge through the back door.

If children are not allowed to express anger but parents are, the stage is set for the martyrdom dragon's takeover. Two-year-olds need to touch, feel, and explore their worlds. If in the course of their explorations they knock over vases or spill milk or draw on walls, so be it. That is part of childhood. However, if they are met with parental rage and emotional abuse over and over again and are not allowed to talk back, they are effectively crushed. No more exploring is allowed, and there is no way to express the frustration of that. The children feel trapped and expect more of the same. New martyrs appear in the world.

Role modeling

Sometimes martyrdom develops through modeling and identification. If children see their mothers passively submit to the beatings of their fathers, and then behind the father's backs the mothers complain and whine bitterly to the children, the children learn martyrdom from these effective teachers. The children see that if their mothers assert themselves, they get beaten. In their own experiences, if they talk back to their fathers, they get beaten, too. There is no solution but to comply and do whatever their fathers dictate. The result is more martyrdom.

Not all children respond in the same fashion. If children have alliances with their fathers, they are repulsed by their mothers' behavior and turn against them too, becoming more like their fathers. However, many children learn to behave in the same way as their mothers because they see how powerful the mother's strategy is. Their mothers torture their fathers slowly and get back at them quietly.

Camille's Tale: A Story of Martyrdom

At the time Camille was born as the eldest child, two important preliminary events had taken place in her family. During her mother's pregnancy, Camille's father had a catastrophic financial setback. His life savings, invested in a real estate deal, were completely wiped out by a swindler who disappeared with the money. As he was a working-class person, this loss was devastating and resulted in his being severely depressed. Also, during her pregnancy, Camille's mother had severe medical problems that manifested in great physical pain and serious debts. This was the environment that Camille was born into: a depressed, angry father and a mother in terrible pain. No doubt, the day of her birth was not exactly a joyous occasion for any of them.

Camille's first few years were difficult. Her mother continued to need treatment for abdominal pain and cried a lot. Her father was stressed and impatient. When Camille began to walk and get into things, her father exploded at her in pent-up rage. Her mother was too weak to protect Camille and instead withdrew from everyone. Camille sustained a lot of verbal abuse from her father. There was no comfort in the home and Camille learned that if she was "good" (nonassertive and compliant), she could avoid her father's rages. Camille became sad and no longer could express herself. The dragon of martyrdom had made its first inroads and was nesting comfortably in her developing personality.

Camille's mother was an excellent role model for her. Camille soon learned from her that life was nothing but pain and suffering and that, as a woman, she could never be happy or get what she wanted. Even though, after a few years, their finances improved greatly and her father was no longer stressed, her mother complained bitterly about her lot in life. Camille's father, now in a better mood, tried to take the family on vacations and attempted to make up for the painful past. Camille and her mother would have none of it.

Camille learned all the little ways to make her father feel guilty. When her father would buy her a toy, she would not play with it but would do her father's laundry instead. She was careful never to laugh or show him that she was having fun. When he came into the room, she would stop smiling and begin to clean up. She learned to deprive him of any comaraderie or good father-daughter feeling. She was making him pay dearly for the early years. She would not forgive and forget.

When Camille was twelve, her mother had a psychotic episode and became hospitalized for several months. Not only was Camille stuck with her father in an uneasy relationship, but she somehow felt responsible for her mother's condition. Subconsciously, Camille felt responsible for her mother's abdominal pain during and after her birth. She also felt that she had brought financial stress to the family by being born. The dragon was wasting no time working on her from within.

The results were twofold. Camille felt totally responsible for causing everybody's trouble, therefore she feared she was worthless in everyone's eyes. As a worthless person, she felt that she deserved no pleasure or success in life but that she should be punished instead. On the other hand, paradoxically, Camille blamed her father for all of these feelings and was committed to punishing him forever by not having any fun. The dragon had taken firm hold and set up house for the long term.

Years went by. Camille left home, attended college, graduated, and went to work as a psychiatric nurse. She was good at this work because of her sensitivity to her clients' problems, and she was able to show them compassion and kindness. Eventually, she married and gave birth to three children for whom she slaved while her husband traveled on business.

The martyrdom dragon saw the marriage and family as an

excellent playground for taking advantage. With all her responsibilities, Camille was having no fun at all. Because her husband was frequently gone, she developed a deep resentment of him but never directly told him of her feelings. She suffered in silence but managed to let him know that she was furious by refusing to enjoy their vacations and by doing everything he wanted in a joyless way, including sex. He was effectively punished without exactly knowing what his sins were. He stopped traveling and tried everything to make life better for her. He entered therapy, developed more sensitivity, and spent much more time caring for the children, all to no avail. He could not figure out what more she wanted and what would make her happy. He was tortured by her.

Camille's husband would offer to take the children out so she could have a massage, but she would always refuse. One time he paid for a massage and set up the appointment for her, but she forgot and cleaned house instead. He took her out to a nice restaurant but of course she did not like what she had ordered and felt sick afterward, so the romantic evening he had planned soured. He arranged a vacation to Hawaii, but she twisted her ankle on the eve of going so they had to cancel, losing their deposit in the process. On another occasion, he planned a trip to Mexico for them, but she made arrangements to work overtime and he was forced to go alone with the children. When they came back, she complained about how hard she had worked while they had had fun.

On Camille's side, she felt that her husband could never do enough to make amends. Somehow, he could never love her the way she wanted to be loved. She truly felt that if he really loved her, he would figure out how to love her right, but of course, she wouldn't or couldn't tell him how, and she would accept nothing from him. Her basic attitude was, "If you were good to me, I'd be happy, but you're not, so I'm not."

Eventually, Camille's husband filed for divorce and she was devastated. It was at this point that she began to gain some insight into the fierce dragon that had hold of her. The children were grown and she had the time to devote to some personal growth experiences. She became involved with a therapeutic support group that was sophisticated enough to see her dragon and confront her on its ownership of her. At first she resisted fiercely by complaining, whining, and trying to make everyone in the group feel guilty, but they would have none of it. She was so desperate for support that she was not willing to alienate the group entirely. She began the long slow process of ridding herself of the dragon of martyrdom. Only after she accepted responsibility for her own behavior and saw her investment in suffering could she begin to turn things around. The battle for her life had begun, and she, for the first time, sensed another way of life that included pleasure and satisfaction.

The Seven Steps of Development
for the Martyrdom Dragon

These steps do not necessarily develop in chronological order.

Step one: The children feel unwelcome to assert
        themselves.
Step two: The children experience a double bind.
Step three: The children hold in anger.
Step four: The children learn to blame.
Step five: The children make others feel guilty.
Step six: The children win by suffering.
Step seven: The children complain to the wrong people.

Step one: The children feel unwelcome to assert themselves.
        The children recognize that their families are somehow not happy with their normal attempts to grow and develop. The children may think, "I am not OK. I seem to be the cause of others' suffering, and I am afraid that I don't deserve to be loved. I am afraid that I am truly worthless."
        The source of the martyrdom dragon is the fear of being

unlovable. This fear is based in the crushing messages of families or environments, usually after the first year of life. The children's first year may be safe and conflict free, but when they develop locomotion and the beginnings of assertiveness, the real trouble begins. Children go through the greatest developmental step since birth during this time. It is the step from total dependence to independent action. The children are no longer totally identified with their mothers but begin to declare their independence as separate unique individuals. This move for independence is troublesome for many parents because it involves more work and it challenges their authority. If Mom and Dad are not secure with their own authority, they will overreact in their attempts to gain control of their children.

Obviously, many events can contribute to parental overwhelm, including poverty, unemployment, exhaustion, medical problems, warfare, other sick children, and divorce. Therefore, parents aren't necessarily to blame for the children feeling unwelcome to assert themselves. They only contribute to a larger context called life.

Belief and decision: "I am not okay. I am unlovable."

Step two: The children experience a double bind.

The children see that if they assert themselves they are damned, if they don't assert themselves they cannot develop.

A few childhood incidents of being unfairly punished or yelled at by parents or siblings are not going to produce the martyrdom dragon. Rather, it is when these incidents become a chronic daily pattern that the dragon is brought home to roost.

Martyrdom is ensured by the notion of being trapped without any alternatives. That is why martyrs are famous for saying, "Yes, but . . ." to any suggestions offered them. They feel so trapped that they cannot conceive of ways out of situations. Therefore, they negate all other possibilities, to the great annoyance of people trying to help them find solutions. Martyrs can defeat most therapists in a short time. When the therapists give up in frustration, the martyrs feel victimized once again and resentful for the lack of help. They are what the late psychologist Fritz Perls called "bear trappers." Martyrs are so powerful that they can defeat even bears.

Belief and decision: "Life is about being trapped. I am trapped."

Step three: The children hold in anger.

The children stop asserting themselves, finding that developing independence only backfires. Later, as adults, they have great endurance and are able to put up with a great deal of disappointment about situations that don't work out. They expect to be trapped in unsavory circumstances and, because of this expectation, that is what they find. Yet their anger builds and turns into an intense resentment that finds indirect expression.

This anger often undermines their health, and they may end up bedridden or suffering from ailments that make them feel even more trapped. They learn to make the most of these maladies, getting people to feel sorry for them because they suffer so much. Yet they are famous for not accepting help, or for working even though they are sick. In this way, martyrs are often held up as shining examples of self-sacrifice and humility. This only feeds the martyrdom dragon because now there are more rewards than ever to continue on its path. For example, parents may be held in high esteem by their churches or communities, but their families, who have to live with them, are tortured.

Belief and decision: "I will never assert myself or fight for what I want."

Step four: The children learn to blame.

The children learn to avoid feeling worthless by blaming someone or something else for their suffering. In all fairness, children who are always blamed and required to pay for the indiscretion of their birth by being "good" have something to be angry about. They are being deeply wounded and shabbily treated. Nevertheless, further damage is done in their lives when they try to redress the situation by blaming others and finding them undeserving as well.

In other words, as with all dragon activity, people under the influence of the martyrdom dragon learn to do the very same thing to others that is done to them. When they blame others, it prevents them from taking responsibility for themselves and therefore robs them of the personal power to make changes and be successful. So, as with all seven dragons, martyrdom creates more problems than it solves. In fact, it produces the things that are most feared: worthlessness and entrapment.

No one likes blamers or whiners. In fact, others tend to lose patience quickly with these people, and unless others are prone to guilt, they try to get away from martyrs. For example, children try to get as far away as possible from their elderly, invalid parents who are pitiful and whiny. The children consider them worthless.

Belief and decision: "It's always other people's fault. Blame them."

Step five: The children make others feel guilty.

Revenge is sweet. Children under the influence of the martyrdom dragon learn to get back at others for what they did, but they do so indirectly. They withhold pleasure and forgiveness. In fact, they learn to never forgive—ever.

Their idea is to develop strategies to make other people realize the damage they have done. The intention of these strategies is to make the other people want to make amends and then to prevent them from ever succeeding. That way, the others feel guilty forever. This is the fantasy behind many suicidal gestures. Many people overcome by the martyrdom dragon attempt suicide or threaten to kill themselves to get others to feel badly for them. These martyrs are not the ones who usually succeed, however. They may feel it is better to remain alive to see the other people suffer. Nevertheless, some martyrs succeed in killing themselves. This is not because they intend to, but because something goes wrong and they are not found in time. Of course, it is much more effective to provoke the other parties into wanting to murder them and then dare them to do it. That way, the martyrs can send the others to prison if they try. And if the others don't kill the martyrs, they can feel horrible that they would have stooped to consider such a thing. Martyrs can provoke even the most peaceful people into murderous rages.

This is why thousands of people could watch and roar with approval as martyrs were attacked and eaten by lions in the Coliseum of ancient Rome. They thought, "Give them what they are asking for."

The fact that the martyrdom dragon never forgives keeps sons, daughters, husbands, wives, parents, and friends tortured forever. When children have martyrs for fathers or mothers, they never feel forgiven for having been born. They may try all their lives to be nice to their parents to no avail.

Martyrs use a very effective strategy for making others feel guilty: they prevent others from ever seeing that they are having fun. That means they try not to have any fun or they creatively spoil the fun for everyone else at an event. There are many ploys the martyrdom dragon uses to get revenge. Martyrs get sick, have accidents, make bad investments, lose money, get fired, get pregnant, crash cars, and burn houses down by "accident." The list is as long as the amount of creativity.
Belief and decision: "Make others feel bad for causing the pain."

Step six: The children win by suffering.

Subconsciously, children influenced by martyrdom learn to make choices that lead to the known experience of suffering. Later in life, they always seem to make disastrous choices and go from one catastrophe to the next.

This is the real tragedy of the martyrdom dragon, because the purpose of life becomes to suffer. This actually becomes an addiction that is very difficult to cure. The experience of pleasure becomes very threatening to these people for two reasons. First, pleasurable experiences bring up the fear of being undeserving and therefore worthless. Secondly, pleasure threatens the careful structure set up to gain redress for pain. If people see martyrs having fun, they are likely to say, "Oh, I guess everything is all right now. They don't need any special attention anymore. I don't have to feel bad anymore about how they were treated in the past."

Winning by suffering means everybody suffers more. The martyrdom dragon ensures that not only victims suffer but that everybody around them suffers, too. Unfortunately, the power of this strategy is so strong that it can infect generation after generation—and entire cultures.

Belief and decision: "I can win by suffering."

Step seven: The children complain to the wrong people.

Martyr children need an outlet for their pain and frustration, so they complain of their plight to people who can't do anything about their problems. Later in life, brothers, sisters, spouses, neighbors, and friends are frequently the ones who hear about the martyr's woes. For example, a wife may have to hear about how awful her husband's boss is, but when she suggests speaking with him, her husband has a million excuses.

As children, these people were punished for asserting themselves, so they learned right away to avoid talking to the people who wounded them. They discovered that it was always safer to let off steam with other people who would feel sorry for them. With their abusers they remained long suffering and noncomplaining. They always deferred to the people who hurt them.

Later in life, these people are so connected to their abusers that they cannot live without them. When one abuser exits, another enters. Acquaintances, friends, and relatives know what hard lives these people have and may at first turn against their insensitive, abusing spouses. They may shake their heads and say, "Poor man, how can he live with such a bitch. He works so hard and she takes him for granted. She's always out with other men." However, gradually, some friends learn to know better: "No wonder she's out with other men all the time, the way he tortures her. Who wouldn't? He's such a victim."

Victims torture their abusers by casting spiteful glances, withholding fun, and destroying their reputations with other people. In this way, martyrs become sadists. Within all martyrs there is a bit of sadist, and vice versa. That is why abusers stick around. They have some martyr in them as well.

The Martyrdom Dragon's Big Lie

The martyrdom dragon wants victims to believe that someone else is always at fault. There is always someone else to blame for their suffering. Martyrs cling to this belief and half of them believe it. However, deep down they don't believe it at all. They are certain that they are victimized because they are truly undeserving and worthless. So no matter how much they blame and complain, they are actually convinced that they do not deserve anything better than a rotten life. The martyrdom dragon is greatly amused by this treachery and enjoys every moment of the great deception.

However, it is very difficult for martyrs to see this. They vehemently fight off any suggestions that this is the case. When they finally do admit to feelings of worthlessness, they still do not want to give up blaming others. They then demonstrate a curious ability to live with this paradox. This habit of blaming is perhaps the last tenacious hold that the dragon keeps on the personality.

The Great Dragon Exchange:
The Slide from Martyrdom to Impatience

Because martyred people hold in their anger, the tension can build up within them to a level of intolerance. When this happens, they can no longer hold everything in and the impatience dragon, companion to the martyrdom dragon, takes over.

They do something about their frustration but do not think it through before they act. The tendency is to burst out in angry tirades. However, they are often unable to sustain this anger, so they then dissolve in tears. This falling apart in a few moments is a hallmark of the quick return of the martyrdom dragon. Martyrs cannot sustain the energy that it takes to carry through a rebellion.

Sometimes people caught in martyrdom make snap decisions to leave jobs or spouses, but because they have not planned these actions, they end up worse off than before and more trapped than ever. They may end up on the streets, homeless with children, whereas if they had planned the action, resources and support would have been available through relatives, friends, or community services. Thus the impatience dragon and the martyrdom dragon work in tandem.

How the Martyrdom Dragon Traps its Victims: The Denial of Neediness

People with this dragon are intensely needy because they require so much empathy and sympathy to justify the wounding that they have suffered. The problem is that it is almost impossible for them to admit their neediness. The dragon has them so entrapped that it simply won't let them. The trap, of course, is fear—fear that if people knew their level of neediness, nobody would want them.

In general, those with the dragon of martyrdom are empathic and have the ability to be quite loving and kind when they are not besieged by the dragon. However, it is very difficult for them to tell the truth about their wants and wishes. Underneath, martyrs genuinely want to be invited to the picnic in the worst sort of way. They want the love and attention that goes with belonging to the crowd. However, they are quite afraid to let anyone see this because they were crushed for having needs as children. They were found undeserving and were forced to earn love by complying.

So when people get around to inviting them to picnics, they refuse, saying they have too much work to do: "You go ahead; have a good time. I just have too much to do here." If the people persist with invitations, the martyrs might just be persuaded to go, but they will not let on that they want to: "Well, all right, if you really want me to, I'll go—just so you won't be angry with me." What they really mean is, "I'd love to go. I've been desperately hoping you would ask me and I am so happy you did. Thank you, thank you, thank you!" Saying this would be way too humiliating and threatening to their entire structure.

The other people may not persist with the invitations but may say instead, "All right, fine, you stay here and get your work done. I'll go on to the picnic by myself." In this case, the martyrs are left behind, absolutely furious and devastated. The dragon within them registers a major victory, however. When the other people return from the picnic, there is hell to pay. They may be punished with silence, spiteful looks, or indirect complaining about sore backs and having to work so hard while "everybody else has fun." When confronted, the martyrs say, "I'm not complaining. I don't have time to complain. My work is never-ending."

Suffering for martyred people is created by their tremendous need for relief, justice, compassion, attention, and love. The suffering also stems from their fear of their own neediness and their effort to disguise it so it can never be known. Their method of getting even with others ensures that others will not be compassionate and loving, but guilty or disgusted instead. The vicious circle is complete.

Stages of Maturity and the Martyrdom Dragon

> **Infant stage:** the extreme victim
> **Toddler stage:** social sheep and pawns
> **Child stage:** martyr who controls with money
> **Adolescent stage:** political martyr
> **Adult stage:** mild victimization

Martyrdom at the infant stage

At the infant level of martyrdom, people take an extreme victim stance with absolutely no responsibility. Many of these individuals are found in prison settings, where they tend to be used and victimized by the more abusive members of the convict population. They are clearly in survival settings.

Martyrdom at the toddler stage

At this stage are all people who allow themselves to be taken advantage of by ruthless cult leaders, sociopathic religious leaders, and dictators who command obedience and lay waste to the population. Wherever people act like sheep and are taken advantage of, there is the toddler level of the martyrdom dragon. Toddler martyrs are also those who go unquestioning to their deaths in the front lines, without adequate arms or ammunition, because their leaders send them for dubious political reasons. At the toddler stage, there is a noticeable lack of questioning or thought before automatically adopting the martyr stance.

Many martyrs are the ready victims of the medical establishment. They are the victims of unnecessary surgeries, the guinea pigs for drugs with horrible side effects, the faithful innocent children of society who do not question their doctor's advice. These people allow themselves to be bankrupted and duped by the institutions and established social structures in which they put all their faith. This includes those who work faithfully for many years with the belief that the company will take care of them in retirement, only to discover that the pension funds have been mismanaged and nothing is left. Many of these people see the signs coming, but fail to question and act in time to save themselves.

Toddler martyrs include the people who buy homes over hazardous waste dumps, on earthquake-prone fault zones, flood plains, or unstable land because they automatically believe that the authoritative contractor who is selling them the property can do no wrong. An investigation into the lives of these people demonstrates a track record of one catastrophe after another.

There are those with little money who manage to avoid such disasters, so it cannot be argued that limited finances are always the source of this problem. Although many people are born to poverty conditions, some people slip into poverty because of the activities of the martyrdom dragon. Poverty happens to be fertile ground for this vicious dragon. Nevertheless, all dragons work the soil of poverty conditions.

Martyrdom at the child stage

As with the self-deprecation dragon, the martyrdom dragon is not prevalent at the child stage because of the nature of the adult child's activities. Nevertheless, the martyrdom dragon finds its way into every level of development. Whereas at the toddler level people experience martyrdom largely as subconscious victimization, at the child level people attempt to make big splashes with their abilities to design regular disasters into their lives. They may use their martyrdom to control their children and make them pay attention to them. They may start out with millions of dollars and dramatically lose their money in a series of actions that bring them headline attention.

The martyrdom of the child level is not the mass catastrophe of the martyr toddlers living on river banks prone to flooding, but is expressed as individual efforts that are recognized as personal life dramas. These are not the victims whose shanties are swept away for the tenth time in floods. Rather, an example of a child martyr is the artful dowager who complains that her wealth cannot buy her good help or that society is going to the dogs because she cannot get her nails done on the weekend. She feels that her sons never visit her enough and are purposely ruining her life with their choice of mates.

Martyrdom at the adolescent stage

The martyrdom dragon at this stage is in its glory because there is so much to be martyred about. Adolescent martyrs can almost legitimately claim that nobody understands them or that life is exceedingly painful on a regular basis. Although all adolescents go through this, those suffering from the martyrdom dragon take advantage of these feelings to dramatize their victim identities.

Martyrs at this level tend to attach their victimization to causes. They are ready to go to prison for life for minor political statements. They lie down over railroad tracks or put themselves in front of rolling tanks to highlight the injustice of situations. Not everyone who engages in this behavior is dominated by the martyrdom dragon. Some are true heroes who make a great difference in the world because of their courage. The adult adolescent martyrs are those who actively seek and find dramatic scenarios in which they can act out their martyrdom. Their causes matter less than their acts. Their track records of victimization tend to identify them.

At the adolescent level, there can be insight. With great discipline, there can be movement to oust the dragon. However, the secondary rewards of martyrdom are so strong that they often overcome people's attempts to gain liberation from the martyrdom dragon.

Martyrdom at the adult stage

At this level, the martyrdom dragon tends to go underground and is not highly visible to others. It creates an internal process that people struggle with. When this process is brought to light, people can often recognize it and fight it off. Adult martyrs have much insight into the ways of the dragon and, although they suffer from its activities, they are not completely run by it all the time.

Adult martyrs recognize that they have great resentment for injustices done to them. They also recognize the feelings of entrapment that come over them, causing them to cave in and comply when they would rather not. Such recognition helps to slay this dragon, but the task is not a simple one.

Many people would not recognize the martyrdom in these

people, but adult martyrs know that they have it. There are not as many rewards in the martyrdom because the pleasure of sympathy from others is missing. Adult martyrs are only able to feel sorry for themselves, and even then, they know too well what they are doing.

How the Martyrdom Dragon Affects Your Life

The impact of the martyrdom dragon on your health

If you are trapped by the martyrdom dragon, you are not necessarily physically unhealthy. In fact, you may be in excellent health. The problem is that illness, aches, and pains are such a calling card for the dragon that you may milk these things for everything they are worth. You may turn a little cold into a withering, bed-ridden, dramatic event. This can obviously hamper healing. However, given the proper motivation, it is amazing how rapidly you can jump out of bed, seemingly miraculously healed.

Angelica hobbled around for weeks on a sprained ankle, gaining sympathy from her spouse and children. They exhorted her to rest and take it easy so it could heal. Actually, they were getting tired of her grimaces and looks of pain as she limped around the house doing unnecessary chores. She rested for a time, but just as she was about to heal, she deliberately helped the neighbor next door carry in groceries and injured her ankle again. The family was desperate. A vacation was coming up soon, and everyone feared it would be ruined by Mom's ankle drama.

Herbert, Angelica's spouse, came up with a brilliant idea. Since Angelica was a fervent Catholic, Herbert arranged for Father Luigi, the church pastor, to pay a visit. The visit was a major success. The next day, Angelica was up and out of bed, setting up flowers and cooking a delicious meal. A miracle had taken place. Her ankle was no longer sprained. Angelica had gotten the special attention she wanted in the way she could receive it.

Since martyrdom thrives on accidents, medical bills can mount for your family if you are a martyr. This is one of the ways that you may exact your toll for injustices done to you: "Make 'em pay. Its not my fault that I'm hurt." In the long run, the martyrdom dragon can ruin your perfectly good health, one of the greatest expenses of this particular dragon. In fact, the costs of martyrdom-driven illnesses and accidents are incalculable if you were to consider the expense on a world or historical level. Imagine the drop in hospitalizations and pharmaceuticals prescribed if the martyrdom dragon were to leave the scene.

If you are a martyr, you may adopt the attitude, "Someone is going to pay for the injustices done to me." Of course, the actual injustices occurred long ago. So, more often than not, the people or groups you make pay have little or nothing to do with your original injuries. This may result in any number of outrageous lawsuits in which you blame everyone and everything for your injustices and demand huge sums of money. However, since you are a true martyr, you may arrange to either lose the cases or end up losing all your money anyway, usually to your attorney.

Two of the greatest playgrounds for the martyrdom dragon are Chronic Fatigue Syndrome and allergies. This is not to say that you have martyrdom if you suffer from these maladies. You may suffer from other dragons, most noticeably impatience, as has been discussed. However, Chronic Fatigue Syndrome and allergies are deadly because they offer you, as a martyr, such a good camouflage for your dragon. You end up with the perfect excuse to say "no" indirectly and blame your body for your inability to comply. These syndromes also make it very easy for you to gain sympathy from a wide variety of people. They can make it possible for you to garner enormous amounts of attention for being ill with a nameless problem that seems to have no solution and that can come and go at whim. When sympathy is not forthcoming and people seem not to "understand," you can feel righteously martyred.

If you have one of these syndromes and feel enraged reading

this, it is probable that you suffer from the dragon of martyrdom
and are experiencing it intensely at the moment. Keep in mind
that the rage comes from a fear of being robbed of the expectation of love. The willingness to suffer with such uncomfortable
symptoms for the sake of a few crackers of attention suggests
deep wounding inside. Much of the energy you expend on med-
ication and treatments would be better spent digging in and
unraveling the dragon.

The impact of the martyrdom dragon on your creativity

As with your health, martyrdom does not necessarily have
to interrupt your creative flow, and yet so often it does. The
martyrdom dragon, like all the dragons, makes its goal the
destruction of your happiness and the creation of suffering.
Therefore, if you derive too much joy from your creative talent,
the dragon will make sure that it is ruined.

> Gloria was a talented artist who spent much of her child-
> hood caring for her alcoholic father. Just after her father
> died, she enrolled in art school and began to excel.
> However, she met her husband within a few months and
> then spent most of her life assisting her husband in a dry
> cleaning business instead of pursuing her art. She claimed
> that he needed her all the time and that she had no time
> left over for her art. Eventually, when her husband died
> and there was a comfortable nest egg, Gloria thought once
> more about pursuing her art. She enrolled in a local art
> course and began painting fine portraits. However, almost
> immediately she came down with an eye infection that
> prevented her from painting.

> Just as she was about to recover, she "by accident" injected
> superglue into her eye instead of the medication prescribed
> by her doctor. Her vision was lost in that eye, making
> painting very difficult. Although she could still make do
> with one eye, she refused, saying that she could never
> paint with one eye.

One of the most obvious ways that the martyrdom dragon stifles your creativity is in your inability to see alternatives. You may feel trapped by circumstances and simply not able to see your way out. Even if you are a highly creative, artistic person, you may become strangely dense when it comes to seeing your way out of a dissatisfying marriage or job. Whereas you may be able to see myriad possibilities for the design of a building or the development of a park, you may be unable to see the course of your own freedom.

The impact of the martyrdom dragon on your presence

When you are afflicted with martyrdom, you are preoccupied with injustice and with claiming restitution. The injustice is in the past and the restitution is in the future. Little energy is left for the present. When you are not focused on the present, you have little presence. Being present is akin to being powerful. If you are a martyr, you do not see yourself as having any power. The power seems to be in other people's hands. Yet those who live with you can attest to the power you have to create suffering. That power is harnessed by the dragon and is not available to support your life goals and higher purpose.

The power is there. Presence exists in potential form. You have everything you need to move forward. The dragon remains the great obstacle.

The impact of the martyrdom dragon on your relationships

The martyr, in feeling victimized, turns even the nicest person into an "abuser." It is not unusual to hear a martyr say things like, "All women are bitches. They take your money and dump you." This martyr may have selected some truly nasty women to be in relationship with. But along the way there were some decent women, too. Yet the easy-going women can be turned into angry, fed-up women when provoked enough. Then they were thrown on the pile of "all those bitches."

The martyrdom dragon, like all the dragons, has the ability

to turn your life into a self-fulfilling prophecy. Your belief in victimization creates the reality of your victimization out of the
raw material of life. The martyrdom dragon is excellent at getting you to select victimizers to be in relationship with. These
victimizers are then tortured indirectly by you. You may tend to
push away truly loving supporters. They do not fit the picture of
exploitation and suffering that you as a martyr need to keep the
dragon happy. On the other hand, the dragon thrives on the
company of other martyrs. They can mutually reinforce your
themes of "ain't it awful" and "nobody loves me, guess I'll eat
some worms."

Perhaps the strongest card in the martyrdom dragon's hand
is the power of the poison called sympathy. Sympathy creates
the false illusion of support and friendship. In reality, sympathy
perpetuates and feeds your identity as a helpless victim.

The impact of the martyrdom dragon on your spiritual life

In many religions, the martyrdom dragon finds a virtual
playground of activity. This is not to say that religion is only for
martyrs. The true teachings behind all religions promise anything but suffering. However, if you are a martyr, you may distort
religion into a platform for pain and a reinforcement for your
follies.

Within Christianity, you can find glory in suffering and
even death for the sake of salvation. You can focus on heaven as
the ultimate recompense for your self-made hell on Earth. You
can take this fixation on suffering to such extremes that it
results in self-punishment and self-mutilation in the hope that
more suffering will offer you redemption. You may not perceive
that much of this is simply more dragon's work.

If you are a martyr you can certainly find reinforcement in
Buddha's fourfold path, a teaching that you can interpret to
mean that life is all suffering. You can use this interpretation as
an excuse to avoid all pleasure and to perform the most rigid
self-deprivations. This is simply more dragon's play. (This interpretation, of course, represents a distortion of the teachings of

Buddha, who taught that it is craving that creates suffering and that life is illusive in nature.)

In Judaism, you can find a basic universal teaching that says that suffering can teach you many things, including moral fiber and discipline. There is great wisdom in this teaching. Yet, as a martyr, you can use this teaching as a justification for your tendency to suffer for later vindication. As a result, Judaism is a virtual feast for the martyrdom dragon. It has converts by the score. Under the influence of the dragon, the basic wisdom of the initial teaching is obscured, and in many cases lost.

In Islam, you can find the concept of the jihad or holy war. Within this principle lies a universal truth: that you must wage a personal internal war against lack of virtue and all the activities of the dragons within you. Yet, once again, you can interpret this powerful teaching to justify external war, with the result that you may be one of hundreds of thousands who are sent to your death based on the notion that martyrdom is good and will result in the certainty of salvation.

How to Transform the Martyrdom Dragon

It may seem that there is no hope of freedom from the scourge of the martyrdom dragon, but this lack of hope is merely the work of the dragon itself. Martyrdom is able to be both healed and erased. The martyrdom dragon can be slain and its energies transformed into life-affirming activities. The road, however, is exceptionally challenging.

The martyrdom dragon is especially artful at moving out of range and making it seem to you that its activities are perfectly justifiable. Because of its ability to cause you to fall apart just as you are about to assert yourself, martyrdom can seem to undermine the strength and determination you need to overcome it. However, all dragons have a weak spot within their horny scales, no matter how secret the place. The martyrdom dragon is no exception. This section describes this dragon's vulnerable spots and how to exploit them. Just reading about the activities of the dragon is quite annoying to it. It thrives on secrecy and remaining hidden. Therefore, you have just struck the first blow. Expect a return thrust. But take heart, for you have begun the battle.

Seven Affirmations to Beat the Martyrdom Dragon

Everything good always happens to me.
I create my own reality.
I am discovering more happiness every day.
I know how to have fun every day.
I always have excellent alternatives and options.
There is a way through every problem.
I am a valuable and worthwhile human being no matter
    what I do.
I am able to speak up for myself.
Life is getting better every day.

Seven Weapons to Slay the Martyrdom Dragon

Weapon one: Tell the truth. Admit that you use the
    strategy of manipulation.
Weapon two: Draw boundaries and hold them. Say no.
Weapon three: Admit your needs and ask for help. Become
    a team player.
Weapon four: Give up the pleasure of sympathy from
    others. Stop complaining.
Weapon five: Take responsibility and choose. See and
    accept alternatives.
Weapon six: Be willing to have fun. Let others see and
    enjoy your pleasure.
Weapon seven: Give up blaming and always being right.

Do these tasks sound impossible? They are not impossible. Are they extremely challenging? Yes, no doubt about it. To win this fight takes exceptional courage. Not everyone who takes up the challenge will win the first battle. But eventually, with discipline, you can succeed. The more power you take back from the dragon, the more powerful you will be. This process begins slowly, like a learning curve, and then by degrees increases in speed until you experience quantum leaps. That is why starting is the hardest thing of all to do.

Weapon one: Tell the truth. Admit that you use the strategy of manipulation.

Martyrdom is a parasite, not who you are at the essence level. You can rid yourself of this unwanted guest only if you see what you are losing to it. Martyrdom is not your friend. You must take responsibility for being a victim if you wish to eliminate it. Martyrdom is the abdication of responsibility for your actions, because blaming is always a lack of responsibility. To say yes when you mean no is manipulative and dishonest. To punish people for believing you adds insult to injury. Say what you mean.

Admitting martyrdom is tough because it brings up your intense feelings of worthlessness at the source of your protective strategy. It means facing your terror of feeling valueless. It also means tackling the rage that accompanies your fear. This rage is directed toward your early experience of having to earn love through compliance rather than deserving love just by being. Your rage must be expressed, not swallowed. This can be done with the assistance of a compassionate, yet tough, therapist. Try not to defeat your therapist by using the strategy of driving her or him insane with your vengeance. Your therapist is not your problem. She or he is your support system and your ally in confronting the dragon. Yes, you can defeat your therapist, but the only winner will be the dragon.

Weapon two: Draw boundaries and hold them. Say no.

The martyrdom dragon gained strength from your involuntary compliance as a child. You learned to be "nice" and "agreeable," saying yes to things you did not like. You had to deserve love and earn love through being servile, and it never worked.

No matter how hard you tried to earn love, you were never deserving enough, therefore you were forced to play by rules that made you lose.

The first step in using this weapon is to admit that being compliant failed. You can't lose by quitting the servile role and telling the truth about how you feel. The next step is to begin the frightening process of admitting to yourself that you don't want to do everything you are asked to do. You must learn to say "no." This means putting your foot down without caving in after two minutes. This takes much practice. You will be tempted to go.back to your old ways of saying "yes," and then complaining indirectly afterward.

Establish clear boundaries. Be clear about what you are willing to do and what you are not willing to do.

Weapon three: Admit your needs and ask for help. Become a team player.

One of the most painful experiences in the world if you are afflicted with the dragon of martyrdom is to admit that you are very needy. Yet, this is exactly what you must do to make progress against the dragon. In fact, you must make a complete confession. Healing comes when you say, "Yes, it's true, I'm desperate for love and I've sold years of my life trying to get it. I'm never going to get love by being good. Never. I'll have to risk disapproval, but I'm going to tell the truth. I need love, and I need help with my chores. Will you help me? I can't do them all by myself."

The martyrdom dragon makes requesting help very difficult. First of all, if you ask for help and get it, your martyrdom strategy is ruined. When you are a martyr, your strategy is not to ask for help but to secretly want someone to notice that you need help. However, you make it exceedingly difficult for anyone to respond. You insist on doing the whole job yourself. If help is given, you may get angry, but if help is not given, you may get angrier still. This makes others crazy.

The martyrdom dragon does not want you to be a team

player. It would rather isolate you to keep the game going. This is what you need to let go of.

Weapon four: Give up the pleasure of sympathy from others. Stop complaining.

All attachment to the poison of sympathy must go. This is a critical step for you to overcome the martyrdom dragon. What makes this so difficult is that you see sympathy as a substitute for missing love. But looking for sympathy and getting it is like being fed cotton candy instead of a balanced meal. It may taste good in the short run but it will kill you in the long run. A steady diet of sympathy is deadly, and the worst perpetrators of sympathy are those also afflicted by this dragon.

Sympathy is obtained as a result of complaining to the wrong people. Often martyrs will go into therapy with specific plans of complaining to sympathetic ears but with no intention of correcting their problems. If their therapists respond and listen sympathetically, they can engage in folies a deux for years. The therapists make an income and the clients make no changes. If the therapists confront the martyrs and offer no sympathy, there is much bitter complaining and spitefulness on the part of the clients. They may attack their therapists for "not helping" and then dissolve into tears.

I once had the experience of a client throwing a sheaf of one dollar bills at me at the end of a nonsympathetic session, saying sarcastically, "There's your money. Hope you enjoy it. Thanks for all the help." She actually thought at that moment that I was the source of her problems because I would not pat her on the head and say "tsk tsk." Of course, she wanted me to feel guilty. The money drifted around the room landing everywhere, but I did not honor her sadism by scrambling to pick it up. I'm sure she planned the dramatic gesture, and unfortunately the satisfaction that it gave her only fed the dragon. I made it a point to buy myself a treat with that money later. I did not want guilt money.

If you are a martyr, you do not need sympathy but you do

need empathy. You need to feel that there is genuine concern from others but that is all. The next step is action. You need to do something. This is the step the martyrdom dragon likes to resist. So, after ruthlessly giving up complaining and sympathy seeking, and seeing them as the poison they are, your next step is weapon five.

Weapon five: Take responsibility and choose. See and accept alternatives.

Taking responsibility for your choices attacks the entrapment you feel as a martyr. Your feelings of being trapped are real. However, the actuality of your being trapped is simply not true. When you are convinced that you are in a prison made by others, you can see no route of escape. The more alternatives you are presented with, the harder you argue that there is no way out. This results in exasperation on the part of those intending to help you, and despair and anger on your part. The secret is that the solutions can only come from you, not from others. You need help in accepting that there is always a way out of your dilemma. However, the way itself is for you to discover, and often the route to discovery is a rocky one.

Your main task is to accept responsibility. Make the discovery that no one is going to save you. You are going to have to take steps and assert yourself even if it means being considered "bad" by someone.

> Frank was in high stress every time he got off the telephone with his mother. No matter what he said or did, he could never seem to please her. According to her, he never visited her enough, and when he did it was for too short a time. He would never reveal to her that he had gone on vacation or had a good time with someone else because this would instantly make her accuse him of neglecting her while he had a good time. In fact, he would often bypass these events just to avoid her disapproval. He worked hard to support his family and felt pressure from his wife to spend less time with his mother and more with his family.

Although he hated to admit it, he would use some of his mother's guilt-inducing strategies on his own wife and children. The dragon of martyrdom had both Frank and his mother by the nape of the neck.

Frank complained to his friends that he had no way out. The only solution he saw was outward compliance with the excessive demands of his mother and trying to please his family by sending them on vacation without him. His friends pointed out that he could risk his mother's displeasure by standing up to her. After all, in thirty-five years he had never succeeded in gaining her approval, so what was there to lose?

Eventually, Frank did stand up to his mother. Faced with losing his family, he made a choice and decided to tell his mother the truth. He told her that he was going to spend more time with his family and that she would just have to be satisfied with his visits when he could manage. To Frank's amazement, his mother did not offer too much of a fuss. She did not like his decision, but it simply proved to her what she had suspected all along: that Frank was not a good son and was not deserving of her love. Frank realized that he could survive his mother's attitude because nothing had really changed about it. He was tremendously relieved. Needless to say, Frank's family life improved.

Weapon six: Be willing to have fun. Let others see and enjoy your pleasure.

The martyrdom dragon is invested in you destroying pleasure for yourself as well as in your using this lack of pleasure to punish others. The antidote is to learn how to have fun and then be willing to share it. This is, of course, easier said than done. If you are a martyr, you know how to avoid fun at all costs. Small wonder, because you were taught that you do not deserve pleasure and can never do enough to earn the right to it. If you have martyrdom, having pleasure is always going to seem like it will bring up the wrath of someone, even if it is the ghost of a parent long since dead. So, to have fun is a very risky business indeed.

Having fun means giving up the fantasy of one day being loved enough. Your strategy as a victim is to avoid fun and keep holding out for love. You do not realize that you are being manipulated by the martyrdom dragon. Your strategy of compliance and funlessness was developed in childhood as a means to survive wounding at that time. What you haven't noticed is that time has gone on and conditions have changed. The truth is that you can have fun and no great disaster is going to strike.

If you have martyrdom on your back, you are so afraid of the consequences of fun that you subconsciously do almost anything to sabotage it. Most often, your strategy is to avoid a fun situation in the first place. However, if you allow yourself to have a little fun, you usually find a way to punish yourself for it soon afterward, even if no one else faults you for it. Therefore, it may not be unusual for you to get sick on or after a vacation or to have a financial disaster following a promotion or business breakthrough. Pain and suffering are known quantities that can be handled, but pleasure is an unknown that could threaten your survival.

The vicious aspect of martyrdom is that so many disasters seem to appear out of nowhere, leading you to believe more assuredly that you have nothing to do with your own suffering. A parent may die two days before your wedding; a tornado may destroy your house just after you have broken your leg; your car may be smashed in a parking lot just as your car insurance is canceled because your check is lost in the mail. You can point to each of these circumstances and say, "But it wasn't my fault. I had nothing to do with it." Yet these strings of catastrophes do not happen with regularity to other people. Why?

The answer is metaphysical. Your belief that you are a victim tends to attract events that confirm your belief. Another way to say this is that like attracts like. Technically speaking, it would be wrong to say that these events are your fault. That would simply be assigning blame. You are not at fault. Yet you are responsible for changing your belief system to attract a different reality to yourself.

The best way to shift this kind of experience is to be willing to have a good time regardless of your fear of consequences and to be willing to have others join you in your fun. With this kind of commitment, the martyrdom dragon eventually gives up. It hates for you to have fun. This dragon is a sadist.

Weapon seven: Give up blaming and always being right.

Blaming is the booby prize. The most you get out of it is a sense of being right. That is not much of a prize. Yet, it is amazing with what tenacity blaming is a part of society. Notice how important the assignment of blame is in politics or in families where children or spouses quarrel: "He did it. No, she did it." It is as if somehow the assignment of blame is going to correct the whole situation. Your strategy as a martyr is to make the other person look bad and yourself look good. In martyrdom, you have a great investment in seeing yourself as good. To admit malice, vengefulness, and pettiness is extremely difficult, but this admission is necessary for your cure.

The real reason behind your blame is your fantasy of emerging as the one who is right and the one who is perfect. This comes from your expectation that you have to earn love by being perfect. You think you have to deserve love or you will be rejected. Since nobody's behavior is perfect, the process of blaming is truly a hopeless one. Blaming will never make you OK. You will still feel deficient and have to try even harder to be good. You may resort to negative strategies to appear good, such as lying and putting on an innocent appearance. The dragon loves the hypocrisy of it all.

Trying to be good can result in serious suffering. Sachi was an only child whose parents had not planned to have any children. Their idea of home was a spic-and-span environment that looked like something out of a television commercial. When Sachi was born unplanned, her parents were not prepared for the natural messiness of a child. She was somehow supposed to eat without slobbering and spreading squished banana all over her clothes and hair. Her natural delight in mashing food and licking her runny nose was met with strong disapproval. Her nose had to be wiped, her bib had to be clean, and her shoes and socks always had to be neatly on. If they weren't, she was considered bad. She had to earn love by being clean.

Faced with the horror of loss of love, Sachi became compliant. She resolved not only to meet her parents' standards but to exceed them. By the time she was ten, she was an extremely rigid little girl who followed all the rules and was totally obedient. Underneath her compliance was a rage that she could not show directly. The way it came out was in her need to be right about everything. Wherever she went, she preached the rules and pointed out if they were being broken. She got a certain pleasure out of catching her parents breaking the rules. This was her revenge.

However, as could be expected, Sachi's schoolmates shunned her, and even her parents found her unpleasant. She was sent to a counselor to be fixed. This convinced her more than ever that she was undeserving of love. Underneath her compliance, Sachi felt completely trapped. She tried to earn love, but no matter what she did she was never deserving enough.

Much later, when Sachi went to college, her parents admitted they had made some mistakes with her and offered to pay her tuition. She refused and put herself through college, living as a pauper, but getting gratification out of punishing her parents. After all, she was right, and they could never repay her for their miserable deeds. Let them die of guilt. Sachi's dragon was in complete control.

The turning point for Sachi came when she, in writing an autobiography for a graduate school program, recognized the failure of her strategy of needing to be right and blaming her parents. At that point she entered group therapy and began to work hard on taking responsibility for her life. Eventually she was able to forgive her parents enough to allow them to help her with graduate school tuition. This represented a major setback for the dragon of martyrdom.

Seven Exercises to Transform the Martyrdom Dragon

Exercise one: Always say yes to offers of help.

Exercise two: Make a practice of admitting error and responsibility.

Exercise three: Practice saying no. Hold your boundaries.

Exercise four: List all choices even if they do not seem attractive. Choose.

Exercise five: Pursue at least one pleasure a day.

Exercise six: List complaints, then burn them.

Exercise seven: Sustain the outward expression of assertiveness.

Exercise one: Always say yes to offers of help.

Martyrdom thrives on denying neediness. Yes, you are needy. Admit it and ask for help. Your challenge is to do it without a whine, a complaint, or any masked blame in your voice. An excellent way is to practice in front of the mirror. When you can stand yourself and feel pleased, you have succeeded.

Eradicate all forms of speech that begin with "You always . . . !" or "You never . . . !" or "Why can't you . . . !" In fact, it is a good idea to eliminate "you" statements altogether and begin all your comments with "I would like . . . !" or "I want . . . !" or "Please help me . . . !" or "I need . . . !" or "I am afraid . . . !"

Form the habit of never refusing an offer of help. Thank the person after help is received.

These exercises are challenging, but when you practice them you will feel more valuable as a human being. This combats the dragon's attempts to make you feel worthless.

Exercise two: Make a practice of admitting error and responsibility.

One excellent way to develop understanding about responsibility is to take a notebook and a pencil and make a list of statements. Begin each statement with the phrase "I am responsible for . . ." Fill in the blank with everything you can think of no matter how absurd you think it is. Your list could include statements like:

I am responsible for my nose . . . ears . . . teeth . . . hands . . . stomach . . . bones . . . and so on.

I am responsible for my sadness . . . anger . . . frustration . . . humor . . . happiness . . . and so on.

I am responsible for my job . . . my marriage . . . my relationships . . . my recreation.

I am responsible for owning my house . . . my car . . . my boat . . . and so on.

I am responsible for the sun . . . the moon . . . the stars . . . the Earth . . . the galaxy.

I am responsible for the trees . . . the grass . . . the animals . . . the rocks . . . and so on.

Make this list extensive. It is an exercise, and it will impact you. You do not have to believe every statement. The level of resistance you have in doing this exercise reflects the extent to which the martyrdom dragon has a firm grip on you.

Responsibility does not in any way mean blame, nor does it imply that you have to solve anyone else's problems. Responsibility implies your ability to respond.

A second step in this exercise is to reverse your habit of always having to be good or right. This is tricky, because the tendency is to fall into feeling worthless if you admit error. That is why you tend to avoid it. The best course of action is to introduce humor into this exercise.

On a daily basis, tell a friend or spouse, or list on paper, your wicked thoughts and actions, no matter how petty. How have you been bad? How did you not comply with your conscience or with someone you know? Being a little bit bad is being human. Celebrate a little.

Exercise three: Practice saying no. Hold your boundaries.

The first version of this exercise is a standard assertiveness-training technique for saying "no." It is best done with friends or partners. Your friends play people who ask you for big favors that you do not want to do. Perhaps they ask to borrow your car for several days or to borrow a large sum of money that you have in savings. They should try to make you feel guilty by pointing out how selfish you are or how undeserving you are. Your job is to say "no" and refuse no matter how hard it gets. If you cave in, you start again. Repeat the exercise until you can sustain the energy to say "no" for good.

The second version of this exercise focuses on your ability to get what you want and not give up. Your friend plays a mechanic trying to weasel out of a shoddy job on your car. You play a person who is returning your car because it is not working after expensive repairs. Your job is to request that the car be fixed and not to take "no" for an answer. You must stick with this request without whining or resorting to blaming or trying to get sympathy. Your partner gives you feedback and tells you if you pass. You pass if he or she is stymied and cannot argue against you any more.

Exercise four: List all choices even if they do not seem attractive. Choose.

This exercise is aimed at combatting your feelings of entrap-ment. If you have martyrdom, you need practice listing your alternatives in a given situation. At first, this will seem almost impossible, so it is good to have someone else pointing out the possibilities to you no matter how farfetched they seem. Your job is to actually consider each alternative without resorting to "Yes, but . . ." The process will bring up rage in you. You may experience hate toward the other person, so it is good if your partner is a therapist trained to handle these emotions. You will feel like blaming your partner for insensitivity at not seeing that the alternatives are impossible. Here is a possible scenario:

Your situation/desire: "I want to go to college but I have all these obstacles." List the obstacles.

Alternatives from your partner: "You could go at night part-time. Yes, you would then not be a perfect mother or spouse. So what!

"You could get a student loan. Yes, you would incur some debt and this might not make your spouse happy. So what!

"You could leave the care of your mother and father to your brothers and sisters for awhile. Yes, you would not be such a wonderful daughter or sister. They might not like it. So what!"

Exercise five: Pursue at least one pleasure a day.

Make a list of pleasures you would like to experience. Your pleasures can include foods, material things like clothes or gadgets, experiences like walks in the park or vacations, spending time with people you like, sex and affection, taking naps, and so on.

Make it a point to do one pleasure a day. Allow nothing to interfere with or interrupt the experience. The dragon will try very hard to ruin it for you or make it seem like you can't have it. You will have ample opportunity to see the wiles and machinations of your dragon. This will be an educational experience.

In order to keep track of the dragon's interferences, make a chart on which you check off your pleasure activity at the end of the day. Be honest. If you allowed a phone call or the kids to interrupt it, you did not pass. You are not allowed to blame anyone or anything for interfering. When you can achieve pleasurable activity five out of seven days a week, you are doing well.

Exercise six: List complaints, then burn them.

First, get your complaints out all at one time and in one place. Grab a notebook and write down something that you want. Next, list all the reasons why you think you can't have it. Let the dragon speak. It is better to control the dragon in a limited space by letting it speak than to let it run amok all the time. See what the dragon has to say. Give it full rein to say anything it wants. Occasionally, repeat the statement of what you want.

For example:

Statement:: "I want to go to college. I am going to college."

Complaints and reasons why not: "I have no time. I work full time. What about my two children? Who will take care of them? I'm too old to go. It is too expensive."

Statement repeated: "I want to go to college. I am going to college."

More complaints and reasons why not: "My spouse won't like it. My parents are aging—I'll have to take care of them. My health isn't so good. I can't climb stairs very well. The car isn't in good shape—we'll have to buy another one. My spouse needs a new car. There will be no resources left."

Do this until the dragon has nothing more to say. Then repeat the statement about what you want. When you feel quite emptied out, make a ritual of burning the pages. You may have to do this regularly for a time in order to make an impact. Your focus can range over a variety of topics.

Exercise seven: Sustain the outward expression of assertiveness.

If you are a martyr, you may have little success in sustaining your point of view or sticking to your guns in the face of resistance. This tendency to crumble or cave in can also be exhibited in your posture. Therefore, standing up straight with your shoulders back and your chest out during a confrontation is a major success. Practice maintaining this posture during a mock confrontation with a friend or therapist. Keep the balance of your weight on the balls of your feet rather than on your heels. Keep your knees bent slightly. Jut your chin forward to help keep you in touch with your assertion. Stick to your guns without resorting to blame, whining, or tears. Mirror work is excellent for this.

The quality of your voice also says a great deal about whether you are coming from a victim stance or a power-based one. Pay attention to the sound of your voice. You can tape your conversation and listen to the tone, quality, and volume of the sound. Is there a whine in that voice? A complaint or blame, perhaps? Is there a helpless quality in it? Work with your voice to create more authority and power in it. You can support it by breathing from your diaphragm. That will shift your voice away from the reedy, nasal quality of the victim stance.

Conclusion

The martyrdom dragon can be beaten. You will have to give up a lot of old habits, but it is worth it. What you will give up is a false way of life, a false identity, and a false persona based on righteousness, blame, sympathy, and suffering. What you will gain is immeasurable. You will find worth and satisfaction in being loved for the first time by your own essence-self. Your expectations of being loved for compliant behavior will gradually cease, and with them so will despair. Despair will be replaced by a sense of having choices, and with those choices will come the personal power to select one or more. You will find pleasure in living and will discover a sense of self that is kind but firm. Best of all, other people will want to have you around instead of finding you a pain in the ass to deal with. You might just find happiness and satisfaction in your old age.

Chapter Seven

THE
GREED
DRAGON

Positive Pole—Appetite
Negative Pole—Voracity

External manifestation

Selfish; grasping; hoarding; depriving; oral; possessive; stingy; devouring; unquenchable; avaricious; voracious; gluttonous; tight-fisted; mercenary; niggardly; covetous; piggish; hoggish; materialistic; participating in a feeding frenzy; anorexic; bulimic; promiscuous; amassing.

Internal manifestation

Deprived; hungry; unsatisfied; craving; ravenous; desirous; empty; insatiable; denying; fearful of losing out; horny; envious.

Examples of situations and conditions that promote the greed dragon

Accumulating version: Western capitalism; government lobbying; advertising and marketing; status symbols; stardom; opulence; lotteries; gambling and gambling meccas; competition; riots, stock markets; the bottom line; corporate raiding; junk bonds; savings and loans of the 1980s; life insurance; sales; yuppies; lawsuits; pornography; bars; the liquor industry; television;

game shows; get rich overnight seminars; scams; theft; fraud; larceny; rape; supermarkets; bulimia; the sex underground.

Deprivation version: Poverty; ghetto life; slums; homelessness; monastic life; asceticism; false humility; anorexia; chastity.

Physical appearance and presentation

The most marked feature of people afflicted with greed is the hungry-eyes look. This predator look in their eyes makes them appear like they would like to consume people. Their mouths can be broad, and when they smile at you, they exhibit almost a grimace. Weight is not necessarily an indicator of greed, but often it is. The look on their faces coupled with their weight is a better measure of it. However, people with greed may be thin, especially if they are bulimic or anorexic. Great swings in weight gain and loss are almost always symptoms of the greed dragon. The most accurate signs of greed are in behavior patterns.

To get a sense of what greed feels like, imagine that you have been in the hot sun in the desert without water and you are parched. As you crest a sand dune, you see a beautiful oasis with palms and a fresh water pond in front of you. Before you dash down to drink, what is the look on your face? What do you feel like? Now imagine that a thick glass window separates you from the water. How do you feel now? What is the expression on your face now? How would you relate to people from this perspective?

The Development of the Greed Dragon

Indulgence and deprivation

The greed dragon has two faces. One face is exemplified by gluttonous, gorging people who want everything for themselves. They help themselves to more than they need at everyone else's expense. The other face is exemplified by deprived individuals who are tightfisted and niggardly and who, as a result, live without the pleasure of anything. These two faces are either played out separately or paradoxically can be seen in the same individual. Such opposing reactions are typical of dragon behavior.

Fixations

The greed dragon differs from the other dragons in that it tends to fixate people on certain areas of focus. In one person, greed may fixate on food and drink; in another, the fixation is on power; and in still another, the greed fixates on information. Many people with greed are fixated on romance and relationships, or simply on attention. Perhaps the most common form of greed is the fixation on money and material goods. The fixation often shifts with circumstances so that, if people are sated for the moment with respect to one object, another object of craving pops up to takes its place. Whatever the fixation, greed follows the same course and takes the same toll. All the fixations involve both selfish desire and feelings of deprivation, no matter how much the people accrue or hoard.

Because deprivation is the source feeling, greedy people greatly fear that there is not enough to go around and that they will miss out on the good things or good times in life. This initiates hoarding behavior that tends to deprive others if there is indeed a limited supply. Greedy people pile up the desired object so obsessively that, in so doing, they lose the friendship and intimacy they so truly need. The dragon scores another victory.

The foundational conditions for the greed dragon are abandonment and loss in early childhood. As with the self-destruction dragon, the abandonment may be the result of a wide variety of conditions. The loved parents may be dead, hospitalized, in prison, traveling, or always at work. The parents may not like or want the children and therefore neglect them. Frequently, the children's mothers are highly dependent and involved in a series of destructive relationships with men that may involve drinking and drugs.

Accepting substitutes for love

The critical feature in the development of greed over self-destruction is the offer of substitutes for love. In the development of the self-destruction dragon, the two ingredients are abandonment and cyclical abuse. In the development of the greed dragon, the two ingredients are abandonment and "substitutes for love."

Substitutes for intimacy come in many forms and can usually be summed up as bribery. The parents feel guilt for not "being there" with their children, and offer sweets, toys, money, the promise of vacations, television, and an endless variety of distractions. All parents resort to these methods from time to time to preserve their sanity. However, for children affected by the greed dragon, this happens as a matter of routine and is not occasional. Rather than the physical nurturing and holding that all children crave, these children, as babies, are given bottles to keep them busy even though they may not be hungry. When touch and contact are withheld, the children accept the substitutes for want of something better. This gradually turns them against their natural instincts. Thus, these children learn to eat even when they are not hungry.

The children learn to expect that they will be given substitutes for what they actually want. Later in life, they actually become suspicious that all things they get are substitutes, even if they are the real things. Offers of good jobs are turned down because they would rather have better ones. Loving friends of average means are ignored because there are promises of excitement in possible wealthy associates. Greedy people ignore or put down things or people that are offered and find fault with them. The available friend is just not loving enough. The good job doesn't offer enough benefits. The gift of a car is scorned because it is dented or several years old. Somehow, what is available is never enough. The result is that what is offered is turned down in hopes that the perfect fantasy will show up. When it does not, these people are left with nothing. The greed dragon finds this most amusing and has a great laugh. Greed creates the deprivation that is so feared. The prophecy is fulfilled.

Rather than having their self-esteem build naturally from physical touch, children threatened by the greed dragon learn to rely on external substitutes to build their sense of identity. The result is that they think, "In order to be me, I must have the object (food, toy). I am desperate for it. It is out there somewhere. If I don't have it, I'm afraid I will die."

Research demonstrates that infant mammals deprived of touch in their earliest days and weeks actually wither and die even if they are given food and shelter. Children know instinctively that they need this basic ingredient of life or they will perish. As they grow, the need for physical touch continues but is not as critical as the first few days of life. Many children receive this nurturing as tiny infants, but soon life events intercede to interrupt the physical contact. Parents become fatigued, fall sick, or go away for any number of reasons. Rather than wither, most children have such a strong instinct for survival that they accept substitutes for contact with their parents. The way is thus paved for the dragon of greed.

The focus on what is missing

Because children affected by the greed dragon spend a great deal of time hungry for food or physical attention, they develop the tendency to fixate on what is not there rather than what is. When they are finally picked up, they are in too much pain or too overwhelmed to enjoy it. So they create the habit of focusing on their hunger and longing for desired objects or substitutes. They also develop the habit of idealizing what is missing or what has been substituted. This becomes a way of life.

The process of feeling deprived and always wanting naturally leads to the development of envy—wanting what others have. These children develop an intense desire, and it seems as if everyone else has desired objects but themselves. Older children create strategies and manipulations to get what others have even if it means taking it away from them, often by theft.

Later in life, these people tend to see the glass half empty instead of half full. The dragon fixates them on what is missing. When good fortune comes to them, they fail to see it. They can only see what is still not there. The grass is always greener somewhere else in the world of those afflicted with the greed dragon.

Three Tales of the Greed Dragon

Josh's story

Josh grew up in a broken home, the eldest of three brothers and two sisters. Josh's father, a traveling salesman, was away from home most of the time, and upon his return he would assuage his guilt by bringing toys and candy for the children. His mother, overwhelmed by trying to raise five children single-handed, left Josh and his siblings under the television's watchful eye most of the time. On many days, Josh and his siblings went hungry. When Josh was ten, his father abandoned his mother for another woman, leaving the family destitute. Occasionally, Josh would spend weekends with his father, who continued his habit of heaping toys and good times on the boy and then disappearing for long periods.

From the age of ten, Josh vowed that he would never be poor or hungry again. He excelled in school and eventually won scholarships to a major university where he majored in business. Within a few short years after graduation, Josh had risen to a position of power within the corporation he helped to prosper. He was known as an ambitious upcoming executive who would stop at nothing to get what he wanted. On the one hand, he was rewarded for his ambition and greed by the rules of the corporate world. On the other hand, he was hated and feared by his colleagues because of his ruthless ability to take over their territories and positions for himself. By the time Josh was thirty, he had become exceptionally wealthy and had an unquenchable desire to accumulate more power and material wealth. He had a reputation for raiding vulnerable corporations and liquidating their assets to further line his pockets.

Josh spent no time with his family, had few if any friends, and could not keep a relationship for more than a few weeks. Those who knew Josh also noticed that he seemed addicted to sex and had endless women at his beck and call. Josh's weight was also known to fluctuate rather radically, as he tended to gobble expensive meals without actually tasting his food. Josh was driven by greed but was not enjoying his life.

Healing for Josh began only after he experienced a series of heart attacks just after his fortieth birthday. His initial response to counseling was a desire to come in five days a week to get fixed so that he could resume his old lifestyle. He tended to fill the sessions with talk and found it very difficult to listen. Then he complained vociferously that he wasn't getting any help and that he felt he could get better treatment with another coun-selor of national reputation.

Slowly, as Josh began to see his tremendous hunger for love and the deprivation around it, he was able to sense the source of his pain and make some progress toward balance.

Clara's story

Clara grew up as the daughter of a diplomat with assign-ments overseas. As a child, she lived in many different coun-tries. Her mother, whose life was constantly disrupted by frequent moving, consoled herself with endless shopping. Clara became used to many beautiful objects being brought into the home from many different countries. She had many exotic toys and dolls and also had the distinction of having a famous father. Yet, Clara had to be satisfied with the excitement of her envi-ronment as a substitute for any real attention or affection from either parent. To make matters worse, the only attention she got from her father was sexual attention. Although she was not physically raped by her father, she became used to his sexual innuendos and caresses that occurred during the time she spent with him. When Clara reached twelve years of age, she grew obsessed with her weight. She would eat so little that she appeared anorexic. Then she would gorge herself and gain weight. This pattern of starving and gorging herself continued for many years but was relieved somewhat as she entered her twenties.

After college, Clara met a young man who was a promising playwright. She was enamored of the potential excitement of his lifestyle and decided to marry him. Soon after they were married, Clara ran up credit card bills shopping for an endless variety of unneeded clothing. When her husband complained and took her credit cards away, she got other ones, built up debt, and hid the bills from him. In addition, Clara's weight fluctuated wildly as she ate, put on weight, and then starved herself to slim down. This became a serious problem when Clara became pregnant and naturally gained weight in the process. The child was miscarried when Clara attempted to starve herself while she was pregnant. After another miscarriage, Clara became pregnant a third time.

By the sixth month of pregnancy, it became clear to the pediatrician that the baby's development was retarded because Clara was not gaining enough weight. The baby was born with a physical abnormality that required intensive care and an enormous amount of time and energy.

By this time, the family was near bankruptcy, and Clara volunteered for counseling only when she was caught shoplifting clothes. She admitted that she had an insatiable appetite for both food and clothing. After she consumed food, she felt horrible and sometimes vomited to get rid of it. After she shopped, she felt regret, and the clothing gave her no pleasure whatsoever. She often returned clothes and had accounts at many stores to keep her habit going. Her husband was fed up, and her friends had long since distanced themselves after failing to get her to admit her problems.

Clara was hungry but was getting no pleasure out of her

addictive attempts to satisfy that hunger. Her healing began with her admission to herself that she indeed was feeling severely deprived inside. She realized that the source of her deprivation was not food or clothes but love.

Margaret's story

Margaret was born during her country's intense involvement in World War II. Her father, a soldier, was gone most of the time. Her mother scrounged for food, clothing, and other items necessary for survival. She did not have enough milk to nurse, and Margaret often went hungry during her first four years of life. After the war, supplies were scarce and life was very difficult until Margaret was eight years old. Margaret used to dream of living in a country where there was plenty of food and everything people could want for satisfaction. Her dreams and fantasies became a substitute for the hardship she was experiencing. As she got older, Margaret developed a burning desire to go to the United States, the land she dreamed would be flowing with opportunity, milk, and honey.

From an early age, Margaret demonstrated talent as an artist. She had a natural gift for design and color coordination. She won several awards in local art competitions. Later, as money became more available, she developed into an outstanding photographer.

In her early twenties, Margaret realized her dream of going to the United States by receiving a scholarship to a prestigious art academy. She excelled in school and became a successful photographer for high-fashion magazines where she garnered high wages. Margaret accumulated material wealth and lived an opulent lifestyle. However, within a short time she grew increasingly dissatisfied and felt that she was not finding the happiness she truly wanted in life.

A friend introduced Margaret to an Eastern-style guru who invited her to join his ashram. She quit her work and gave all her possessions away. She existed on boiled vegetables and gruel, proclaiming that this was the proper way to live. But Margaret was not happy, and she grew tired of the ashram members, who seemed to quarrel and fight on a regular basis for the guru's attention. She even found herself enjoying being his favorite devotee, so she felt it was time to quit. After leaving the ashram and living for several years as an ascetic, she met a successful filmmaker whom she married. Margaret found herself back in an opulent lifestyle again. She resumed her photography, but each time she was up for an award or a promotion she would deliberately quit or not submit her work. She stated that there was too much ego in awards and success. After several years of society living, she divorced her husband and followed a hippie musician out to the West Coast to live on the land. She was broke and on food stamps but proclaimed to her friends that this was the right life to live.

Although Margaret feigned bliss living as a hippie, she was no happier than she had been before. She felt frustrated with the lifestyle and the lack of ambition in the people around her. She naturally fell into organizing craft fairs and local art shows. Everything she touched became instantly successful. Yet each time she showed signs of erasing her poverty, she would quit inexplicably and move on to something else, claiming she was afraid she would become bored. Her friends and family would tear their hair with frustration because they knew they would have to support her with more loans, money that she could go through in a twinkling.

Margaret had talent, the Midas touch, and the ability to support herself well. However, she was out of work most of the time, on the dole, and had nothing to show for her ability and talent. Margaret was terrified of success and did everything in her power to sabotage it. She was terrified of her hunger, her wants and desires, and the emptiness she felt when she experienced success. So instead she created deprivation, thinking that somehow this was better than having something. In reality, deprivation was what she had come to know and be familiar with from her earliest childhood, but it did not lead to happiness. She was merely playing out an old theme like a broken record, and creating hardship for herself and those who loved her.

Margaret began to study with a Buddhist teacher who helped her to see her patterns. She learned that neither having nor not-having leads to happiness. The true source of happiness for her lay in realizing her talent and expressing her natural ability whether it led to wealth or not. The road to happiness was blocked by the greed dragon that had been playing havoc with her life for decades. She had to face the pain and fear of her hunger as well as the fantasy that somewhere, out there, was the great and final meal that would satisfy all her desires.

The Seven Steps of Development for the Greed Dragon

Step one: Abandonment and deprivation fuel the children's hunger.

Step two: The children accept substitutes for affection.

Step three: Desire for the substitutes takes over.

Step four: The children feel entitled to the substitutes and blame others when the substitutes do not satisfy.

Step five: Acquiring the substitutes reminds the children of deprivation.

Step six: The children focus on what is missing rather than on what is available.

Step seven: The missing objects are never found.

Step one: Abandonment and deprivation fuel the children's hunger.

Deprivation is firmly imprinted in early childhood. "I'm hungry. I'm starving. I've got to have it." This is the intense feeling inside these children as their experience of deprivation of food and/or affection becomes a way of life. In terror and pain, the children become desperate for relief of any kind.

Belief and decision: "Life is about wanting relief desperately."

Step two: The children accept substitutes for affection.

After long waits, the children become aware that substitutes are being offered. At first, the toys are refused, the rubber nipples and plastic bottles are pushed away, the unknown people are frowned at. However, as hunger for affection, food, and stimulation mounts, the substitutes are eventually accepted. At that point, the children fantasize that the substitute objects are the real thing; otherwise they will not survive. The children become split. At one level, they know they are getting substitutes, not as good as the real things. At another level, they make believe the substitutes are the real things. In other words, they go into denial.

Belief and decision: "The real thing is never going to come along. I'll take what I can get and pretend to like it."

Step three: Desire for the substitutes takes over.

Fixation occurs and acquiring begins. The children begin to intensely desire substitutes. Eventually, these substitutes develop into fixated objects that may be concrete or abstract, including food, attention, sex, information, power, money, gold, property, jewels, corporations, territory, influence, spouses, experiences, and collector items.

Belief and decision: "By collecting and hoarding this, I will never be hungry again. Acquiring is a relief."

Step four: The children feel entitled to the substitutes and blame others when the substitutes do not satisfy.

The children feel that the world owes them what they are looking for. To them, it seems entirely reasonable to demand or grab. That is why they can eat all the cookies and milk and leave everybody else with none. They simply cannot get out of their own needs enough to put themselves in other people's shoes.

The problem is that, as adults, it is very hard for people afflicted by the greed dragon to see that they are the ones responsible for breakdown of relationships when they grab, demand, or act possessive. Their tendency is to blame others for not supplying the needed attention. This blame is misplaced. Their resentment goes back to the original offenders who may be long dead.

Belief and decision: "I have a right to what I am missing and I don't care who pays as long as I get it. It's their fault that I am hungry."

Step five: Acquiring the substitutes reminds the children of deprivation.

Acquiring results in pain. The objects of desire are thus rejected. Each time the children are successful at acquiring the desired objects, they are reminded that these objects are only substitutes and not the real things. Thus, rather than being satisfied, they are fueled even more to search for another object-meal-love-drink-toy to satisfy them. They are again sated only for moments, and then they begin to cry in pain. The objects are rejected or ignored as purveyors of satisfaction. The search for other objects eases the pain temporarily. The new objects may be identical to the previous objects.

A variation of this theme is that the children reject the substitutes and then refuse to search for new objects. Searching for new objects is just too painful. The children fear their own great hunger and desire, so they try to keep their needs suppressed. They settle for living without what they need, but the hunger goes on and on. Often, they try to prove that they are above the hunger or have controlled it. Later, this can lead to lives as renunciates or ascetics. Many people, controlled by the dragon of greed, opt for life in religious orders. That is why churches and temples often become so opulent and wealthy. The greed dragon is busy at work anyway.

Belief and decision: "Whatever I get, I won't like. It isn't the real thing. I need another one." Or "I quit. I'll do without. You see, I need nothing."

Step six: The children focus on what is missing rather than on what is available.

This step is the development of the famous "grass is greener" syndrome. It is also the source of the emotion of envy—desiring what others have. Later in life, others always seem to have what greedy people are personally missing. That means that others become the object of their intense interest or even obsession. Greedy people follow others around, scrutinizing them and finding ways to intrude into their lives. They may even fall into the fatal attraction syndrome. If they succeed in entering other people's lives, they may ruthlessly take what they want and then cast the people out.

Greedy people are unreasonably demanding of others' time, energy, space, and generosity. They are abnormally possessive within relationships. They become furious if their partners spend time with other people or devote energy to their children or jobs. They want every moment, and even then, they are upset if their partners do not appear to attend to them every second. Thus, the time spent with partners is stressed and filled with resentment, even though the partners try as hard as they can to be accommodating. Eventually, the partners are driven away by the demands, and the greedy people are left with nothing.

Belief and decision: "Whatever I have is not what I want. Other people have what I want. I'll have to take it."

Step seven: The missing objects are never found.

Panic sets in, then despair. No matter how hard children affected by the greed dragon look, hoard, possess, take, want, and wish, they do not get what they want to fill the hole. When these children miss the cuddling and nurturing of loving parents in early childhood, they grow into adults for whom no amount of food, money, sex, or power is ever going to make that up. These are forever unsatisfying substitutes because they are the wrong ingredients. They are like salt instead of sugar in a recipe.

Yet the greed dragon would have people believe that they need these objects.

Underneath the surface denial, a horrible truth keeps trying to penetrate the awareness of these people: "My efforts are truly hopeless; the substitutes are useless. The external world will never fill my needs." As this truth tries to penetrate their consciousness, terrible anxiety sets in. The people redouble their efforts to satisfy their needs, even at risk of life and limb. Panic sets in, and seriously addictive behavior may result. When the panic fails to produce satisfactory results, the truth dawns and despair takes its place. This is why the denial is so strong. Nobody wants to feel such despair.

Belief and decision: "If I tell the truth, I will have to admit that what is missing in my life can never be found. It's better to lie to myself."

The Greed Dragon's Big Lie

The greed dragon wants people to believe that just one more of anything will bring a feeling of satisfaction. One more drink will do it for the night. One more corporation taken over will produce relief and make everything OK. One more lover will be the right one. One more cookie will cure the hunger. In their obsession with obtaining the next thing, greedy people tromp on what they already have and destroy it. They end up with less than they had before. They end up with nothing. This is the greed dragon's great lie.

Hungry, overweight children constantly ask other children if they can have bites of their sandwiches, sips of their Cokes, or pieces of their candy bars. They always take too much. Soon, the other children learn to avoid these greedy children and sneak away when they see them coming. Rather than getting what they want, the greedy children drive everyone away and get nothing at all.

Greed produces the deprivation that fueled it in the first

place. This is the terrible irony produced by the greed dragon. Most people who allow the greed dragon to dominate their lives die lonely, impoverished individuals. They experience the creation of their worst fear: to die unloved, uncared for, unhappy, and unfulfilled. They did it to themselves.

Although Howard Hughes died having money, he certainly died with nothing else. He was a lonely old man unable to enjoy his fortune. This, of course, is the theme of Charles Dickens' *A Christmas Carol*, in which Scrooge is on his way to a lonely death before he mends his ways. This is the classic tale of salvation from the greed dragon.

Greedy people do not enjoy their money, their food, their power, and their relationships because they are too worried about losing these things and they are too focused on getting more of them. One of the easiest ways to identify greed in people is to see whether or not they actually enjoy what they have accumulated.

The Great Dragon Exchange:
The Slide from Greed to Self-Destruction

Myths and fairy tales are replete with themes of greed leading to ultimate self-destruction. This is also a powerful theme on television soap operas and in Hollywood films such as the James Bond series. In all these stories, greedy people are so intent on getting more power or wealth that their judgment fails them and they make foolish choices resulting in their demise. The reason this is such a popular theme is that it is so true.

Too much food leads to loss of control over weight and results in heart attack and death. Bulimia and anorexia, the spin-off problems of greed, destroy the body. Similarly, too much alcohol and too many drugs damage the body beyond repair. Gambling often results in the total loss of all possessions as well as the destruction of personal relationships. Hitler's greed for power, fueled by the deprivation created by the Treaty of

Versailles, led to ultimate disaster for himself and his country. The examples go on and on.

Excess always leads to loss of control and destruction. Therefore, what often begins as greed ends in self-destruction. The panic of greed not satisfied can lead to despair. Both the panic and the despair are dangerous responses. The panic leads to serious errors of judgment while the despair can lead directly to suicide.

Since greed is so often associated with addiction, especially alcoholism, it frequently leads to destructive and abusive behavior. The majority of child abuse, including violence and incest, is alcohol related. What begins as greed ends in destruction.

After the greed dragon has its way with people, it passes the empty husks of these people to the self-destruction dragon for the final coup de grace. These two dragons like to work together in this fashion. They perform a one-two punch.

Stages of Maturity and the Greed Dragon

Infant stage: ruthless, savage survivalism
Toddler stage: addiction and local corruption
Child stage: hoarding, amassing, and flouting
Adolescent stage: jealousy and hunger for love
Adult stage: spiritual materialism

Greed at the infant stage

Greed at the infant stage manifests as an absolutely ruthless, "me-first," survive-at-all-costs attitude. This is an ultimately selfish point of view that states, "To hell with everyone else." Following are some examples of the infant approach to greed: A person lets an entire village perish so he or she can personally escape the enemy. Someone steals the entire food supply of a family in winter in order to eat. A person kills someone else's spouse in order to take the spouse for him- or herself. Someone commits an endless stream of rapes and murders until caught, imprisoned, or killed. An ancient tribal king in Fiji eats over one thousand of his own subjects to satisfy his appetite for human flesh.

The greed dragon performs its most heinous deeds through those who never grow beyond an infant's emotional development. The voracious appetite of people who do not recognize other human beings as sacred is truly dangerous.

Greed at the toddler stage

Greed at the toddler stage is most often fixated on food. Weight problems abound. Toddlers are weaned from their mothers' breasts and naturally try to establish independence. Part of their independence is being able to feed themselves. The problem is that toddlers don't always know when to stop feeding themselves, especially when it comes to candy and desserts. They still require parental guidance to eat healthy foods in the appropriate quantities. Many adults, stuck at the toddler stage, become hopelessly addicted to sweets because these desserts are like mother's milk to them. Their adult supervisors are the small army of counselors, doctors, and professionals who monitor their weight. Of course, nothing works because the weight problem is the result of deprivation at the most instinctive level. The sweets are substitutes that are hard to give up for people too undeveloped to have insight into the source of their problem.

Adult toddlers fixated on power are the individuals who amass power at the small pond level. They are, for example, the local clan leaders, chieftains, sheriffs, or mayors who want all the emulation and control for themselves. Toddlers always want credit and attention for what they accomplish. They want Mom and Dad to notice them and give them praise. Greedy adults, acting as toddlers, try to attract the attention of more powerful politicians or lords who will notice them and give them local rewards and favors. Some small countries also do this by trying to attract the attention of their large, prosperous, parental neighbors.

Since toddlers are interested in learning society's rules, they almost always arrange to get caught by the law (parents). Eighty percent of all bank robbers are caught by the law. Yet bank rob-bery is perpetrated over and over again, even by those who have done it before, and even by those who have already been impris-oned for years. Uncontrolled greed for unearned money usually leads to toddlers performing primitive, impulsive acts that get them caught. More sophisticated individuals know how to acquire plenty of money without the risks associated with bank robbery.

Adult toddlers almost always flout their newly acquired power or stolen goods to the point that they are ratted on, caught, and jailed. The boys just have to show off their stolen car to all their friends and brag about the heist. They spend their stolen money wildly, attracting as much attention as possi-ble. Or, after a blatant drug deal, a ghetto kid pays cash for an expensive new Italian sportscar to broadcast his success. In this fashion, toddlers always arrange to get caught for their greed. They want to be stopped, because they fear their own out-of-control impulses. They continue their crime sprees until they are stopped. In a society that refuses to stop them, they are out of control and deeply anxious.

Greed at the child stage

Greed at the child stage is usually fixated on power, sex, and money. Children want to excel and flex their newly discovered skills and muscle. Therefore, adults acting as children do not arrange to get caught like toddlers do. Greedy adult children try to acquire and amass in such a way as to wrest everything away from competitors and become ultimately powerful. They want the complete success of being the wealthiest people around, the most attractive people in society, or the most politically power-ful people in the land. Nothing less will do. Their ambition is to become the unparalleled stars of Broadway or Hollywood who can command the highest fees, have anyone they want, and who listen to no one. In these ultimate children's fantasies, they are free of parental guidance and do what they please.

Greedy adult children like to collect sexual conquests like

others collect coins. They often retain keepsakes of their conquests as badges of honor. The greed has them going through a
series of partners without regard for their partners' feelings or
sensitivities. Their sexual conquests are treated like objects to
be left behind in favor of new objects. Some people even spe-
cialize in their collections, such as rock-star groupies or female
followers of athletes in major league sports. Greed at this level
contributes to the spread of diseases such as AIDS.

Greed at the child level has the most consequences for the
environment and the masses. When a few people amass such
wealth or power, they often enjoy depriving others in the
process. Their decisions are far reaching and may effect the lives
of thousands of people. When a corporate mogul decides to
move his manufacturing base overseas to make more money,
thousands of employees may lose their jobs. When a nation's
leader makes the decision to invade another country for its
resources, millions of lives are put at risk.

Greed for personal power often concentrates itself at the top
echelons of political power in the world. For example, a world
leader, greedy for power, may refuse to step down even when a
transfer of leadership might mean salvation for the country.
Adult children's greed in action is apparent in the behavior of
many leaders in national and international politics.

Greed at the adolescent stage

Adolescent greed is more often concentrated in the area of
social relationships. Adult adolescents are extremely jealous or
very possessive in their relationships with spouses and significant others. They have great needs for love and affection, and
they sense that the satisfaction of those needs will come from
other people, not so much from money or things, as adult children believe. In this respect, adolescents are more sophisticated
than their child counterparts.

Even so, the greed dragon is disastrous in relationships
because it slowly but surely pushes the needed people away.

People under the influence of this dragon drive their families away by constantly demanding all their time, loyalty, and attention. Adult adolescents often go from partner to partner seeking satisfaction in love, only to drive their partners off time and again. The greed dragon tends to make these people's lives look like soap operas with their intense intrigues, jealousies, and fights over attention.

Some adolescent greed shows up in drinking problems and eating disorders. Often, alcoholics are extremely emotionally draining and demanding in relationships. Anorexia and bulimia are also common ailments among adolescents because their underlying issue is sexual attractiveness. Adult adolescents are prone to ongoing bouts with these greed disorders.

Greed at the adult stage

Greed at the adult stage is often fixated on experiences or knowledge. These people are insatiable travelers and collectors of adventures. They have a fear that they will die too soon to experience everything they want to do or be. The greed backfires on them in that they are never able to go in depth into anything because they always move on before they finish what they were doing. They feel perpetual dissatisfaction with their lives because they are not able to ground themselves in anything.

I had occasion to meet some of these individuals during my early college teaching days. Since I taught in the evening for a chronologically older group of students training for a second career, I met many people who simply could not settle down to do anything with their lives. They were drifters, always looking for something but never finding it. Many had been to India or to other countries of the world in pursuit of spiritual enlightenment. They collected gurus, teachings, and practices like so many stamps. They did not stick with these studies. Since they were looking for "the answer," they did not have the motivation to develop emotional relationships with others. Relationships

were seen as too distracting. For these people, looking for the
"the answer" was a substitute for the real thing: self-respect and
unconditional acceptance of themselves and others.

Greed for knowledge operates in a similar fashion. Greedy
adults are constantly distracted by something else they want to
study, so they fail to complete their current interests. In this
way, some people become perpetual students who are never able
to declare their majors or train for professions. The greed results
in its nemesis: little to show for the great investment of energy,
time, and money.

When I first began teaching, I had a student in a graduate
psychology course who was so interested in the lecture material
he could not keep himself from interrupting the class with questions. Questions would follow more questions until other class
members began to complain that he was interfering with their
learning. Rather than getting more information, the class was
actually getting less. The greedy student badgered me before and
after class, bombarding me with questions. He even got hold of
my phone number and called me at home for more information.
I felt smothered by him but was torn because I did not want to
discourage his interest. However, when papers were due, a curious thing happened. This student's paper showed no compre-
hension of the material. He was so distracted by what he wanted
to know that he never listened to the material. He ended up
with less education than the rest of the class and a teacher who
was annoyed with him.

How the Greed Dragon Gets You in the End

The greed dragon can be quite insidious, for it always leads
to having, doing, and being less than before. Not only do you
fail in the long run to acquire more, but you lose what you had
to begin with. The harsh lessons of this dragon always involve
the pursuit of substitutes, and ultimate loss as a consequence.

To the extent that you are unconscious of the activities

of this dragon, you are completely run by it. Without insight, you are doomed to play out the age-old moral drama of greed.

How the Greed Dragon Affects Your Life

The impact of the greed dragon on your health

The impact of greed on your health is obvious. Consuming too much is the scourge of modern Western culture. Anything consumed beyond moderation becomes a destructive force, and Westerners consume too much of everything. A great percentage of medical problems have their source in food and drink disorders as well as in the inappropriate consumption of drugs. Both anorexia and bulimia have serious health consequences that often lead to death.

Eating disorders involve rejection of yourself, anger, and a cycle of deprivation and self-gratification. When you starve yourself in anorexia, you are saying, "I am undesirable at any weight. I must not eat so I can lose weight and get what I want: love and attention. There is no weight that is acceptable. Therefore, I will starve until I die and then I won't have a problem." If you are bulimic, you experience a cycle of eating and purging. The eating is gratifying, it temporarily relieves tension, and it is often a release for a great amount of anger and frustration. You may say, "I hate being deprived. I can't stand it. I'm going to have as much as I want of anything." Immediately after splurging, you experience remorse as well as self-rejection: "I'll lose love. I better lose weight. I am unacceptable." Your purging begins with vomiting and then the cycle moves on to rebellion and eating again.

However, food is not the only thing you may overconsume. Greed causes you to risk everything for the sake of acquisition. This acquisitiveness destroys the health of society and culture as well as your own life. Cultures that consume more than their share of Earth's resources doom themselves and other cultures to natural disasters and eco-destruction. Greed on a national scale ruins the health of smaller economies around the world. A small country that gives up its diversity to provide a single cash crop to meet the needs of a developed nation is courting disaster. Whose greed is this? The small country's or the developed nation's? Perhaps both.

The impact of the greed dragon on your creativity

The greed dragon waylays your creativity by making your acquisition goals more desirable than your expression goals. In their times, the great masters might never have produced their great masterpieces had they been more concerned with greed.

Greed fixates you on acquiring substitutes rather than on releasing your true self-expression. If you are a greedy creative artist, you are going to go for the big ticket items when it comes to your artistic expression. Recently, Hollywood has been fixated on creating sequels to known successes rather than striking out into the unknown territory where true creative expression lies. In the arts, the tried and true is the death knell of creativity.

The hallmark of greed is the substitute of artifice for something with true artistic value. If you are a greedy seascape artist, you may churn out variations on a theme, day after day, to lure the pocketbooks of tourists at the seashore. If you are a pulp fiction writer, you may pump out formula look-alike novels in lieu of real literature. Currently, greed is rampant in the creative arts, and satisfaction is at a low point.

Perhaps the most dismal of all results of greed in the arts is the inflation of masterpieces for their investment value. The world's outstanding artistic masterpieces are often under extreme protection and hidden in vaults where no one can see them because they are worth too much to their owners.

Sexuality is intimately associated with creativity. If your greed fixates on sexuality, it tends to divorce it from its creative qualities and drive it toward obsession. Under these conditions, your sexual fantasy life fixates on a narrow focus like body parts or related objects such as articles of clothing. Sometimes your fantasies revolve around a specific scenario or series of steps—like a dominant mistress with black boots who methodically spanks you. You are then driven to acquire the object of your greed until you can experience it over and over again, like a pigeon at a feeding station. If you are sexually obsessed, you may collect or hoard objects that are fantasy related, to the exclusion of real relationships. The problem is that your hunger for satisfaction is never satisfied and your obsession gets stronger and stronger until it drives you into a frenzy.

The impact of the greed dragon on your presence

If you are under the influence of greed, you may not be able to be truly present with others. Your attention is somewhere else rather than with those you are relating with. You are concerned with acquiring someone else's attention because you have already acquired the attention of those with you. Imagine trying to talk in a satisfying way to someone who has not eaten in a week or is extremely thirsty. His or her thoughts are on the next meal or oasis. Imagine trying to be intimate with someone who is already planning the strategy of the next sexual conquest, since he or she has obviously already conquered you. The alcoholic is not present and neither is the drug taker. If you are not present, you have little presence either. Presence is the result of focusing your attention on what is immediate, not elsewhere.

The impact of the greed dragon on your relationships

If you are a greedy person, your demands in a relationship are great but your willingness to satisfy the needs of others is limited. You want everything from your partner, including affection, attention, understanding, and sympathy. You resent the slightest inattentiveness or insensitivity demonstrated by your partner or mate. You desperately need the love of your mate but are resentful and hostile toward her or him for not always delivering what you need. Your resentment undermines the relationship while your greed drives your partner away.

In more committed relationships, you may become unfaithful in order to punish your partner for failing to deliver, or you may be unfaithful out of your greed to find a more attentive partner. Your spouse may then become unfaithful just to get away from you. Relationships cannot tolerate greed for long. Greed is designed by its very nature to ambush relationships and destroy them. The two are by nature incompatible.

The impact of the greed dragon on your spiritual life

The paradox introduced by the greed dragon is at times most obvious in the spiritual realm. Greed and all of the other dragons infiltrate all areas of life, and religion and spirituality are no exceptions.

Hunger for spiritual truth sometimes becomes a voracious consumption of religious teachings. If you are bitten by the dragon of greed, you may collect gurus and spiritual teachers like so many butterflies. Yet, no one teacher is ever the right one, and you may keep searching and searching but never finding. Every other week you convert to something else.

If you are in a spiritual community, you may be greedy to be in the presence of the guru at all times. You may compete fiercely to see if you can be closest to the guru or the favorite of the cardinal, bishop, or pope. I was once nearly trampled by people rushing to get the choicest seats to see a visiting guru. This did not appear to me to be enlightened behavior.

There are historical examples aplenty of those who climbed the ladders of power and influence within their spiritual communities. Their greed was fixated on power, and these people made sure they sat at the right hand of the guru or in the seat of greatest influence.

Spiritual materialism has been around at least as long as religion. The idea that you can collect brownie points for heaven or buy forgiveness through donations and contributions to a church or temple has greed at its source. If you are a greedy soul, you may believe that a more expensive ritual sacrifice insures salvation. The notion that you get to heaven by demonstrating material success is another distortion based on greed.

Yet greed has another form that is harder to see. If you are controlled by greed, you may try to handle it by repressing it or denying it. Greed has a self-depriving aspect to it. Therefore, you may try to control or hide your greed by joining a religious order, taking a vow of poverty or chastity, choosing to live as an ascetic, or eschewing the pleasures of the world. You may sermonize and preach against "filthy money and sex" and extol the virtues of living without them. Yet a closer inspection may reveal that greed is actively present in your everyday affairs. You may profess to be a servant of this god or that, but you enjoy hobnobbing with the rich and famous, generously sampling their sumptuous feasts and parties. You may be a professed pauper who ends up with a weight problem and an ample girth.

Currently, many priests of the Catholic Church are being accused of both child sexual abuse and having sex with members of their congregations. This is a classic example of the greed dragon at work. These individuals promised society to do something that was beyond them, which was to remain chaste. Their deprivation led to a hunger for sex that undid them in the end. Perhaps the promise to be without gratification is simply unrealistic for these people.

While individuals within religious organizations take vows of poverty, the organizations often grow rich and are at times obviously greedy. The people of a small, poor village may give everything they have to help build an opulent temple or cathedral. Icons and vestments are gilded in gold and the stout priest is finely arrayed while the people dress in rags and go to bed hungry.

Many a church has turned its greedy organizational eyes covetously on the government treasury and has warred with kings over the control of power and wealth. A greedy organization is simply an organization controlled by individuals within whom the greed dragon has gained control.

Although the greed dragon has corrupted religions and clergies, and infiltrated itself into individual spiritual development, there are, of course, many people with spiritual convictions untainted by greed. These people often come into conflict with those who are run by it. This makes for great drama.

How to Transform the Greed Dragon

As with all the dragons, there is a way to "starve" the dragon of greed. If you do not starve it out of your life, it will feed on your vitality and life energy until you die of starvation. There are good examples of those who did not fight greed but allowed it to run rampant in their lives: Howard Hughes, Adolph Hitler, Jim and Tammy Bakker, Ferdinand and Imelda Marcos, and Leona Helmsley, to name a few. Scrooge from Dickens' A Christmas Carol was saved because he made the choice to transform. This story contains valuable clues to the overthrow of greed.

You can choose addiction, sadness, and endless suffering or happiness, productivity, and serenity. Not everyone chooses the latter because the dragon of greed is so seductive and hypnotic that many choose to follow it and become ensnared in its lies. Some sense the danger and have the insight to fight back. Fighting back involves recognizing that there is a way out and becoming committed to that disciplined but liberating process.

Your arsenal to combat greed is diverse and at times may seem paradoxical or contradictory. It takes a great deal of maturity to understand the nature of these paradoxes and to avoid losing your way.

Affirmations to Beat the Greed Dragon

I have everything I need or want in order to be happy.
I love to share what I have with others.
The more I give, the more I get.
I thoroughly enjoy everything I have.

I am confident enough to face my sadness.

I no longer feel the cravings I used to have.

I am powerful and no longer need to blame others for anything.

I am completely satisfied with what I have.

Seven Weapons to Slay the Greed Dragon

Weapon one: Acknowledge that greed is a problem and get help.

Weapon two: Recognize your greed's fixation on substitutes such as food, power, and sex.

Weapon three: End the search. Surrender. Face your feelings of despair.

Weapon four: Recognize your true source of satisfaction.

Weapon five: Learn to give to others. Give up blame. Take responsibility for your life.

Weapon six: Be kind and generous with yourself.

Weapon seven: Recognize what you already have. Enjoy your wealth.

Weapon one: Acknowledge that greed is a problem and get help.

Create plans to end greed now.

The first major weapon in your fight against any dragon is becoming aware of it as an enemy. At first, you may not even recognize the greed dragon in your life. Then you might see it, but not yet see it as a problem. Acknowledging and targeting greed as a major player in your life will help you understand the entire structure of your process. It will also help you identify what substitutes you have learned to crave. Your craving is a key feeling to identify within yourself. Another key feeling is the lack of satisfaction that comes when you get what you have been craving. If the object of your desire has to be renewed time and again, you have a problem with greed. If you have a food disorder, you also have a problem with the greed dragon. Your problem may be severe enough to warrant professional help. The alternative is failing health and possible death.

If you have a great fear of actually getting what you want, you may have trouble with greed as well. Notice your tendency to arrange events so that you never get what you want. Begin to be a close observer of your greed process. Be aware of its presence as an enemy.

Weapon two: Recognize your greed's fixation on substitutes such as food, power, and sex.

What is it that you crave? Is it something to put into your mouth, like food, dessert, candy, soda, alcohol, or chewing tobacco? Or do you want more influence in the world? Do you lust for power and dominance? Does the greed dragon make you ruthless in pursuit of power? Is your greed fixated on relationships, so that you want everyone's heart, mind, and soul? Do you become obsessed with people and have to have their love and attention? Do you have to have sex all the time to know you are cared about? Is your craving for material things like money, cars, clothes, and jewelry causing you to buy two of everything just in case? Are you a shopping addict who cannot control your impulse to acquire? Do you overspend and then deprive and punish yourself for your transgression? Is gambling hurting you and your family?

These fixations are the substitutes you accept for what you are really looking for. Notice how your craving and lust keep you tortured. Notice how you feel cheated because it seems like everyone else but you has what you want. Notice how you are never neutral about the object of your desire. You always feel intense about your fixation, and your behavior goes all awry whenever you are faced with either having what you want or lacking it. Often you feel shame about your relationship to it.

A major method for identifying your substitute or addiction is recognizing it as something that preoccupies you most of the time. For example, people with food addictions think about food and where to get it and how to avoid being detected almost all of the time. The same is true for those who search for the object of their sexual desire.

Weapon three: End the search. Surrender. Face your feelings of despair.

This weapon is hard to pick up and even harder to use. Tremendous strength and courage are needed to face the fact that, whatever it is you are craving, it is simply not the answer. Your next piece of candy is a brief, relieving fix, and with it, you make the dragon bigger. Giving in to the dragon over and over again only brings ruin. The solution is to give up, to surrender, to quit. This means that when you feel a craving, recognize that what you are craving is a poison in the form of a substitute. Few people, when they come face to face with this fact and have no more denial, actually take the poison. The secret is to tell the truth at the moment of truth.

If you resist the temptation to satisfy your addiction, you will feel a terrible hopelessness that has been lurking under the surface for a very long time. This hopelessness has to do with the fact that, deep down, you know that the substitute you are about to indulge in will fail to satisfy you. You feel hopeless because your original painful deprivation happened a long time ago and you have never accepted it. You have been resisting and fighting it off for years. However, resistance is an ineffective strategy in the long run because it always creates more of what you are resisting. This is a fundamental postulate of martial arts: Resist and you get hurt.

Weapon four: Recognize your true source of satisfaction.

Identify what is behind the craving for your substitutes. You will never find out what it is as long as you indulge in your addiction or obsession. Only by denying the urge to "act out," as psychotherapists call it, can you discover the real source of your hunger. The real source of hunger is twofold for human beings. Your first hunger is for real food and affection from "the one"— Mom, or whoever is like a mom. If as an infant you went hungry or were deprived of physical touch, that was an experience of great physical suffering and pain. Your pain says, "I long to feel full and warm inside my body. I long to feel warm and safe outside my body. I want to know I am welcome and part of a family."

The second source of your hunger is spiritual. As Victor Frankl suggests in *Man's Search for Meaning*, all people, no matter how loved they were as children, have deep desires to know their place in the cosmos, to know the meaning and purpose of their lives. Another way to put this is that you want to feel connected, to know that you belong and have a place in the universe. You may not know that this is the true source of your hunger, so you seek substitutes that never satisfy you. Eventually, you discover that the uncovering of a spiritual life satisfies your craving. This is how you can be cured of your addictions. If you are fixated at a younger level of development, this spiritual unfolding may involve your conversion to a religion with a moral code that gives you structure. If you are functioning at the adult level, your spiritual blossoming may have nothing whatsoever to do with a religion. It may involve an expanded philosophy of life, the study of metaphysics, or a life-changing realization about your true purpose or the meaning of your life.

The ultimate source of your happiness is your recognition and experience of true relationship with your deepest self, with others, and with all of nature. In order to accomplish this experience of true relationship, you must have no conditions or judgments, just unconditional acceptance. When you achieve this experience, you will have no addiction and no suffering.

Weapon five: Learn to give to others. Give up blame. Take responsibility for your life.

The greed dragon gets you to blame your dissatisfaction on others. You feel you are deprived because others have what you want and you have to wrest it from them. You act like Scrooge and deprive others of that you want. You may not offer compliments or bonuses, or be generous. Since whatever you perpetuate on others always ends up happening to you, sooner or later, being a depriver always results in more personal deprivation for yourself.

The only solution is to turn the whole thing around. This means catching yourself when you blame others and making it a point to eliminate this habit. You must take responsibility for your life. The fact that others have things means you can have them also. Think of life as a win-win proposition. The secret is in giving. When you are generous with your money, money is not hard to get. When you are generous with your love and your time, you end up with more of both. When you delegate power, you become powerful in the process. The basic principle that fights off the greed dragon is "What you give is what you get." Read *A Christmas Carol* by Charles Dickens. He knew.

Weapon six: Be kind and generous with yourself.

Be a kind and generous mother to yourself. Watch for the fear of losing control and the fear of getting what you want. Also, watch for indulgence in substitutes.

Just as learning to give others what you want produces results in your relationships, you must learn to be generous and give to yourself to eliminate the greed dragon. Greed often produces self-deprivation. The very thought of being kind and generous with yourself can bring up anger, sadness, and fear.

The anger is about having to do kind things for yourself. The tendency is to feel that someone else ought to satisfy your needs. The sadness is the realization of the depth of your deprivation and how long it has been going on. When you are hungry and you get a little bit to eat, you may feel more tortured than if you get nothing. The tiny portion reminds you how hungry you really are. Thus, if you are kind to yourself, you may recognize how unkind you have been all along. This is painful.

The fear is that if you begin giving to yourself a little bit, you may go out of control and become a raving maniac, hurtling toward self-destruction. You may feel that perhaps it is better not to loosen the tight reins you have held on being generous with yourself. This message is what the greed dragon always sends to you in order to keep control. The truth is that you already deprive yourself and then sometimes rebel and binge to excess out of a need for gratification. The secret to healing this pattern is to neither deprive yourself nor to binge but to consistently live normally. Easier said than done.

Weapon seven: Recognize what you already have. Enjoy your wealth.

Acknowledge and learn how to enjoy what you have. Notice your tendency to reject it: First, you feel hunger for something and you go looking for it. Then, when you finally get it, you are disappointed in it. It is not like your fantasy. So you reject it. You must understand that it is never going to be like your fantasy—ever. If you do not use and celebrate what you already have, you will tend to neglect it to the point that you lose it. Then you end up with nothing. This is the theme of countless country music and blues songs: "I had a good woman but I threw her away for another. Now I'm singing the blues."

The secret to defeating the greed dragon is giving up your search for something better. Greed does not want you to enjoy yourself. Greed does not want you to love your man or woman. Greed does not want you to be without craving. "But if I don't desire something better, I'll never make any progress," you might say. There is just enough truth in that to make you blind to the dragon. Yet, desire for evolution is quite different from craving. Craving hurts. Craving leads to uncontrollable behavior like eating binges or theft. The desire to evolve is natural, like the desire to be happy or the desire to take a walk.

Seven Exercises to Transform the Greed Dragon

The following exercises will help you defeat the greed dragon. These exercises are not a substitute for professional help, but they can be adjunctive.

Exercise one: Identify the object that you crave.
Exercise two: Make a list of everything you have already
accomplished.
Exercise three: Give something nice to yourself that you
have always wanted.
Exercise four: Make a list of everything you think you need
in order to be happy.
Exercise five: Make a list of all the things that you won't
let yourself have.
Exercise six: Closely examine an object that you crave.
Exercise seven: Seek help from a professional.

Exercise one: Identify the object that you crave.

As you think about the object of your desire, notice the
physical sensations you feel in your body. Focus on the place
where you feel the most sensation. Allow yourself to have
images, visions, or memories from the past. Go over these in
detail. They are clues to the source of your feelings. They may
be upsetting and make your craving stronger for the time being.
That is just the dragon getting uncomfortable with your scrutiny. Have discipline and persist. Allow yourself to express any
emotion that arises from the imagery. With the expression of
emotion, your craving will decline. This is best done with a
guide, counselor, or facilitator.

Exercise two: Make a list of everything you have already accomplished.

Make a list of everything you have, including material
things, talents, relationships, abilities, and savings. Give thanks
for these things. Realize that in order to keep these things you
need to be generous with them and share them with other people. This is challenging, because the greed dragon wants you to
believe that you are deprived and have nothing to share. It
wants you to hoard what you have.

Get in the habit of sharing yourself with others. Share your
time, your energy, and your money. However, do not exaggerate

and give everything away. This will just result in a backlash. Keep plenty for yourself.

Exercise three: Give something nice to yourself that you have always wanted.

Make sure that you get the best of what you want, not a look-alike or copy. Your gift can be a small item like a Swiss army knife or a pair of nice earrings. If you have funds, it can be a more costly item. It should be something that you will use a lot. Every time you use it or wear it, feel glad that you bought it.

Too often, the greed dragon prevents you from enjoying the things you have because you are too busy looking for the next thing. Enjoy to the maximum what you have. When you have used up or worn out something you have, you can replace it with a new or better one.

Exercise four: Make a list of everything you think you need in order to be happy.

These can be material things, relationships, or capabilities. Look this list over carefully to make sure it is complete. Now make a list of all the things that in the past you thought would make you happy and that you eventually acquired. Go way back into your past. Did the new bicycle make you happy? Did the new car make you happy? Did your first wife or husband make you happy? Did anything that you ever thought would make you happy succeed in making you happy for very long? Compare your list of the past with your list for the future. What makes you think the future list will be any different? Can it be that you are fooling yourself?

Exercise five: Make a list of all the things that you won't let yourself have.

Please include the foods that you try not to let yourself have but fail to keep from eating. Include everything that makes you feel guilty. Observe your guilty feelings closely. Notice the physical sensations in your body when you feel guilty. Notice that the guilt associated with an object makes you want it more than ever and makes acquiring it more satisfying. Now imagine obtaining the forbidden object and consuming it, using it, or having it. Notice the feelings of remorse that follow your enjoy-ment of it. The remorse is one of the subtle controls of the greed dragon. It keeps the pattern going. If you really enjoyed the ice cream and then did not feel bad afterward, you would actually begin to regulate your eating of it. Feeling bad only ensures its position as the forbidden fruit. You will then go for it again and again, because people cannot resist forbidden fruit. When you make it all right, you take the energy out of the pattern of desire, guilt, and remorse and eventually it ceases to be.

Exercise six: Closely examine an object that you crave.

Be with your craved object and get to know it. Then con-sume it or use it with awareness, taking your time. Your craving exists because you are unconscious about the thing you crave. For example, you may tend to eat without paying attention to the flavor and texture of what is in your mouth. If it is food you crave, then follow the yogic exercise of chewing each bite one hundred times before swallowing. In other words, experience thoroughly what you crave. Guilt robs you of the enjoyment while you are acquiring and consuming the object of your desire. Slow way down.

If you feel greedy for sex, then don't rush it when you are in the midst of it. Examine it closely, in great detail. Or, if you crave power or money, savor the power or money in front of you instead of rushing past them for more. For example, pay cash for something you want to buy. Count each bill and enjoy the power of it as it brings you something you wanted.

Notice that this is not an exercise in taking pleasure in sadistic acts. Enjoying the power of hurting other beings brings serious consequences to your own happiness.

Exercise seven: Seek help from a professional.

Seek help from a professional who has a true understanding about how the greed dragon works. This person needs to have tackled his or her own demons with addiction. Group work in this matter is very helpful. Learn to accept the support of those in the group. Shame about greed is a big obstacle that keeps it going. Hiding the effects of the greed dragon on your life only perpetuates the dragon's activities. Hiding feelings of shame only extends them. Communicating the shameful feelings takes the power out of them. Through communication, shame evaporates and the greed dragon shrinks.

Conclusion

The greed dragon works with the self-destruction dragon. Together they can deliver a one-two punch that can knock the vitality and life completely out of you. If you struggle with the greed dragon, then you are fighting with the self-destruction dragon as well. Read the exercises for erasing that dragon and this will help to keep both dragons at bay. The best way to approach this is to tackle self-destructiveness first, because it is so life threatening. When you have succeeded at this, you will develop an appetite for life and everything it has to offer. This appetite can cause problems, too, because it can so easily be taken over by the greed dragon. Then you are stuck again. That is why you have to work on eliminating both dragons.

Chapter Eight

THE SELF-DESTRUCTION DRAGON

Positive Pole—Sacrifice
Negative Pole—Suicide

External manifestation

Reckless; daredevil-like; dangerous; delinquent; frantic; rampaging; precarious; death-defying; imprudent; wild; violent; foolhardy; hazardous; fatal; deadly; excessive; dejected; uncontrollable; self-mutilating; ruined; addicted; controlled or controlling.

Internal manifestation

Out-of-control; hopeless; despairing; devastated; wretched, inconsolable; futile-feeling; anguished; worthless-feeling; defeated.

Examples of situations and conditions that promote the self-destruction dragon

Wars; drugs; bars; ghettos; poverty; alcoholism; unemployment; the underworld; the Mafia; prisons; much military activity; much police work; the military-industrial complex; guns; drugs; prostitution; sadomasochism; violent pornography; the world of gambling; professional athletics (especially boxing);

rodeos; many mental hospitals; street gangs; stunt work; race car driving; some heavy metal and rap music; duels; revenge; violent motorcycle gangs; anorexia; bulimia; crime; skinheads; Ku Klux Klan.

Physical appearance and presentation

Persons afflicted by the self-destruction dragon often have eyes that appear desperate, wild, or bloodshot. They may have numerous self-inflicted scars and tattoos on their bodies. (However, not everyone with a tattoo has the self-destruction affliction.) On the other hand, self-destruction can mask itself behind professional appearances or high-society personalities. It is not unusual for self-destructive people to feel panic and desperation behind their in-control personas. This dragon does not lend itself to trying on for size.

The Development of the Self-Destruction Dragon

Socioeconomic status and abandonment

No other dragon has such dire consequences as the self-destruction dragon. Sooner or later, if unchecked, this dragon leads to sure death—either by slow, gradual means or by instant, violent means. This dragon is deadly because it turns people against themselves. It turns rationality upside down by getting people to think, "Only through death can I survive." The self-destruction dragon can be seen in addictions, wild living in the fast lane, dangerous risk taking, antisocial violent behavior, anorexic or bulimic activities, and attempts at suicide, successful or not.

Most people who are self-destructive come from very specific backgrounds. Not all are poor and abandoned children of crack cocaine addicts; some come from the most prominent homes. There are specific ingredients that can be found in a range of settings that contribute to this deadly condition. The key ingredient is emotional abandonment from the earliest age.

The second ingredient is emotional or physical abuse or punishment. This punishment is either spontaneous, and does not relate to misbehavior, or it far outweighs the children's crime. When these two ingredients come together, the results are tragically predictable: they neatly pave the way for the entrance of the self-destruction dragon. These two ingredients may be present in the homes of almost any social class of any culture. There is almost always one parent afflicted with the same dragon, but in a few situations this is not so.

Poverty, social distress, unemployment, mental illness, alcoholism, and drug addiction contribute heavily to self-destruction in children. That is why the children of disenfranchised social groups so often embark on self-destructive behavior. Yet there are poor families of minority populations who raise healthy and happy children. And there are wealthy families of the highest pedigree whose children commit suicide at an alarming rate. That is because emotional abandonment and physical abuse of children is not confined to the ghetto.

When parents are alcoholic or their consciousness is absent due to the heavy abuse of drugs, their children are, de facto, abandoned. When parents are in prison, there is often no one to offer guidance and love in the home. The children may spend much time on the streets coping with abuse and violence. When the parents come home from prison, the children may be subjected to more severe abuse from these despairing parents. Children of the well-to-do are often no better off, because their abandonment is the result of the extensive drinking, traveling, or constant social engagements of the parents. Even middle-class children are afflicted with abandonment when both parents work long hours and are unavailable for nurturing. However, abandonment alone is not enough to invite this particular dragon in. Abandonment may alternatively produce the activities of the self-deprecation dragon, or even the stubbornness dragon. What causes abandonment to turn in the direction of self-destruction is the additional ingredient of abuse.

Random physical abuse

The clincher for the creation of self-destruction is the presence of violence, in the form of emotional and physical abuse, in addition to the presence of abandonment. Also, the emotional and physical abuse must violate the laws of reason. If children are hit for breaking household objects of value, the children at least know why they are being punished, even though there is never a good enough excuse for striking children. However, if children are repeatedly struck for no other reason than that their parents are drunk and in foul moods, then the children's sense of fairness and understanding of cause and effect are totally destroyed. This same scenario of abuse can take place if the parents are mentally ill and have fantasized that their children are evil or bad and must be punished.

Unreasonable punishment

If a child spills a glass of milk and is sent to his or her room without dinner and confined there all the next day, this punishment violates the child's sense of justice that the punishment should fit the crime, if in fact what the child did was a crime at all. Children in such situations learn that life is totally unpredictable. Sometimes they are completely abandoned, and sometimes they are brutally treated, for no understandable reasons. They can make no sense out of life like this. This kind of life is not worth living.

The cycle of abandonment and abuse can reach extreme proportions. I have worked with adults who as children were tied up, beaten, burned with cigarettes, urinated on, raped, made to perform unspeakable perverted sexual acts on adults, made to kill animals, forced to sleep with corpses, and so on. Unfortunately, there is no limit to the human imagination when it comes to torturing children. The consequences are the same in most cases: the children become vulnerable to the dragon of self-destruction. Once the self-destruction dragon takes over, the children often turn their violence outward in the form of vandalism, assault, and criminal activity.

To make matters utterly confusing, occasionally people will embark on courses of self-destruction without any of the conditions described above. People are mysterious creatures, and there are always exceptions to every rule. Therefore, the dragon of self-destruction sometimes finds footholds in people, especially during the adolescent years of peer pressure, despite their childhood upbringing. I believe the choice to allow the self-destruction dragon entrance always rests with the individual.

Stan's Story: A Tale of Self-Destruction

Stan was wealthy by any standards. He traveled extensively on a whim and lived a first class lifestyle. He belonged to the most prominent social clubs, drove an exotic car, and dressed in the finest apparel. Stan was also a cutter—that is, he sliced himself with shards of glass until he bled profusely. This usually took place in the dead of night after a bout of drinking and mixed social drugs. Stan felt desperate constantly, and he was clearly actively suicidal. He was obviously out of control, and he terrified himself on a regular basis with the thought that on any given day he could finally go over the edge and kill himself with his cutting and drug abuse.

Stan grew up the eldest of four children. His father was an extremely successful corporate raider and business mogul, and his mother a socialite and hypochondriac. Both his father and mother drank heavily and were physically abusive when they were home. Stan grew up with a succession of nannies because his parents were always traveling. At age six he was packed off to boarding school. For the next ten years, he was shunted around the world, from one school to the next, because of his behavior problems. He was, for all practical purposes, abandoned. Periodically, he was also physically and sexually abused—at home by his father and at school by a male instructor. To cope, he learned to control people and manipulate them for his own purposes. This gave him a sense of the control he did not feel he had over his own life.

Stan began to drink as a child and learned to cut and tattoo himself by age eleven. He adopted the abusive behavior of his parents toward himself. His father bailed him out of a number of brushes with the law for petty theft and truancy during his pre-teen and teenage years. He adopted abusive behavior toward others as well. His grades were miserable and his education was bought by his family's big contributions to the private schools he attended. Stan had no motivation for school and knew he would inherit a fortune by the time he was twenty-one.

Stan was always an overweight child with rather plain features. He hated his looks and made no pretense about them. He felt he could not compete in the appearance competition of his upper class. He essentially turned against himself because he saw his life as meaningless.

When Stan was twenty-five, he inherited an even greater sum of money and began spending it wildly. However, he did not enjoy this in the least. He cut himself every day and drank over two bottles of wine a night, in addition to taking sleeping pills. He was rushed to the emergency room on three occasions to have his stomach pumped. On one occasion, he cut his wrist too deeply and had to be treated by a doctor. He saw psychia-trists on and off for years but never made a commitment to work, so there were no results.

When Stan came in for therapy with me, he was so desper-ate and frightened that he was more motivated than usual to work on himself. Even though he was desperate, he could not help from insulting me and trying to abuse me by criticizing my office, my clothes, my fees, and anything else he could attack. He came to one session drunk, and he tended to spend a fortune on shopping right after the sessions. I had to be very tough with him at first and lay out the rules very clearly about attendance and sobriety. He constantly wanted to interrupt his therapy to travel to parties in Paris and Madrid, and I warned him that I would not work with him if he didn't take the therapy seriously and dedicate himself to it. Grudgingly, and with much complaining and attacking, he complied. The work was long, hard, and painful for both of us.

Stan threatened to abandon me repeatedly, just as he had been abandoned. He tried to abuse me, just as he had been abused. He abused and abandoned himself. But gradually, with discipline and growing self-respect, he decided to live rather than die. He slowed the cutting and eventually stopped. The drinking continued to be a problem for a longer period, but eventually that stopped as well. His life really turned around after he became involved in a philanthropic social cause that demanded his time and commitment—and yes, his money as well.

Whatever the reasons and foundation for self-destruction, whether it be violence or abandonment or simply choice to let it in, people can rid themselves of this unwanted guest with a set of specific steps.

The Seven Steps of Development for the Self-Destruction Dragon

Step one: The children are abandoned.

Step two: The abandonment results in loss of structure.

Step three: Emotional and physical abuse occur.

Step four: The children turn against themselves.

Step five: The children fear loss of control.

Step six: The children learn that gaining control is vital to survival.

Step seven: The children no longer value life. Death seems better.

Step one: The children are abandoned.

Infants and small children affected by the self-destruction dragon feel the absence of primary loving forces that provide security and nurturing. For the infants, this is like being in the midst of a terrific storm with no shelter from the cold, wind, and rain. If the abandonment is too severe from the beginning, death can be imminent. If there is sporadic nurturing, death can come more slowly through the dragon of self-destruction. This may take many years.

Research shows that children of parents who commit suicide have a much greater probability of committing suicide themselves. This is because of the abandonment factor coupled with the children's notion that suicide is seen as a viable option, a way out.

Abandonment is one of the two critical ingredients in the formation of a self-destructive pattern. The abandonment begins in infancy when the basic sense of trust vs. distrust is established. The consequences of physical abandonment and emotional abandonment are the same for infants: the formation of distrust in the world and distrust in their ability to cope with life. The reasons for the abandonment are not significant. Whether the parents or guardians are absent because of mental illness, hospitalization, suicide, alcoholism, drug addiction, death, warfare, poverty, partying, or for business reasons, the consequences are the same. If the abdicated positions are filled by loving grandparents, older siblings, or stable and loving foster families, the consequences can be eliminated or the intensity of the self-destructiveness mitigated. Too often, however, the children are left to languish without nurturing adults to care for them. The key ingredient is that the children feel and experience abandonment, whatever the reason for it.

Belief and decision: "I am all alone and the world is scary. I am too small to fix this."

Step two: The abandonment results in loss of structure.

Without primary caregivers, the infants and small children experience that no one is in charge of their environments and no one is in charge of their bodies. They may lie in their own feces or urine-soaked diapers for hours. When they are hungry, cold, frightened, or sick, no one comes. There is no one to pick them up, hold them, and give them a sense that someone is in control of their situations.

Thus, the dragon of self-destruction has its opening. With

no one else in charge, the dragon takes over because it sees no competition. The dragon says, "I'll be in charge; I'll take over as the parent. Give that child to me and I'll provide the structure." However, the stage is not yet set for the dragon's takeover. First there must be some abuse to complete the foundation.

Belief and decision: "No one is in control. No one is in charge. There is no structure. I am abandoned."

Step three: Emotional and physical abuse occurs.

Children suffering from self-destructiveness often are subjected to unfair, irrational punishment or pain. This pain may be inflicted because of the sadism, mental illness, or perversion of their guardians or because of a rigid moral code that their parents follow. Whatever the reason, the abuse amounts to an undermining of any sense of fair play or reasonableness in life. The children's inner sense of justice is destroyed.

> Fred, a convict doing a life sentence for the murder of a policeman, recounted the following story of his earliest years, "My father was a burly merchant marine who was home only partially and absent for long periods. He was a brawling drunk and was in and out of jail for disturbing the peace. Mother was a frightened mouse of a woman who was always at work trying to meet the needs of the family. When father was home, she cowered and could not be counted upon for any protection. From time to time, in a drunken rage, my father would remove his belt and lash us kids viciously for no other reason than to teach us that life was not a bed of roses and we'd better get used to it." Fred took that teaching to heart. Abandoned and beaten senseless for no reason, he fled home at age thirteen and embarked on a life of prostitution and crime.

Belief and decision: "My guardians are abusive and out of control. I am not in control because I can't stop them. The world is a hostile place."

Step four: The children turn against themselves.

Children almost always adopt the behavior they see in their primary guardians. There is vast research to show that if parents are abusive to their children, the children tend to be abusive as well, either toward themselves, others, or both. The children identify with their aggressors and think, "If they beat me, I must be bad, or they wouldn't beat me." Small children cannot conceive of the possibility that adults can be wrong.

Those afflicted by the self-destruction dragon are often just as destructive to other people. However, some people are only self-destructive and never intend to harm others. This difference occurs due to their maturity level.

The children's next thought in this process is, "If I am bad, then I must be punished. So I'll make sure I am punished." Sometimes the conclusion is, "If I am bad, then I am bad to others. I'll punish others, too." These conclusions are still not the whole story, for there are yet more twists to the self-destruction dragon's steady takeover of the entire personality.

Belief and decision: "I am bad. I should be punished. I'll punish the world, too."

Step five: The children fear loss of control.

First, by virtue of abandonment, the children sense that no one is in charge or in control of their environments. This is terrifying to the infants because survival is at stake. The infants are helpless, and if there is no one to assist or nurture them, death is a real possibility.

Secondly, as the infants grow and develop into young children, they see that their parents or guardians are out of control much of the time. Their parents may be chronically drunk, stoned, crazy, or sadistic. They fly out of control without provocation. As a result, the children become even more terrified of loss of control. Since the children have no model for controlled behavior, they also feel out of control. Gaining external control becomes a life-saving proposition. Internal controls remain elusive.

Belief and decision: "My parents are out of control. I am out of control. My life is threatened."

Step six: The children learn that gaining control is vital to survival.

These children are raised in unpredictable atmospheres where there is no adequate guidance. The result of this is a terrible split in their personalities. When older, they often turn to drugs and alcohol for solace from their terrible environments or as a response to peer pressure, which they cannot resist. The awful consequence is that these children lose control and become addicted.

This process deserves closer examination. First, the children take over the job of abuse from their parents. They identify themselves as bad. They think, "If I am bad, I deserve to be abused. Therefore, I will abuse myself. By abusing myself, I have more control over the situation than when I am being abused randomly." They believe they have more control if they take over the job of being destructive. They become control addicts.

These people afflicted with the self-destruction dragon go a step further. They form the habit of proving they are in control of death. Alcoholics are known for their insistence on having control by saying, "It's all right, I can still drive after five Bloody Marys," or, "I can handle another one." This, of course, amounts to major denial, and eventually the result is loss of control. Not only do these people lose control of their bodily functions through overdose, but they may lose control of their cars and end up dead. The loss of control results in brawling, sexual abuse of children, spouse battery, self-injury, and loss of jobs, to name but a few of the dire consequences.

People taken over by the self-destruction dragon are known for taking dangerous risks to prove they have external control over their environments. They race cars or planes to the limit of control and engage in daredevil stunts to see how far they can jump motorcycles or stay on wild Brahma bulls. They may gamble everything in a game of cards or roulette. The addiction helps them prove to themselves that they are always in control, but they never actually believe it. They must repeat the risks over and over again because the proof never lasts. They may win these contests and make a name for themselves, but invariably they lose badly when they push too far. They lose control in the long run and prove their worst fear—that indeed they are out of control.

Belief and Decision: "I must be in control at all times. I must prove to myself that I have this control. I will control the abuse."

Step seven: The children no longer value life. Death seems better.

The dragon of self-destruction seals these children's fates when it creates the final paradox: "Have control at all costs," the dragon says. But it also says, "Life is not worth living." In adolescence, these people test their self-control over and over again in self-abusive ways. Their surface idea is, "I'll prove I have control and I'll beat death." Yet underneath this surface thought is the more insidious one: "Life is not worth living." Thus, people afflicted with the self-destruction dragon head inexorably to a final conclusion: "Death is better than living." For these people, death is always a suicide, whether it looks like an accident or not. The irony is that deliberate suicide is the final act of control: "I'll kill myself. Nobody else is going to do it for me." All this can be reversed with conscious attention and desire.

Belief and decision: "Death is better than life. I'll kill myself."

The Self-Destruction Dragon's Big Lie

The dragon of self-destruction leads people to believe that more external control is the answer to all problems. Nothing could be further from the truth. Although the lay person's view of mentally ill people is that they are wild, crazed, and murderous, the truth is that more patients are in mental hospitals because they are over-controlled than because they lack control. Obsessive-compulsive people who spend all their time washing their hands are actually suffering from over-control. In a paradoxical way, this one behavior is out of control, although the rest of the personality is held in rigid over-control.

Many professional athletes and rock stars rise from extremely dysfunctional backgrounds. It is their very striving for complete external control that makes them so good at what they do. Yet this desire for control can never be totally satisfied as long as the dragon remains in charge. For, along with the need for control can come sabotage from the dangerous "life is not worth living" belief deep within the subconscious. The fabulous control of the athlete on the ball field can turn into a total loss of control at the hands of alcohol or cocaine, resulting inevential loss of skill, rape and violence.

The promise that external control can save the day is a lie. External controls never make up for the needed internal personality structures that guide productive living. External control is excellent for the mastery of many athletic and engineering feats, but it is no substitute for a deep sense of meaning, self-guidance, and confidence that do not have to be proven over and over again.

The Great Dragon Exchange:
The Slide from Self-Destruction to Greed

The dragon of self-destruction is intimately associated with the greed dragon. These two dragons have many mutual qualities, not the least of which is addiction. People who are dominated by one of these dragons often exhibit signs or symptoms of the polar dragon. For example, self-destructors often cannot control their appetite for food, drugs, power, or lust. They often live wild lives of excess in every arena, only to die of their excesses sooner rather than later. The wild excesses act as distractions from their deeper feelings of despair.

When people with self-destruction begin to recover from their feelings of despair, they often display a tremendous appetite for life's activities. This can be a healthy sign, but it is fraught with danger because appetite can lead to loss of control, resulting in excess. Those dominated by the self-destruction dragon can be tossed over to the greed dragon and then back to the self-destruction dragon again and again. This cycling of binge and despair is quite common in those afflicted by these dragons.

Self-Destruction: The Dragon of Panic and Despair

A hallmark of the self-destruction dragon is the feeling of panic that is almost always reflected in afflicted people's eyes. Although drinkers and drug takers often have bloodshot eyes, even those who are self-destructive in other ways display the reddened-eye effect. Their eyes appear panicked and wild, as if they are looking everywhere for an answer that is not forthcoming. This is the look of addicts who are desperate for a fix. The key word here is desperate. Self-destructive people feel desperate for a resolution of their pain. However, too often their idea of resolution is a drink, a fix, or a self-destructive act.

When the self-destruction dragon has firmly established itself, a second look appears in the eyes: the look of despair. The look of panic relates to being out of control. The look of despair relates to the feeling that life is not worth living. These looks can replace each other depending on the situation. To become acquainted with the look of despair and the look of panic or desperation, visit a part of town where winos end up and you can see these looks in their most exaggerated forms. Keep in mind that there are many people living more ordinary lives with less intense versions of these looks. With a little discernment, you can see the looks in their eyes as well.

Adolescents frequently display minor or extreme versions of the panic and despair of self-destruction. Some flirt with these symptoms for a time and then move out of them entirely. This is

almost a natural part of these hormone-charged years. However, other adolescents experience full-blown self-destruction
that is truly life threatening and, unless erased, may become a
lifelong pattern. For an unfortunate number, the pattern may
end suddenly in self-imposed death.

Stages of Maturity and the Self-Destruction Dragon

Maturity has much to do with the way self-destruction
appears in external behavior. The earlier the maturity stage at
which people are fixated, the more probable it is that violence
and destructive behavior toward others will accompany their
self-destructive acts. The older their stage of maturity, the less
violence toward others and the more internalized and self-
directed their behavior will be.

Infant stage: criminal insanity
Toddler stage: wanting to get caught; gangs
Child stage: short life in the fast lane
Adolescent stage: suicide
Adult stage: self-sabotage

Self-destruction at the infant stage

At the infant stage, there are few controls of any kind within the personality, therefore, behavior tends to be out of control
in all areas of experience. The world is experienced as "me" and
"not me." And since "not me" is perceived as hostile, "not me"
is attacked with vigor.

Those with self-destruction fixated at the infant stage are
perhaps the most dangerous people on the planet because they
are in a state of total fear, they are out of control, and they are
in attack mode. Since their activities are so outrageous, they are
often killed by police at the scenes of their crimes or incarcerat-
ed in the most extreme manner. Many of these people are
among those considered criminally insane. Total behavioral
control is the only thing that works for these people because
that is the only thing that makes them feel safe.

Since they are in a total state of despair, adult infants do not care what happens to them as a consequence of their acts. They welcome death, either by their own hand or by the hands of those trying to stop them from committing more damage. Even when jailed or hospitalized, they tend to inflict damage on those around them and, of course, on themselves. Their self-destructiveness is usually physical, self-mutilating, and revolting to others because it is so primitive. They are equally savage with their victims.

Self-destruction at the toddler stage

At the toddler level, there is a need to become socialized and civilized, yet there is still much fear of the big outer world. Therefore when toddlers are self-destructive, they are waving red flags to others saying, "I'm in trouble. I need attention. Please stop me from banging my head or picking at my skin."

People fixated at the toddler level also act out violently toward others when they are being self-destructive. Their violence is geared to get them caught so that they can be stopped, eprimanded, and ultimately paid attention to and taken care of.

Since toddlers are interested in rules and regulations, self-destructive adult toddlers play out their experiences in a cops-and-robbers format. They become involved in gang and Klan activities, in petty local crimes, and in bribery and corruption at the lower levels of government and society. Their self-destructive activities may or may not involve drinking or drug taking but they are always geared to attract the attention of others.

Self-destruction at the child stage

At the child level, self-destructive behavior is often masked by achievement and external success. The wild, destructive behavior of entertainers may win them the attention of media and bring them closer to stardom. The fear of loss of control and the dangerous risk taking of self-destructive athletes can, for a time, bring them acclaim on the ball fields or racetracks, but the risk taking ultimately destroys them. This kind of behavior attracts fans and accompanying wealth but does not bring a sense of control, safety, or meaning to life.

Hard drinking, fast-lane living, and mega-partying are all hallmarks of the adult child's self-destructive routines. The self-destruction dragon is at its wildest and most attractive at this maturity level. In a way, it is least recognizable because it is not seen as a problem and it is obscured behind success. Adult children do not want to address their self-destruction and therefore seldom ask for, or receive, help for their problems. When they do receive help, it seldom sticks, because they are not psychologically sophisticated enough to have insight into their behavior.

The self-destruction dragon often pushes people at this maturity level into destructive behavior toward others. When they crash their cars they usually take others with them to the hospital or the morgue. When they embark on insane military strategies, they may be responsible for the wasteful deaths of many soldiers and civilians. Property and the environment suffer terrible devastation at the claws of this dragon. Whole countries can be laid waste or led into bondage because of the decisions of self-destructive adult children.

Self-destruction at the adolescent stage

Self-destruction at the adult-adolescent level is perhaps the most self-devastating of all. At this stage, people's destructive behavior is much less directed toward others and almost entirely inflicted on themselves. This is the level of the most consciously chosen suicides, the most self-defeating drug and alcohol abuse, and the most driven self-destructive behaviors. Unlike adult children, adult adolescents usually avoid success and suffer pain over their lack of control in relationships. Their romance with the self-destruction dragon is a much more private affair.

Because adolescence is much more sophisticated than childhood, people possessed by the self-destructive dragon at this level are much more amenable to help. They have insight into their self-destructive behavior and are aware of its damaging effects. In fact, much of their self-destructive activity is an obvious cry for help to friends and relatives. When and if they get help, it is more likely to stick and succeed than it is for adult children. On the other hand, because they are more insightful, they tend to feel more psychological pain and are therefore more likely to feel like committing suicide.

Self-destruction at the adult stage

The self-destruction dragon does not make many inroads at the adult level of maturation, and when it does it is usually confined to the period of life prior to thirty-five years of age. Adults, of course, are more capable of throwing off the trend of self-destruction because of their insight, understanding, and capability. Nevertheless, when disappointed by life or let down in specific relationships, they may exhibit self-destructive drinking or self-sabotage. This behavior does not often result in suicide, and the destruction is confined to themselves rather than directed toward others.

Adults are the most likely to take advantage of assistance and counseling, and they tend to apply what they learn quickly and effectively. They are not prone to remain in counseling for long periods of time but tend to use therapy as a tool to clear out the self-destruction dragon once and for all.

How the Self-Destruction Dragon Affects Your Life

The impact of the self-destruction dragon on your health

The self-destruction dragon is the ultimate disaster for your physical health. Smoking, drinking, eating, drug taking, or anything done to excess destroys the organs of your body beyond repair. Even a genetically healthy body cannot stand up to reckless treatment forever. Self-destruction can be slow suicide, designed to eventually kill off your body. On the other hand, the self-destruction dragon more often leads to direct suicide. Even if your body is very healthy, it will not tolerate a jump out of a twenty-story building or a handgun blast in your temple.

The impact of the self-destruction dragon on your creativity

Many of the most artistically creative human beings have succumbed to the forces of the dragon of self-destruction: Vincent van Gogh, Ernest Hemingway, Jim Morrison, John Belushi, and Marilyn Monroe, to name a few. In fact, an inordinate number of creative people kill themselves and cut short lives of prolific creativity and artistic expression. The reason for this is that the energies of creativity and destruction are like two sides of a coin. One slides into the other and needs its opposite in order to exist.

If you are an artist, you know that to create something new, something else must be destroyed. A white, blank canvas is destroyed when the first paint is applied. An old building is razed to make way for an architectural wonder. A wall is destroyed to make way for a view. Destruction opens the door to the most creative of forces. Waves of creativity wash over cultures following devastating wars or natural catastrophes. Witness the rebuilding of countries following World War II and the recovery of Japan after its decimation by atomic bombs.

If you are gifted creatively, you are also the most sensitive to the strength of the destructive force. If that force comes under the power of the self-destruction dragon, you may twist it into a deadly suicidal force rather than use it as a partner of creativity. You become a suicidal person, and your creativity is destroyed rather than enhanced.

If you are a creative person, you need the most social support because of your gifts and your tendency to be manipulated by the self-destruction dragon. Yet modern Western societies tend to discourage creative expression in their children through ridicule and lack of support. When you are artistic, you are more sensitive, and you need more love and affection than average people in order to remain productive and expressive. Certainly emotional abandonment and abuse have undermined more than one creative genius. If you believe that self-destructiveness is necessary for creative genius, you are listening to the dragon.

The impact of the self-destruction dragon on your presence

Your fixation, if you are caught by the self-destruction dragon, is fear of loss of control. When you are fixated on fear, you can have no presence or charisma on the playing field or stage. Athletes on the playing field exercise control over the ball so well that they are momentarily able to let out the fullness of who they are. The same is true for actors with stage presence who demonstrate control of their craft. However, in their ordinary social lives they may lack this same control. In their desperate striving for control, they bolster themselves with alcohol or drugs, thus destroying their presence of mind. A jockey, brilliant on horseback before cheering thousands, may become a retiring drunk at a party in his honor.

The ultimate loss of presence occurs if you commit suicide, for then you get rid of yourself entirely. You have no more presence of any kind.

The impact of the self-destruction dragon on your relationships

Self-destruction causes you to destroy your relationships in several ways. First, you try to control your relationships so you can have control over yourself. Since most people do not like being controlled in the long run, your partners leave. Second, your addictive behavior, whether it be gambling or drug abuse, causes others to eventually abandon you. They do not want to experience the pain of losing someone they love or the torment of being abused. Friends and relatives may abandon you before you can abandon them by committing suicide.

In the end, the only people left in your life if you are well known may be leeches and sponges who make a living from the carcass of their deteriorating idol. Elvis Presley was an example of this.

The impact of the self destruction dragon on your spiritual life

Like all the dragons, self-destruction has infiltrated religious thought over the ages. Some spiritual traditions preach the value of destroying your old self so that you may be born anew. This usually means giving up your old values and embracing a new set of beliefs designed by a given religion. Sometimes this new set of beliefs effectively destroys your creative expression by prohibiting dancing, singing, playing, sex, and expressive dress.

If you a are self-destructor, you may be attracted to a religion that professes a strict code of living and has rigid rules about proper behavior. You may see in that religion a structure that promises to control your out-of-control behavior. While this may work for a time, in the long run you may not deal with the source of your self-destructive tendencies, and you may experience serious setbacks that cause your expulsion from the group. Many individuals in Jim Jones' cult who committed mass suicide in Guyana formerly had difficulty controlling their behavior.

Other traditions have included in their teachings a belief that if you die defending your faith you will achieve eternal salvation. This teaching has allowed self-destructors over the ages to carry out numerous destructive acts in the names of their religions. The Crusades were a case in point, as were the waves of human suicide in the Iran-Iraq war. In the Christian tradition, the crucifixion of Jesus has inspired many people to justify their self-destructive acts as spiritual acts rather than the suicides they may be.

The Buddhist tradition teaches destruction of your ego in order to discover enlightenment. If you are self-destructive, you may twist this teaching into meaning that self-destructive acts are spiritual in nature. I knew a seriously disturbed young man who, upon reading and misinterpreting some Buddhist writings, began to burn himself with cigarettes in order to transcend ego-induced pain. He suffered infections that had to be medically treated. Many people over the centuries have afflicted their flesh by beating, whipping, scarring, or crucifying themselves to serve their gods or religious beliefs, only to have these actions burst out of control and result in their deaths.

Some Native American spiritual practices such as the Sun Dance of the Lakota Sioux also involve mortification of the flesh. Is performing the Sun Dance an act of self-destruction or an act of spiritual development? This is a question that is not possible to answer because for each individual the answer may be different. For some individuals, performing the Sun Dance is undoubtedly an act of great spiritual significance. For others, twisted by the self-destruction dragon, it may be a desperately disguised method of trying to control self-destructive tendencies in themselves only to inflict greater self-damage. Some Sun Dancers have died during the ceremony.

What is being discussed here is not the validity of religious beliefs but the interpretations that have led many people to self-destruct in their name.

Ultimately, if you are engaged in self-destructive acts, you are searching for meaning to your life, and that search is always a spiritual one. The healing of self-destruction always involves some kind of spiritual renewal or an awakening of spiritual values. If you are self-destructive, you are searching for the path to enlightenment; you are simply looking in the wrong places.

How to Transform the Self-Destruction Dragon

The ultimate cure for self-destruction, brought on by the self-destruction dragon, is death. In the most bitter irony, the parasite that destroys its host dies, too. The dragon of self-destruction loses its host at the moment of death and can play no more. However, there is another way to get rid of this parasite before it can play its full hand.

Slaying the self-destruction dragon early is crucial because of the time factor involved. Sooner or later, self-destruction is going to lead to suicide or death-by-crash if something is not done to get rid of it. That is why it is so deadly.

There is a subpersonality within each person that has a self-destruct theme. This is not unnatural because it can be found all over the animal kingdom. A scorpion surrounded by flames will sting itself in the back and kill itself rather than be burned to death. Human beings will do likewise in their own way if they sense that the alternative to dying at their own hands is much more painful. Humans readily choose death for political reasons, for principles, for values, or to save the lives of others. In most people, this perfectly natural self-destruct subpersonality sleeps unless extreme conditions call it forth to influence events. In people who struggle with control problems, the self-destruction dragon has garnered this subpersonality for its own twisted purposes.

Your challenge is to set this subpersonality free to act in a normal way and to drive out the self-destruction dragon. You must come to terms with abandonment, face childhood abuse issues, and learn that life can be lived happily without necessarily having total control over it.

As with all the dragons, the most effective way to deal with the self-destruction dragon is to face it squarely and directly. You need to face it down without denial, without projection, without blaming, and without avoidance. This can be terrifying. But it is done every day by courageous human beings.

Affirmations to Beat the Self-Destruction Dragon

I am able to find value and meaning in my life.
The pain I have experienced helps me to help others.
I choose to live no matter how hard life is.
I have enough control to choose my actions wisely.
I have enough strength of character to admit my
    limitations.
I am powerful enough to ask for help.
I have a wonderful support group of people who care
    about me.
I am strong enough to let go of the need for control.
I am able to be a friend to myself.
I have the courage to live simply without high drama.
I have learned to respect myself and others.

Seven Weapons to Slay the Self-Destruction Dragon

Weapon one: Realize that life is sacred and has ultimate meaning.

Weapon two: Admit you are out of control and ask for help.

Weapon three: Admit that being in control is the big issue.

Weapon four: Set your sights on realistic goals.

Weapon five: Clean up the messes in your life.

Weapon six: Admit and face your abuse of yourself and others.

Weapon seven: Admit and face the issue of abandonment.

Weapon one: Realize that life is sacred and has ultimate meaning.

The urge to self-destruct and behave in ways that do violence to your self-preservation is foreign. This urge does not come from yourself, nor is it natural to feel this way. This urge comes from the activities of your enemy, the self-destruction dragon, that you have allowed to take up residence in your house of personality. Self-destruction is a lethal virus that can be purged with strong intention, brutal honesty, and hard work. There is no easy way out. If you do nothing, death is the inevitable result. Instead, search and create beauty. Align yourself with people who respect life. Seek philosophies that speak of the sacredness of life.

Weapon two: Admit you are out of control and ask for help.

Admit that something is seriously wrong in your life and that it is clearly too much for you to handle by yourself. You need help. One of the symptoms that shows you the truth is that you feel panicky and desperate much of the time. It is not a personal failure to need help. Having problems is only human, but it is a sign of courage to ask for assistance.

Weapon three: Admit that being in control is the big issue.

Realize that you fear losing control and that you are out of control much of the time. To gain control, you are abusive with yourself and often with others. You wreak havoc on others' lives because you are too afraid to admit that you are out of control. Being out of control is not bad, nor is it anybody's fault. It is simply a reality. Trying to be in control is a strategy you developed for survival purposes when you were very young. The way to gain control is to give up pretending you have it when you don't. You will find that you can survive without being in control of your external environment. However, you can gain some measure of control over your own reactions.

> Frank was a talented musician who showed promise of being quite successful. He had a charming personality and could talk his way through anything. When it came to borrowing money from well-heeled friends to start a band, Frank found it easy. As Frank began to become successful, his drinking accelerated and he engaged in frequent cocaine binges. He mistreated his girlfriend to the point that she refused to see him anymore. He began a series of abusive relationships with women who were into the drug culture. Gradually Frank became less and less reliable. He failed to attend rehearsals and eventually even performances. The band that at first had made plenty of money and recorded five albums, deteriorated and broke apart. Frank owed money to everyone but had blown his wealth on drugs and foolish speculations. His solution to the problem was to move to another city to avoid those he had borrowed money from. This became his regular pattern. He attempted to stage comeback after comeback, always with other people's money. He was completely out of control, yet he thought he was in control of his life. To be able to carry out this charade, Frank became an expert in major denial. He refused to admit that he had a problem. To others, his problem was as obvious as the nose on his face. Frank eventually took care of his problem the fast way. He shot himself fatally in the head. If he had admitted his probem, he could have sought help and lived.

Weapon four: Set your sights on realistic goals.
Proving self-control over and over again is depleting. It is important to play and work for pleasure rather than constantly straining to prove yourself only to explode into self-destructive patterns when the tension gets too high. People afflicted with the self-destruction dragon typically aim unrealistically high. Interviews with self-destructive teenagers and adults show them to have goals way out of line with the realities of their lives. A teenager completely hooked on drugs plans to make the baseball hall of fame, when a realistic goal would be to have a steady job and be off drugs within a year. An unemployed adult ex-convict on probation plans to start a hotel chain, when finding a place to live and supporting himself would be more practical.

Weapon five: Clean up the messes in your life.
If you are self-destructive, you most likely create messes in your life, from romances to friendships to business-related disasters. Your pattern is to create success and then to not follow through on the details or to sabotage the deal or relationship by getting distracted by something else. This usually results in a trail of broken hearts, disappointed former friends, angry creditors, and people left holding the bag. What you need are commitment, perseverance, and the choice to see through the details, even if it means facing discomfort and upset. Cleaning up the mess means paying off debts, communicating to others, keeping appointments, and following through even when there are obstacles.

Weapon six: Admit and face your abuse of yourself and others.
You must return value to and respect your body above all else. Make it a priority to take care of your body through appropriate exercise, good food, proper rest, and regular hygiene. Often the dragon of self-destruction pushes you to exhaust yourself through wild living to the point that your body does not feel good to live in anymore. A toxic liver, depleted immune system,

and overstimulated nervous system are uncomfortable to live with. When push comes to shove, it is easier to contemplate killing off a wasted body than a healthy one. Keep your body happy and healthy, and your spirit will enjoy its experience.

Essential to respecting your body is facing the issue of abuse in your past and present. Many self-destructive people gloss over the abuse of their childhoods or deny it outright. Abuse may be physical or emotional in nature. Often, abuse can appear as neglect, screaming, or physical sadism. Abuse is an outrage and the ultimate in lack of respect. All forms of abuse must be faced honestly, and your feelings must be expressed. More often than not, your feelings are rage and, more deeply, despair. Despair is the hardest emotion to face because it has been vigorously denied.

Denial is so strong that mental health professionals have often found it necessary to take a heavy-handed approach to patients with self-destruction to get them to face their feelings. This is effective as long as human respect is always paramount along with the treatment.

Just as your self-abuse must be looked at, your abuse of others is important as well. This means coming to terms with the harm and pain that you have inflicted on others in your self-destructive lifestyle. What people have you discarded? Taken advantage of? Run roughshod over? What people have cared for you and had faith in you only to be ignored or walked on by you? Amends need to be made, apologies delivered, and debts repaid.

Weapon seven: Admit and face the issue of abandonment.

No matter what the cause or extenuating circumstances, abandonment, even if unintentional, is extraordinarily painful. Abandonment is so serious and impactful that newly born animals shrivel and die if they are given food but deprived of touch and comfort. Abandonment is critical to the formation of self-destructive patterns. It is how the dragon finds its first toehold in your personality. If you are abandoned by significant others at a young age, you tend to abandon yourself and your life later on, unless you get help.

Abandonment of yourself leads to suicide, slow or fast. Facing your abandonment can be devastating but is critical to destroying the dragon. All healing is paradoxical in nature. When you face your abandonment and realize you are alone, you recognize your relationship to others and the importance of that contact. You are then able to begin truly relating.

Seven Exercises to Transform the Self-Destruction Dragon

> **Exercise one:** Assess yourself.
> **Exercise two:** Make a list of your life goals.
> **Exercise three:** Make amends.
> **Exercise four:** Recall your abandonment.
> **Exercise five:** Recall your abuse.
> **Exercise six:** Gather a support team.
> **Exercise seven:** Assist others.

Exercise one: Assess yourself.

> Ask yourself the following questions:
> Do I feel panicky and desperate much of the time?
> Do I have frequent episodes when I seem to lose control of my actions and feel chagrined afterward?
> Is my life a mess?
> Do I seem to be running from something all the time?
> Do I have to make frequent excuses to other people for not following through?
> Do I often feel that life is not worth living?
> Do I think about killing myself often, or feel that I would be better off dead?
> Am I isolated from other people, and do I feel basically alone?
>
> If you answered "yes" to as few as three of these questions,

you have a problem with the self-destruction dragon. This is the time to admit that you have a problem and that no one is going to save you unless you take action. Taking action means seeking professional help and making a commitment to see it through. You have become an expert at running away. You can stop and reverse the pattern.

Exercise two: Make a list of your life goals.

While making a list of your life goals, ask a friend to tell you what is realistic and what is grandiose. Work on the list until you have a set of goals that is clear and reachable given your current situation. The goals need to be modest. That is why the affirmation, "one day at a time", is effective for recovering alcoholics. There is a tendency to rush ahead and get overwhelmed by trying to tackle too much all at once. Then you are out of control again and have an excuse to self-destruct. Do not give the dragon this option.

Exercise three: Make amends.

Form a realistic plan to pay off debts that are payable and to right wrongs that are fixable. If people you owe are deceased, then pay charities that you feel represent their values. You are never free until you psychologically atone for your outstanding debts. If you are lucky, you will be forgiven by the occasional creditor. If not, you owe.

Apologize to people who have been offended or hurt by you. You can do this in the form of a letter or a telephone call or a personal meeting. Remember that words are cheap, and actions taken to repair damage are worth a lot more.

Ultimately, you need to forgive yourself for succumbing to the dragon. That is a human experience that can teach you a great deal about both human frailty and human strength of character.

Exercise four: Recall your abandonment.

Make a list of all the experiences of abandonment you can recall from any time in your life. As you remember these events, go over them in your conscious mind and recall the feelings that you had at these times. This takes courage, because the dragon does not want you to remember the feelings. The dragon would rather that you run away and create havoc for its own entertainment. As you recall your abandonment, the dragon will push you to create still more alienation in your life. Look out for sabotage. Take a look at how you push others away so that you can reproduce the rejection and abandonment of your past. See how this gives you a sense of control. If you stay in a relationship, you don't always know what the other person is going to do. Thus you risk feeling out of control.

The dragon of self-destruction does not want you to be in intimate relationship with anyone. That way it has you all to itself. You are not in control as long as the dragon is in complete control of you.

Exercise five: Recall your abuse.

Make a list of all your remembered experiences of abuse at the hands of others during your life. Do not be hesitant to recall very early experiences in your life. Remember that abuse is anything that makes you feel less than a human being or takes away your choice in a serious way. Being beaten with words, or belts, or inconsistency in love are all forms of abuse.

Notice how you have incorporated this abuse and how you now treat yourself with the same careless, disrespectful approach. A dog that has been beaten becomes unpredictable and vicious on occasion. Notice how you have become that way. Winning trust from an abused animal takes time and patience. You need that as well. However, for the time being, you cannot be trusted either. You need a sponsor to help you stay out of trouble at first. You can eventually let go of this benevolent disciplinarian when you have made some progress. Choose your sponsor well. She or he must demonstrate balance.

Exercise six: Gather a support team.

Make a list of all the people and situations that contribute to your self-destructive behavior. The dragon tends to push you toward people and events that contribute to your suffering. The people are either self-destructive themselves or they get off on watching you self-destruct. Your fans can be your worst enemies in this regard. Identify your enemies and make tracks away from them. Surround yourself with people and situations that promote your self-respect and affirm your life. Get yourself a sponsor, a role model, a teacher, a therapist, or a support group that is firm but compassionate. Make sure that person or group has the moral fiber to tell you the truth and confront you when you need it.

Make use of stepping stones. A spiritual community may offer you temporary assistance. Beware of religious groups and organizations that seem to offer you an answer but actually wish to use you for their own selfish purposes. You will eventually need to graduate from any such group because it is only a stepping stone. In the long run, you need to take responsibility for your own life. Find your true family. They are not necessarily your blood relations. They are people who care about you enough to be tough with you and loving at the same time.

Exercise seven: Assist others.

As long as you are in the dragon's control, you are not in a position to help anyone else. Any attempt to do so is pure hypocrisy and self-deception. However, when you have demonstrated to yourself that you have silenced the dragon for a considerable length of time and have become life affirming instead of self-destructive, you are ready to sponsor someone else. Sponsoring someone is a way of repaying what was done for you. You repay your own sponsor by sponsoring someone new. By assisting others, you keep yourself dragon-free.

Conclusion

It is crucial to transform the self-destruction dragon. When you learn to release its grip on you and liberate the power it holds, you literally find a new life. A step in the right direction is to slide toward the positive pole of the greed dragon, which is appetite. When you develop an appetite for life, you want to live. The challenge is to develop the best kind of appetite, which is not for addictions, but an appetite for truly satisfying relationships and growthful experiences.

Chapter Nine

THE STUBBORNNESS DRAGON

Positive Pole—Determination
Negative Pole—Obstinacy

External manifestation

Unyielding; contrary; unbending; set in one's ways; pigheaded; hard-shelled; headstrong; uncooperative; unpersuadable; mule-headed; immovable; ungovernable.

Internal manifestation

Inflexible; tenacious; relentless; willful; fixed; stuck; perverse; hard-core.

Examples of situations and conditions that are stubborn in nature or that promote the stubbornness dragon

All cultures; all societies; all governments; all militaries; all orthodox religions; the use of force; political domination; oppression; dictatorships; rapid change; dominating and controlling and/or impatient parents; arguing; coercion; resistance; police; laws; torture.

Physical appearance and presentation

The stubbornness dragon creates tension in several parts of the body. In the jaw, this tension appears as a buildup of mass just in front of and below the ear line. Over time, this tension can interfere with the inner ear and reduce hearing capability. Tension in the jaw means tension in the pelvis because the two have a reciprocal relationship. This stress translates into a lack of mobility in the pelvis. Painful tension can also be found in the lower back muscles, which may lead to back trouble. Tension in the feet and ankles is the result of literally digging the heels in.

Physical characteristics of stubbornness may vary greatly. When it is mild or deeply buried, stubbornness has no obvious appearance. In most cases, stubbornness is obvious in the jaw line and in the overall set of the body. Since stubbornness reduces flexibility, People afflicted by it may move stiffly, almost as if at military attention. They have a tendency to fold the arms tightly across the chest as if saying, "You may not pass here."

To get a feel for stubbornness, clench your jaw tightly, squeeze your buttocks, lock your knees, curl your toes, fold your arms over your chest, and say through clenched teeth, "You can't make me," or simply, "No."

The Development of the Stubbornness Dragon

The fear of sudden change

The first root of stubbornness is the fact that children under age seven are not prepared for sudden changes in plans. Dominant parents or guardians, wanting to be in total control of their families, or sometimes just in a big hurry, often do not realize the importance of communicating upcoming changes to small children. The children are not told, for example, that they are to be dropped off at a relative's house for the weekend. To the adults, these are ordinary scenarios that no one should need to adjust to. To the small children, these are big and possibly frightening events. Their relatives' houses may seem alien, and everything familiar like the bathrooms and the kitchens are in different places. The children, not capable of abstract thought at this age, have no way of preparing for these sudden changes of environment without the familiar faces of their parents. In a flash, they are dropped at their relatives' doorsteps. Their parents leave in a hurry, wave goodbye, and are off for the weekend.

At first, the children are overwhelmed, so unprepared are they for such changes, even if their relatives are nice. Not only do the children experience deep loss and betrayal, but they learn to recoil at their new experiences because they are associated with pain. Little by little, as these events accumulate, the children develop a distrust of sudden change deep inside themselves. This distrust formulates itself into a kind of basic resistance to change of any kind. Their bodies develop deep tensions in the muscle groups around the jaw, back, pelvis, and feet. These muscles say, "No, I'm not going anywhere. I'm staying right where I am." This is similar to a donkey with a load on its back, digging in with all four feet as a merchant tries to get it to go forward. Eventually, the muscle groups develop a pattern of habitual tension; they are in a constant state of resistance. This tension allows an opening for the dragon of stubbornness.

Later in life, these people, now in the firm grip of the stubbornness dragon, may not say "no" to change with their words, but their bodies say "no" for them. Their jaws are set, their pelvises locked, their backs tense, and their feet braced against forward movement. Their arms are folded tightly across their chests, and they are inflexible and unspontaneous. They say "no" to everything just to buy some time for inner consideration. Only when they have gotten used to new ideas might they say "yes" to them.

Exploitation

The second source of stubbornness in children is exploitative parents, guardians, or teachers. The children may have talents that give them pleasure, such as music or playing ball or skiing. Their parents or coaches notice these talents and decide that they need development. They move in and take control of the children's pleasures by demanding and requiring endless hours of practice or study. The children must then perform in competitions and win for the satisfaction of the adults.

The parents and coaches may agree to withhold ordinary pleasures such as playing with friends if the children do not perform perfectly. The pleasures that the talents once brought are destroyed in the process. Deep inside, the children rebel by making a lifelong decision: "Never let them take over like that again. Never give them even an inch. Never let anyone do that, ever." Thus, the stage is set for obstinacy and rebellion in all situations that appear to threaten autonomy.

The unfortunate consequence of this exploitation of children is that they may turn their special talents off forever or sabotage their natural skills in order to avoid being controlled and exploited. The stubbornness dragon wins by destroying the people, not the problems.

Controlling parents

The third source for the development of the stubbornness dragon is thoroughly controlling parents or guardians. These adults rule with iron fists and allow their children no options. "Just do it. No back talk. You don't have a choice," is what the children hear again and again. The children are forced to sit at their tables until they have eaten every one of their peas or all their porridge. They are put on potty schedules and made to sit on toilets whether they are ready or not. They are robbed of any options or choices that would help build their integrity and feelings of competence.

With these scenarios, the natural personalities forming

within the children are frustrated. Growing children want to test themselves in the world. They want to have certain choices. For example, they want the freedom to choose between chocolate and vanilla ice cream. Later in life, they move toward more complex choices that bring greater burdens of responsibility. Children know instinctively that having the right to choose is important for developing personal integrity. When simple choices are prevented and children are told, "You will, or else," the children resist being robbed of their power and integrity.

Here is where the stubbornness dragon makes its appearance. Just as with unpreparedness for change, the children develop tension in certain muscle groups. If the children are prevented from protesting the orders by being shouted down, diminished with withering stares, or threatened with dire consequences, they remain silent but say "no" with every fiber of their bodies. Their bodies shout, "No, you can't make me. I won't do it." Sure enough, the children, through quiet resistance, often win in the long run. They learn that quiet defiance is effective against bullying. They learn the strategic value of passive resistance. The dragon takes over.

The defiant stand called "stubbornness" becomes integrated into the personality by adulthood. By the time stubborn children grow up, they are deeply distrustful of authority of any kind. They react with rebellion to anyone trying to tell them what to do.

Stubborn adults may appear on the surface to be relaxed people, but when confronted with sudden change or apparent authority, the dragon comes forth with a vengeance. These people's response to authority or perceived authority is often inappropriate and may cause conflict or loss of opportunity.

In the following example, John is speaking to his wife, Kathy, about going to college:

John: "You know, honey, you really should go back to

school and get that degree. It would make getting that position you want so much easier."

Kathy, getting tight: "I'm not interested."

John: "But it's the practical thing to do. Why not?"

Kathy, getting angry: "Leave me alone. I'm not going and there is no way you can make me go."

John: "But I'm not trying to make you go. I'm just offering a suggestion and trying to find out why you don't want to. It would be helpful."

Kathy, shouting and slamming door: "I won't, I won't, I won't."

John does not perceive himself as an authority over Kathy, but she responds to him as if he were. She is taken over by the stubbornness dragon and is rebelling against old scenarios in which she was deprived of choice and was told what to do. She responds to any suggestion with antagonism and rebellion. She is projecting heavy authority onto John, and the result is a blueprint for conflict and unhappiness.

The anger Kathy displays actually covers fear. She is afraid her freedom is going to be taken away from her. She is afraid that she won't be able to choose freely and that she will somehow be forced to do something that she may not want to do. In fact, Kathy, although very bright, has avoided college for the very same reasons. She is afraid that she will be told what to do by the professors and that she will become a spineless cog in the college machine. Ultimately, she is afraid that someone will push her into a sudden change that she does not feel ready for. Going to college has to be her own idea in her own time. This, however, is a rigid position to take, and chances are she is too rebellious to ever get to college. Her world is sharply curtailed by this stubborn pattern.

The Story of Thomas: A Tale of Stubbornness

Thomas was brought up in a home with mixed parentage. His dominant German father ruled with an iron fist. He was from the old country and felt that children should be seen and not heard (arrogance dragon). The children were told what to do and not given any choices because he believed that children were to be taught total obedience. Thomas's mother was a highly active and impatient woman (impatience dragon) who basically submitted to her husband and was always in a rush to meet the many obligations dictated by Thomas's father.

Therefore, Thomas as a young child never quite knew what would happen next. There was no communication. He was given no warning about when or where he would be dropped off at the baby sitter's, and he was given no notice that mealtimes would be changed. He developed a kind of ongoing anxiety that manifested in his sucking his thumb continually and pulling out his hair in little patches, something that infuriated his father. Thomas was ripe for takeover by the stubbornness dragon.

His father's attitude did not affect Thomas as an infant, but the older he got the more conflict arose between the two of them. By the time Thomas was two, that difficult age of developing autonomy, his father declared total war on his tantrums and willfulness. Thomas was made to sit at the table until all his food was eaten, was forced to stay in his room for lengthy periods, and he lost all privileges when he did not do exactly what he was told. When Thomas was older, the wars between him and his father were about his grades in school and his choice of friends. Thomas's father, a labor union leader, took the position that there was to be no negotiation whatsoever. When Thomas failed to attain an A average in school, he was punished by not being able to see any of his friends until that grade was achieved. Although, like all children, Thomas tried to get his mother to intercede, she was too submissive to stand up to her husband. She simply told Thomas that discipline was the way his father showed he loved him.

Although Thomas appeared to grow up as healthy as any other normal child, he developed layers of hard muscle, like steel plating, in his back and in his jaw. He also developed the habit of grinding his teeth at night, so that in the mornings his jaw ached and he had to see the dentist for worn and cracked teeth. The dragon had made powerful inroads into the core of his personality.

In high school, Thomas excelled at football and was praised for his determination on the field. However, he was recalcitrant and rebellious, and in his senior year he was kicked off the team for refusing to follow the coaches' orders. His relationships with his peers were rocky and often ended abruptly when Thomas would inexplicably get angry, clam up, and refuse to talk about what was troubling him.

Thomas managed to avoid the military and succeeded in finishing college, although he battled with his father over his choice of a major. Because he was on scholarship, he did not have to do what his father wanted, which was to study medicine. Instead, he pursued a major in geology and went to work for an oil company, a job that required frequent moving. The abrupt changes that his job required provoked his fear and stubbornness, and after a quarrel with the head office, he was out of a job. For a time, Thomas jumped from job to job, but they always ended the same way, with a quarrel with the boss. Thomas developed a reputation for being hard to work with and rebellious against authority. His stubbornness dragon assumed complete control.

Thomas struggled through a series of relationships with women, but they usually failed when Thomas complained that the women were too bossy and were always trying to tell him how to live his life. He ended up with a very submissive woman who looked unusually like his mother. They had two children and, not surprisingly, Thomas became inflexible as a father. He was just like his own father, something that he tried to deny at all costs.

When Thomas was thirty years old, he was seriously injured in a fall resulting from his refusal to wear a safety line while working on the roof of his house. He was immobilized for a time in the hospital and then received considerable massage and physical therapy on an outpatient basis. During his long convalescence, Thomas became acquainted with his body as never before. He discovered that his muscle tension worsened his condition and that his tendency to resist the physical therapist's suggestions only caused him terrific pain. He was forced to confront a personality style that not only hindered his healing, but actually heightened his pain.

After a painful period, Thomas began to give up his rebellion. As the physical therapist worked on his tense muscles, he could feel himself letting go. With that choice to surrender to his body's needs, Thomas at one point felt a rush of tears. Sobbing, he began to recall the memories of rebellion against his father and his fear of change that kept his body so tense. For the first time, Thomas had the dragon on the run.

This marked a significant turnaround in Thomas's life. He became determined to release himself from the terrible tyranny of stubbornness. In letting go of his resistance, Thomas discovered his true self. No longer was he exactly like his father. He practiced flexibility, not only in the movement of his physical body but in his relationships with others. He began to learn the art of give and take and compromise. His long months of convalescence and talks with the physical therapist had a profound effect on him. Instead of seeing his accident and recovery as a nightmare, Thomas began to see them as a lifesaver.

With these powerful realizations came changes in his relationships with his wife and children. As Thomas relaxed, his wife, Wendy, found the opportunity to discover a greater assertiveness within herself. His children delighted in their new father—the warmer, more flexible, and playful man behind the suit of armor.

Thomas had beaten back the stubbornness dragon and vastly reduced the dragon's hold on his personality. However, he continued to discover little pockets of stubbornness that cropped up when he was confronted with the intense stress of sudden change or authoritarian people. When a policeman gave him a traffic ticket, he felt his back begin to get tight, but with internal attention, he released his back and let it relax. Thomas was now in the driver's seat of his life.

The Seven Steps of Development for the Stubbornness Dragon

Step one: The children are subjected to sudden changes without adequate warning or preparation.

Step two: The children are not allowed to make personal choices.

Step three: The children are excluded from family choices.

Step four: The children grow resentful and fear the loss of integrity.

Step five: The children learn to resist all forms of external control.

Step six: The older children lose the ability to distinguish between force and suggestion.

Step seven: The older children internalize the struggle and resist themselves.

Step one: The children are subjected to sudden changes without adequate warning or preparation.

Parents or guardians are often ignorant of the importance of communication with their small children and the need to prepare them for coming changes. Sometimes parents get into a pattern of withholding future plans from their children because they want to avoid upsets. For example, the parents know that if the children are told that they are going out of town, the children will create a big fuss. To avoid the fusses, the parents just wait until the last minute and then drop the children off in hurried getaways. While such tactics may serve to avoid unpleasant scenes, they are actually disservices to the children. No one says parenting is easy, but these shortcuts to avoid pain create bigger problems down the road.

There is no need to warn children weeks in advance because children do not think that far ahead. However, telling them of plans a day or two in advance is possible and desirable.

Occasionally, children are caught in emergency situations and neglected due to the nature of the crises. If parents or siblings have an accident and are rushed to a hospital, relatives may neglect to fully inform the children, or they may try to protect the children by telling them white lies. This is a bad policy and simply does not work in the long run. Children are not stupid, and they know psychically when something is wrong. They need to be told what is occurring. In the absence of facts, children's fantasies work overtime in their attempt to piece together what is going on. Often the children reach erroneous conclusions such as that they caused accidents because they were bad. Communication can release children from such guilt. If children know what to expect, they learn to trust change and to understand that life is full of unexpected change that can be accommodated.

Belief and decision: "Change is frightening and a threat to my survival. I need to resist it."

Step two: The children are not allowed to make personal choices.

These children are unilaterally told what to do. However, children build personal power by making choices. These choices begin with small things such as whether to reach for toys or not.

Gradually, the choices involve more complexity, such as whether to go outside or whom to interact with.

Children develop a sense of body integrity. They want to choose what food to put inside their bodies and when and where to touch themselves. The children say, "This is my body and I should be able to do whatever I want with it." If the parents say, "You have to eat everything on your plate" or "I never want to see you touching yourself there again," the children's sense of personal integrity is violated. When children are given choices such as "You can either eat a bite of potatoes or a bite of peas," at least they are given the power to decide. Certainly children can be taught that scratching their genitals at the dinner table is poor manners by society's standards. However, this leaves the children with the choice to touch themselves in private. After all, their bodies are their own.

Belief and decision: "I am being robbed of my power over my body by those in authority. I am not allowed to have my own self. Authority is bad."

Step three: The children are excluded from family choices.

Children developing stubbornness are given no say about decisions that affect their whole families. They are expected to go along with whatever has been decided without regard for their feelings. The children are exploited because their own decisions play no part in family choices.

As toddlers grow into childhood, they naturally feel a desire to exert greater influence on their environments along with their growing bodies. They want to be able to choose whether to go on a family picnic or go to the zoo. When children are never included in these decisions, they are robbed of the experience of feeling that they have the power to make a difference in the world. How are they supposed to grow up to be movers and a shakers if they don't practice that skill? When they are always forced to do what their parents say, they conclude that authority is a rotten idea. Their energy goes into resentment instead of empowerment. This is especially true if they are forced to perform for controlling parents or teachers without being included in the decision to perform. A young boy, forced by his father to win baseball games at all costs, feels the loss of personal power in a game he once loved.

Belief and decision: "I have no power. I have no influence over the environment. I'm always being forced and controlled."

Step four: The children grow resentful and fear the loss of integrity.

Rebellion in these children can arise either from a lack of preparation for sudden changes, which is a fear response, or from having no say in their lives, which is more of an anger response. The net result is the same: rebellion and resistance. This is the point when the dragon of stubbornness truly takes over. The children become mules: unmanageable, difficult, and obstinate.

Little do their parents know that they have made these little monsters themselves. They do not realize that their children, in order to preserve their own sense of integrity, are resisting for their lives. The children fear becoming spineless, submissive wimps who cannot fend for themselves in the world. To counteract this, they develop very hard spines that will not bend. The more resistive the children become, the more their rigid parents respond by digging in. They become locked in power struggles.

This situation produces the most absurd punishments. One parent decided that, since her child loved cheese, the cheese was the cause of her child's rebellion. The child was deprived of cheese from that time on. In this scenario, the parent became a child also, using irrational and childish ploys to win. Since the child looked to the parent to be rational, the child lost all trust in the parent.

The rebellion is often absurdly oppositional. One instructor teaching psychology at a state prison encountered an exceptionally stubborn prisoner. To make a point, the instructor asked the

class to stand up. Of course the stubborn prisoner remained sitting. Then the instructor told the prisoner to sit down. Of
course, he stood up with everyone else. The prisoner and the
whole class got the point. Stubborn people can be controlled
and manipulated easily by telling them to do the opposite of
what you want them to do.

Belief and decision: "Resist authority at all costs in order to
preserve integrity."

**Step five: The children learn to resist all forms of external
control.**

To survive, these children must hold the line on external
control at all costs. They utilize the phrase, "Over my dead
body." In order to resist such formidable figures as parents and
authorities, the children create jaws, backs, and legs of steel.
Their muscles say, "You'll never break me. You'll never make
me. I'll never give in. You have to kill me first." The children
become totally inflexible and unable to compromise or give
and take.

In this way, stubborn children or adults get locked into certain choices that cause them terrible consequences. If other
people dare them to do something dangerous and they agree,
they cannot back down for any reason, even if it becomes apparent that they could die. Although this behavior is also self-
destructive, its roots are in stubbornness.

This tenacious stubbornness is the source of many forms of
attachment to patterns and set plans that make stubborn people
so infuriating to deal with. Once people controlled by the stubbornness dragon get it into their heads that they are going to do
something, almost nothing can deter them.

> Mary made plans to go dress shopping for a social occasion
> on a Saturday well before the event. When Saturday came,
> a blizzard struck and the roads were frozen and hazardous.
> Mary's husband tried to dissuade her from going, citing the

dangerous driving conditions and the ample time to shop in days to come. However, she was not to be deterred. She was convinced that her husband was trying to control her and make her stay at home just as her mother used to do. She chose to go shopping and, on her way there, wrecked the car and only miraculously escaped injury.

Belief and decision: "I can't back down, whatever happens. I can never give in or I'll die."

Step six: The older children lose the ability to distinguish between force and suggestion.

As they get older, children affected by the stubbornness dragon lose the ability to distinguish between small changes and big disasters. After countless experiences of sudden change and bruising authority, the children become highly sensitized to anything that smacks of the possibility that they might lose their choice. They learn to say "no" to all suggestions, just in case. This serves two functions. First, they protect themselves against "bad" authority. Second, they protect themselves against suggested changes that might not be in their best interest. However, once the stubbornness dragon is in control, they can no longer tell the difference between friends offering suggestions and direct orders from authority figures. They can no longer distinguish between the harmless suggestion to paint the kitchen and the painful disaster of losing house and home. They become inflexible and unable to flow with the constant little changes that make life dynamic and interesting.

Belief and decision: "Anything that even remotely looks like I'm being told what to do is bad. I must instantly rebel or say no."

Step seven: The older children internalize the struggle and resist themselves.

This step is the coup de grace of the stubbornness dragon because what started as a defense mechanism becomes the cause of great suffering within people. Stubborn people can suffer from their stubbornness even though no one else is making them do anything.

> Henry decides to accept a job that doesn't pay well and turns out to have serious drawbacks. The foreman is a drunk and abuses Henry verbally on a daily basis. Henry says to himself, "I made my choice and now I'll have to live with it." Friends and relatives suggest that maybe there is a better job out there for him, and he even gets an offer of a better job with higher pay. But Henry doggedly refuses to change jobs. He feels he must outlast the foreman and that he must stick with his decision or die trying. It feels that if he quits, he is admitting that he can't take it, and he is afraid he will become a spineless weakling. Therefore, he must stay. The only one hurt is Henry.

> Henry comes down with a cold but stubbornly refuses to admit it. He does not take care of it, and he gets worse until he finally catches pneumonia and is hospitalized. The stubbornness is internalized. He can't give in to the voice inside of himself that says, "Go home and go to bed." That voice is too much like the voice of his mother and father who always told him what to do. The main victim is again Henry.

Belief and decision: "Now that I've made my decision, I'll have to stick with it, right or wrong."

The Stubbornness Dragon's Big Lie

The stubbornness dragon wants people to believe that by resisting authority and refusing to change they are more powerful. The seduction of stubbornness is that they are fooled into believing that they are more powerful than everybody else because they stonewall and stop the action. Stubborn people get a secret gleam of joy from their habit of refusal. They believe the dragon's message that through stubbornness lies their salvation and ultimate victory. Victory, however, is mostly hollow. In the end, although stubborn people may prove to everyone else that they can't be budged, they lose the goodwill of friends and colleagues. Other people begin to turn away from them, not wanting to deal with such difficult, inflexible people.

Stubborn people end up alone, victorious but isolated. The dragon has lied to them. This is no victory at all. Rather, it is the blueprint for loneliness and despair. Sadly, retirement and nursing homes are filled with stubborn older people who are warehoused by their relatives who no longer want to deal with their inflexibility and recalcitrance. These older people listened to the dragon and were sold a bill of goods. They end up losing warmth and love in their old age. What they win is emptiness of spirit and their worst fear—loss of freedom to choose.

The Great Dragon Exchange

The stubbornness dragon is different from all the other dragons because it stands alone and is not paired with another dragon. However, although this dragon is inflexible, people under its influence can slide easily from it into the claws of any of the other six dragons. For example, people can be stubbornly greedy, stubbornly self-destructive, stubbornly self-deprecating, stubbornly arrogant, stubbornly impatient, stubbornly martyred, and of course stubbornly stubborn. Following are examples of the ways stubbornness can slide into the other dragons:

When people are locked into stubborn decisions or attitudes, they can easily become arrogant about their position: "I'm right. They're stupid and wrong."

They can also slip into stubborn self-deprecation and refuse to budge from their positions: "I'm worthless, and no one is going to tell me otherwise."

They can slide into impatience with everyone who tries to change their minds: "Get out of my way. No one is going to stop me."

They may easily feel martyred by their stubborn choices: "I made my decision and now I'll have to stick with it. I have no other choice."

By the same token, their position may be quite self-destructive: "You can't make me leave my home, fire or no fire."

Stubbornness can even demonstrate aspects of greed: "I'm going to take it all and nobody is going to stop me."

Therefore, the stubborn dragon has its own unique hazards to look out for. When two dragons work together in concert, people are in for some big trouble. Yet, the dragons can be overcome with awareness and effort.

The Wonderful Stubbornness Dragon

Often people think that stubbornness is an endearing trait, or they talk about it as if it were cute. Someone might say, "Oh, little Johnny is so stubborn," as if that were a sign that Johnny is going to grow up to be a strong person. Nothing could be further from the truth. Stubbornness does not make someone strong; it only undermines them and makes them weak. Any behavior based on fear, like stubbornness, only makes fear grow.

Sometimes people fool themselves by saying, "Well, if I hadn't been so stubborn, I never would have succeeded like I have." This is just another form of self-deception. The truth is that stubbornness never helps; it only hinders. People do not have to be stubborn to be persevering or to have discipline and commitment. These traits are independent from stubbornness because they are not based on fear. These self-deceptions are perpetrated by the stubbornness dragon to make sure it is firmly entrenched. After all, it wants to survive by controlling all of people's behavior.

Stages of Maturity and the Stubbornness Dragon

Infant stage: autism and catatonia
Toddler stage: skinheads and reactionaries; the far right
Child stage: good old boys; the Mafia

Adolescent stage: radical leftists and rebels
Adult stage: self-defeat; internal rigidity

Stubbornness at the infant stage

At the infant stage, stubbornness shows up as a complete refusal to communicate or deal with any other human being. This rigidity can manifest as a refusal to eat or a refusal to talk so that the people have to be institutionalized for the better part of their lives. These conditions are called autism and catatonia.

Stubbornness at the toddler stage

Stubbornness at the toddler stage appears in the form of tantrums and defiance: complete rebellion against authority in the most blatant of ways. Adult toddlers are gang members who see how far they can push or break the rules before they are arrested and imprisoned. They are individuals who defy all authority and end up as survivalists, neo-Nazis, skinheads or Ku Klux Klan members. Their position is that nobody is going to tell them what the rules are or how they can live. They fight to the death before allowing themselves to be caught.

These people may appear to be self-destructive, but they are actually stubborn; they refuse to give in. They resist change and want to turn the clock back to the old days. They don't like newcomers and they don't want to have to get used to them. They are actually terribly frightened of change and feel ill prepared to handle it. That is why they resist so much.

Stubbornness at the child stage

Stubbornness at the child stage is more sophisticated. Stubborn adult children are highly successful people who win financially and influentially by resisting the rules. They get pleasure from breaking every rule in the book in sophisticated ways and getting away with it. They get rich by circumventing tax laws and paying off politicians and lawmakers. They pride themselves on never playing by the rules and yet still winning. However, they tend to be very conservative; they do not like change.

Good examples of these adult children are members of the Mafia who break the social rules but keep the traditions of the family. They want women to be submissive and men to be aggressive. They do not like change, and in fact are afraid of it, yet they live their lives in defiance of authority.

Stubborn adult children are corrupt police and politicians who break all the rules they can while appearing to be rule followers. They have a tendency to be very conservative in their viewpoints, and they resist any changes in the status quo. For example, these politicians may accept bribes and cater to big business by overlooking environmental laws; or they may work actively to prevent minorities from gaining political footholds. They operate under the "good old boy" system. They keep the status quo but defy the laws of the land and do what they want to get ahead.

Stubbornness at the adolescent stage

At the adolescent level of stubbornness are the social reformers and radical members of minority political movements. These are angry people who want to overthrow the system. They want to bring down the big, bad, corrupt father government and replace it with their own liberated version.

Stubborn adult adolescents tend to be highly vocal and challenging, unafraid to be the sole demonstrators at opposing political rallies or the lone hecklers at speeches given by politicians in power. They see themselves as righteous and representing the great hidden masses who are too cowed to complain. They are clearly on missions. However, if they succeed in bringing about reforms, they soon find other soapboxes to carry on their opposition to new tyrannies.

These people are married to their oppositional stance. In this way, they, too, are afraid of change. They are afraid to change their positions or their oppositional style, and they are afraid to grow up and move on to other things. While they want change in the system, they do not want change in themselves.

They are afraid of it as much as all stubborn people are. Their lives are torturous and their suffering intense.

Stubbornness at the adult stage

Stubbornness at the adult level is internalized. It is not so obvious on the outside because the struggle is within. Stubborn adults fight their battles by engaging in internal dialogues. They do not wear coats in the cold because the internalized voices of their mothers say, "It's cold. Wear a jacket." If they twist an ankle, they force themselves to walk anyway because they do not want to give in to the tyranny of a sprained ankle. The result, of course, is a worse condition.

Although their stubbornness can appear admirable to others, it is actually an exercise in defeat. Their rebellions against internalized tyrannies, are designed to fail. I worked with a man who refused to wear a tie, no matter what the occasion. I myself dislike wearing ties, so I did not fault him for this. Not wearing a tie was his own personal rebellion against imposed authority. However, the result was the loss of good jobs, the alienation of a friend who asked him to be best man at his wedding, and the inability to attend many social occasions where a tie was mandatory. The question is, what did he win? A sense of personal integrity? At whose expense? The fact is that there are other, more effective ways of preserving integrity or making a contribution in the world. The inflexibility of stubbornness keeps people in the minor leagues.

How the Stubbornness Dragon Gets You in the End

Stubbornness is designed to protect you from sudden, unexpected change that could be threatening to your integrity or your life. Stubbornness buys you time. When you say, "No, I won't do it," you slow the action down so that you have a chance to change your mind. Later, as you get used to the idea, you may decide to say "yes" on your own terms. That is the strategy behind stubbornness as it applies to fear of change.

However, too often the other people in your life won't wait for you but go right on ahead with their plans. That means you not only have a sudden change on your hands, but you lose out as well.

A woman lived in a house on land that was in the direct path of a major highway being built. The state was buying up all the land in the path of the highway, offering market value for each parcel. On the one hand, this was very difficult for the people who were selling, but on the other hand, the highway was already under construction and the time for fighting the project was over. The woman, governed by the stubbornness dragon, refused to sell. She hated change and liked even less people trying to tell her what to do. The state eventually offered her three times what her property was worth, but she refused to sell. Finally they gave up and built the highway around her small parcel.

Many people admired the woman for holding out until she won. She became a kind of local hero. However, did the woman really win anything at all? Her land plummeted in value and became worth virtually nothing because of its proximity to the highway. Her peace and quiet was shattered by the noise of trucks and heavy traffic. Her view of the hills was gone, and all the reasons she liked living there were no longer valid.

However, in her mind, even though she now hated living there, she thought she had won. This is the typical sting of the stubbornness dragon. People think they win, but really they lose. The woman tried to stave off change, but it happened anyway. She defied authority, but it won her nothing but misery. Later, she wished she had sold, but it was too late.

One man refused to vacate his house when he was warned of the imminent eruption of Mt. St. Helens in Washington state. He stubbornly refused to go, saying that nobody was going to make him. His stubbornness caused him to defy the local authorities, and the next day the volcano erupted. Later, no trace of him or his home could be found. They were buried under tens of tons of lava and ash.

Who is to say who was right? Maybe this man knew it was his time to die. Or maybe he would have lived longer had he not been so stubborn. However, defiance of authority just for the sake of defying it is a losing proposition. This man's strategy was to preserve his integrity against bullying. However, no one was trying to bully him. The authorities were simply trying to save his life. Defiance of authority sometimes results in people being killed, as many prisoners of war have observed. The ones who aren't stubborn live to tell about their experiences.

Many criminals can attest to the fact that resistance to authority only tends to attract it to you more strongly. What you resist you create. What you are afraid of, you bring to you. The dragon of stubbornness brings you what you fear the most: sudden change and greater authority.

How the Stubbornness Dragon Affects Your Life

The impact of the stubbornness dragon on your health

As described in the previous section, stubbornness can lead to your early demise. Imagine the results of stubbornness if you are captured by ruthless enemy soldiers during a war. If you want to live, you must do exactly what they tell you instantly, or you are executed on the spot. If they say march, you march. If they say sit, you sit. If you do routine military service you know this need for obedience to authority as well. Defiance of your superior officer can bring terrible consequences in boot camp. It can mean punishment that is bad for your health, such as being "volunteered" for hazardous duty.

There are also more mundane consequences of stubbornness on your health. Stubbornness affects your back muscles, jaw muscles, pelvic muscles, and feet muscles. Chronic muscle tension in these areas can wreak havoc on your body. Chronic tension in the masseter muscles of your jaw can cause TMJ syndrome (temporomandibular joint syndrome), a problem that affects many people. Bruxism, the problem of grinding your teeth at night, can cause loss of your teeth and gum disease. Tight back muscles can pull your vertebrae out of alignment and compact them together so that the discs rub, wear, and rupture. Tight back muscles can also tear more easily in sudden lifts, causing a loss of mobility and chronic back ailments.

Tight muscles in your pelvis can limit the blood supply to this region and pinch the nerves so that pleasure is cut off and numbness takes its place. Tight anal muscles can create bowel movement problems and even result in hemorrhoids. Foot tension ultimately results in walking problems and the need for special shoes or braces. There is absolutely nothing healthy about stubbornness. Yet it can fool you into making you think you need it to survive.

The impact of the stubbornness dragon on your creativity

If you do creative work, you know that creativity flows best when your body is relaxed and in a state of surrender. That is why there are so many creative breakthroughs when people are seated on a toilet letting go, or lying in a bath of warm water. When your body is locked into defiance and tension against fear, how can your creativity flow? Creative breakthroughs don't occur when you grind your teeth or fold your arms tightly across your chest and say "no." This is the opposite of creativity. Creativity demands expansion. Stubbornness is contraction.

The impact of the stubbornness dragon on your presence

Stubbornness represents a fear of sudden change. Therefore, if you are stubborn, you have anxiety about what could happen in the future. This robs you of your attention to the present moment. When you are not present, you have no presence. Likewise, when you resist authority, you are locked into a conflict with whoever or whatever happens to represent local authority. This makes you mechanical, because you respond to authority with a predicted response. There is a stimulus, and you have a response. Your authority button is pressed and out comes your defiance, just like a vending machine. When you operate mechanically, you are not present. You are not acting with the flexibility of a human being.

Only dragon-free people can have the true presence of a Mahatma Gandhi, a determined Mother Teresa, or a serene Buddha. Presence is what replaces the dragon when you dump it. With presence, there is no limit to what you can accomplish.

The impact of the stubbornness dragon on your relationships

Stubbornness is particularly destructive when it comes to your relationships with others and with yourself. Because the stubbornness dragon causes you to rebel against authority, when you are under its influence, everything looks like a possible threat to your personal freedom and independence. You may refuse to participate in events or interact with others because you don't want anyone telling you what to do.

If you are stubborn, you may be poor at compromise and inflexible in your dealings with others. You tend not to cooperate well, and this gets in the way of your working with a team. If you are a stubborn manager, you may be hated by your employees. Unhappy employees manufacture poor products, are often sick, and work more slowly. In fact, a stubborn boss makes for stubborn employees. Each side digs in and refuses to negotiate. The result is a strike.

> Joe owned a construction-materials outlet with a staff of fifteen employees. He was a stubborn man and refused to listen to anyone's suggestions about how to improve his operation. He paid an average wage but offered no benefits to his staff. The employees petitioned him for a retirement plan and some medical benefits. Business was brisk, and he could have afforded the benefits, but he hated having any-

one tell him how to run his operation. He adamantly refused, and the staff felt that he was being unreasonable. Eventually, after total frustration, they went on strike. Joe, backed into a corner by his stubbornness, steadfastly refused to negotiate. As the strike dragged on, everyone lost money and the public was inconvenienced. A major chain saw its opportunity and opened a modern, larger store nearby.

Since they offered benefits, they scooped up the striking staff. Before long, Joe was out of business. He won the battle but lost the war.

When two stubborn people tangle, the results can be both humorous and tragic. I once worked with a couple who had not slept together in the same bed for over five years. After a big argument, during which both sides dug in, Carl, the husband, bedded down on the couch and remained there for years. Neither side would give in. However, neither person could quite remember what the original fight was all about.

The stubbornness dragon can play havoc with your sexual relationships. If you are stubborn, you may not want to try any new sexual behavior, and you may be quite physically armored against the other person. Your partners may have to walk on eggshells to avoid doing anything that displeases you. They risk the silent treatment and withdrawal if they intrude on your sense of integrity.

The consequences of stubborn behavior in the family can be tragic. A ten-year-old girl angered her stubborn father by refusing to eat her vegetables at dinner. He told her he would not talk to her again until she ate all her vegetables. By the time I worked with them, the girl was sixteen years old. Although she and her father lived in the same house, neither one had talked to the other since that day when she was ten years old. This was extreme behavior and very childish, but it happens every day with sad results. Happily, therapy helped them reopen their communication. The episode illustrates how stubbornness in a parent often imprints stubbornness onto a child. All the dragons work this way. They teach children through the actions of the parents and guardians.

The impact of the stubbornness dragon on your spiritual life

Spiritual leaders teach expansive philosophies that are backed up with their own actions. These philosophies are soon translated into dogmas by loyal followers, who then create orthodox religions that offer behavior control for millions. Religions have hierarchies of authority, bureaucracy, and wealth, and they have an intense need for self-preservation. Since these structures tend to become fossilized rather quickly, they resist change that could be threatening to their survival. This resistance to change is one of the core ingredients of stubbornness. Therefore, most religions teach stubbornness by modeling stubborn behavior.

Since it is in the nature of things in the physical world to change, stubbornness represents an unnatural resistance to the natural order. Stubbornness is based on fear; and fear, not spirituality, is something many religions perpetrate. Stubbornness can only be an obstacle to spiritual awareness, for spiritual awareness requires an inquiring and open mind, not a fearful and closed mind.

Sometimes the automatic response of your body is to protect itself from threats by attacking and possibly harming other human beings. Your spiritual awareness represents the higher authority within you as an individual. Your higher spiritual authority, coming from within you, can override your primitive bodily response and call for communication instead. However, if you are stubborn, you may resist all authority, including that voice coming from within you. You may say to that voice, "You can't tell me what to do." Your tendency would be not to listen to that voice from within that has greater wisdom. The stubbornness entraps you at the primitive level of response. It effectively prevents your spiritual awareness.

How to Transform the Stubbornness Dragon

Stubbornness is the one dragon that can appear impervious to change, but like all dragons it is subject to transformation. However, it is one dragon that it is best not to attack head on, because it will only dig itself in deeper. Stubbornness must be melted, not hammered and cracked. You must release this dragon slowly by seeing the larger context of your situation. In this way, your fear is overcome and you see that you are not truly threatened by what is taking place. You can release stubbornness with kindness, compassion, and gentle guidance.

The following weapons may be challenging to use, but they are not harsh and jagged. They are related to releasing, accepting, listening, relaxing, and going with the world instead of against it. If you are stubborn, this list of weapons may sound paradoxically more like a list of tortures. In a way, they are like tortures. They need to be, because letting the dragon control your actions can be very comfortable. All you have to do is respond mechanically and the rest takes care of itself. You do not have to take responsibility for yourself. On the other hand, letting the stubbornness dragon run the show is certain to impede your progress toward growth, and it will definitely limit your happiness.

Affirmations to Weaken the Stubbornness Dragon

I am an excellent listener.

I always take advantage of the opportunities that change brings into my life, even the ones that are painful.

I always admit when I am wrong, which is often.

I enjoy implementing suggestions and advice.

I am secure in the knowledge that I can count on knowing what to do.

I learn a lot from my failures.

I have the courage to admit when I am wrong.

I am learning the art of compromise.

It is smart to listen to other people at times.
I like to do new and interesting things.
When I say "yes" to others, I learn a great deal.

Seven Weapons to Transform the Stubbornness Dragon

Weapon one: Learn to be flexible.
Weapon two: Learn to say "yes."
Weapon three: Express yourself openly.
Weapon four: Listen with an open mind.
Weapon five: Come to terms with authority.
Weapon six: Embrace change.
Weapon seven: Admit your mistakes and accept failure.

Weapon one: Learn to be flexible.

If you are stubborn, you are as inflexible in your thought processes as you are in your responses to external events. This inflexibility also manifests in your physical body. Therefore, you must learn flexibility in all three spheres: thinking, doing, and being.

There is a bumper sticker that addresses inflexible thinking. It says, "Minds are like parachutes—they only work when they're open." Having an open mind means considering the possibility that a concept presented to you could be true or have potential. You do not necessarily have to agree wholeheartedly with the concept to have flexible thinking. You can simply weigh the idea without rejecting it forthwith.

I once studied with a Zen master who spoke very little English. He used to say, in true Zen form, "Keep 'don't know' mind." This meant, don't jump to conclusions and think you know something automatically. If you are stubborn, maybe there is something new and fresh that you have not considered before. Be present with your reality. That way, you are closer to sensing the true nature of things. When you think you know, or you close your mind to new possibilities, you become fossilized and stop your growth.

Flexibility in your body translates eventually into flexibility in your mind. The reverse is also true. Stubbornness makes your body tight, armored, and protective. Your mobility is restricted and you cannot do much. By stretching and limbering up your body, you have a greater range of responses to changes that you are inevitably faced with. This is one of the great teachings of the martial arts. If you brace yourself for blows, you risk injury. If you are flexible enough to step aside, you gain the advantage. The momentum of attackers can then be used against them.

Weapon two: Learn to say "yes."

When you are more flexible with what you do, you say "yes" to people more often. You try new things, eat new foods, and go new places. You are vital and alive. Being stubborn closes off the world and ruins many possibilities. When you "keep 'don't know' mind," you are open to the possibility of discovery, adventure, and evolution. When you leave stubbornness and fear behind, you do much more with your life than if you cling to the stubbornness dragon.

Saying "yes" to suggestions and taking advice from knowledgeable sources are effective means of succeeding in the world. If you are in a position of authority with others, sometimes the most knowledgeable people are your employees, because they deal with front-line problems that you may not be acquainted with. Listening to them and saying "yes" to suggested changes can make nonprofitable, stale situations more flexible and therefore more successful.

Weapon three: Express yourself openly.

Often, procrastination is a mask for stubborn behavior. You may keep saying you will do something and then never get around to it. For example, you may never pick up your clothes. Your roommate asks you many times, and although you agree to do so, nothing happens. Chances are the stubbornness dragon is in charge of you. Your actions reveal your underlying attitude: "No one is going to tell me what to do." You need to learn to speak the truth from the outset. Say to your roommate, "I don't want to pick up my clothes." This is the starting place for further communication, because at least the truth has been told. Compromise can then follow.

If you are stubborn, you need much practice in communication. You need to learn how to express your feelings, especially your fears. You cannot be pushed, however. You need to proceed with this learning slowly.

Weapon four: Listen with an open mind.

The silence of stubbornness is its most deadly attribute. Silent opposition can lead to conflicts that last for long periods without resolution. The silent treatment—the refusal to listen—is sometimes a purely stubborn response. (It can also come from martyrdom and be used as punishment.) Not surprisingly, if you are stubborn, you may develop hearing loss. Not hearing can result from not listening to others over the years. The clamping of your jaw can actually interfere with the sensitive structure of your inner ears. If you want good hearing in your old age, learn to listen when you are younger.

Weapon five: Come to terms with authority.

When you resist something, you become it. If you make a habit of resisting oppressive authority, you become oppressive yourself in the long run. You become the authority oppressing others. This may be one of the hardest things for you to see with clarity. For you as a stubborn person, authority is the enemy. So what happens when you become the authority? You tend to see anyone who disagrees with you as the enemy.

If you are under the control of the stubbornness dragon, you have no inner authority and are afraid.

To erase stubbornness, you must accept authority. First, develop the ability to listen to your own inner authority. This builds stability and character from the inside out.

When you feel secure and balanced, you can accept appropriate authority from the outside because you are not afraid of it.

You have inner confidence. Therefore, when a traffic cop directs traffic in an emergency, you do as you are told for the common good. You are not afraid of losing your integrity over such a small matter because you are used to listening to sound authority from within yourself.

Weapon six: Embrace change.

There is a saying that "only one thing is constant in this world, and that is change." Change is inevitable in your external environment: friends and relatives move away, neighborhoods change, cars wear out, jobs shift, and pets get old along with people. To compensate for the anxiety that change can bring, you may try to hang onto old things and old habit patterns. You cling to old hairstyles, clothes, music, attachments, attitudes and belief systems. In addition to trying to halt change from without, you cement your inner world together to try to prevent change from within. The result is painful. You are terrified to see gray appear in your hair, or you cannot cope with your child marrying outside your race or religion. You are in pain yourself, and you create pain for the people who love you the most.

To resist change is useless in the long run. Change must be not only accepted but desired, just as you would desire to see your plants flower or your children grow. When you are an effective human being, you embrace change and take the position that no matter how painful it is, there is an opportunity in it.

> Jack thought the world had ended when he learned that his closest brother and roommate had shot himself in the head. This change was irrevocable for Jack. No matter what he did, he could not bring his brother back. So strong was Jack's denial that he refused to even enter his brother's room or deal with his belongings for months. He did not like change of any kind in his life, and this was one change he did not want to accept.

> However, Jack's grief was great, and this motivated him to seek help. With the help of a counselor, he began to deal

with his brother's death. He went through all the classic feelings: denial, guilt, anger, and finally acceptance. Eventually, he went through his brother's things and cleared them out of the house. Then he began to consider even bigger changes. He sold the house and moved to a more appealing neighborhood. With this change of perspective, he began to see how his job was not satisfying him anymore. He set wheels turning to change offices and responsibilities. The change in offices led him to meet Margaret, the woman he later married.

As Jack made changes in his environment, he also began to see how his resistance to his mother's scattered, spontaneous lifestyle had resulted in his own choice for a stuck and unchanging existence. In an indirect way, Jack's brother's suicide had helped him to discover a new life.

Weapon seven: Admit your mistakes and accept failure.

If you are controlled by the stubbornness dragon, you hate to admit that your choices are mistakes. You try to prove indefinitely that you are right. Therefore, you often throw good money after bad in cantankerous drives to demonstrate your rightness. You don't change a bad business decision in time to save the business from bankruptcy court. You don't call back your troops from a deadly trap after committing them to battle. You decide to quit a relationship after a quarrel and refuse to make up even though you love the person intensely. You cannot go back on your decisions no matter what, because to do so would be to lose face. Not only is this exceptionally painful for others, but you suffer unnecessarily with your decisions for a very long time. Saving face is saving only a false sense of your personal integrity. This face is a facade and, at its worst, a false sense of yourself.

Admission of error is critical for you to erase your stubbornness. This involves looking fear in the face. If there is anything that is hard to do, it is admitting to yourself that your stubborn stance is based on fear, not strength. This is an act of supreme courage. Admitting your mistakes allows for reconciliation, renewed communication, growth of relationships and the saving of resources, money, and even lives.

Admitting failure leads to growth because, through failure, lessons are learned. If the dragon of stubbornness had its way, children would not learn to walk because falling down is a failure to walk. To save face, the children would have to sit all their lives. This borders on the absurd, but then, stubbornness leads to totally absurd acts.

Many stubborn doctors consider the deaths of their patients to be personal failures. Therefore, they either abandon their patients before their inevitable deaths or they hook them up to machines and create a technical semblance of life that is little more than suspended death. Erasing stubbornness involves letting go: letting go of a patient with grace when that is appropriate; letting go of a relationship when it is clearly dead; letting go of a job or a business when it is no longer viable.

Seven Exercises to Transform the Stubbornness Dragon

Exercise one: Identify your worst nightmare scenario.
Exercise two: Identify rigidity in your body.
Exercise three: Learn to listen.
Exercise four: Follow the leader.
Exercise five: Admit error.
Exercise six: Learn to be fluid.
Exercise seven: Let go of structures and set patterns.

Exercise one: Identify your worst nightmare scenario.

This is a writing exercise. The goal is to get in touch with your hidden fear.

Identify a situation involving a perceived change that is out of your control—one that you have resistance to. Write a list of all the worst case scenarios that come to mind when you contemplate the new event or situation. As you write them down, a pattern will emerge that reveals the fear you harbor over this change.

For example, the situation you identify may be that you are told to relocate by the company that employs you. Write down your worst fears involving the move. Then observe exactly what it is that is so negative about the experience. Do not dwell on the nightmare scenes; simply get them out.

Exercise two. Identify rigidity in your body.

Sit quietly in a comfortable chair and, after taking several deep breaths, begin to identify the areas of your body where you experience tension or tightness. Usually, you will find that these are chronic areas of tension such as your jaw, neck, back, buttocks, or feet. Select one area to focus on. Describe the area's size, shape, color, temperature, and texture as you focus on it.

When you have successfully described this area of your body to yourself, get more creative. Allow words to come to your mind that label the area. Allow mental pictures or symbols to show themselves to you. If you are particularly visual, let yourself watch movies that spontaneously appear as you focus on the tense area. These images will always relate to the concerns and fears you store in the area of focus. The movies may be replays of memories, or they may be more symbolic in nature. Sometimes, when you do this exercise, faces or names may appear in your imagination that relate to early experiences of your life. These may tell a story of an earlier time in your life when the dragon of stubbornness got its grip on you.

Exercise three: Learn to listen.

You need a partner for this exercise. Sit down with your partner and have your partner tell you something he or she is having difficulty with in terms of relating to you. Normally, this is something you resist hearing. Every couple of minutes, repeat everything your partner said to you, including the feelings behind what he or she said. As part of this exercise, do not argue. Simply feed back faithfully what was said, along with the phrase "I understand." For example, you might repeat to your partner, "I understand that you are upset with me because I do not like to spend time with your friends or have them over for dinner. This makes you feel that I do not value you."

If you find this exercise too difficult, begin with a subject that is not as intense as a relationship problem. You can work up to personal issues.

Exercise four: Follow the leader.

For half a day or a day, follow a trusted partner's instructions without resistance. The partner should make suggestions to you that break the ordinary routine you follow together. These sug-gestions can include activities that you ordinarily say "no" to. The idea is to closely observe your feelings and inner responses as you go about saying "yes" to the suggested activities. If your partner is already your sexual partner, and if sex is involved in his or her suggestions, then do what your partner asks for a change. Try to stretch yourself. However, it is important that you use your discretion as to where your limit is.

A variation on this exercise is to simply take a day and do an entirely new set of activities, things that you would not ordi-narily do. This requires no outside partner.

Exercise five: Admit error.

This is another writing exercise. Make a list of all the big mistakes you remember making in your life. Or, you could limit this to all the mistakes you made in the last year. Recall when you did not take another's advice—to your detriment. What were the consequences? Recall when other people had better ideas and suggestions for you. Recall those times when you did not follow your own inner counsel and what results that brought you.

Exercise six: Learn to be fluid.

Find a quiet space where you will not be interrupted for a period of time. Sit comfortably with your legs and hands uncrossed and your spine straight. Close your eyes and focus your attention on the image of a running stream. Become a leaf floating down the stream and sense where the current carries you. Then imagine that you are a bird flying with a flock. Follow the flock's course without trying to control where it goes. Become a fish swimming with a school under the sea. Or lope along with a pack of wolves in the frozen north and sense their spontaneous experience. Use any image that appeals to you and learn to follow a fluid unplanned course. Do this many times.

Exercise seven: Let go of structures and set patterns.

This exercise is meant to help you release attachment, something that stubborn people struggle with. Notice the set patterns in your life that you are particularly reluctant to give up in order to accommodate someone else. Make a point of giving up a routine and sense what you experience around this letting go. Do you feel anger, fear, relief? Change your set plans in the middle of the day simply to do so and experience the result. To do this most effectively, it is best to listen carefully to the little voice inside you that makes suggestions. You might consider this voice to be your intuition.

Conclusion

The stubbornness dragon derives from the fear of sudden change, the curse of exploitation, and the damage of overcontrol in childhood. As with all the dragons, stubbornness can be erased only if it is recognized as the enemy. If you have it, you yourself must take the responsibility to remove its grip on your personality. Perhaps more than with any other dragon this is true, because no one can tell a stubborn person to let go of stubbornness. If you release it, you will not be rendered weak. On the contrary, you will be more empowered than you have ever been in your life. Such is the nature of challenging the dragon and winning.

Chapter Ten

THE DYNAMICS OF DRAGON-CONTROLLED AND DRAGON-FREE RELATIONSHIPS

Making Essence Contact

The previous chapters described how each dragon operates: its development, takeover, and domination of every aspect of life. These chapters also listed each dragon's vulnerable points and the steps needed to transform the dragon's negativity into a positive force.

This chapter looks at the interaction between the dragons of two people in a relationship. This interaction and play of dragons between people is unfortunately much of the story of the human race. Without the dragon drama between people, there would be no wars, coups, executions, massacres, takeovers, lies, rapes, pillaging, crime, oppression, or any of the other ills that have caused the human race to suffer for most of its relatively short history.

Transforming relationships

As the human species matures, the dragons' territory will be gradually encroached upon and eventually eliminated. Even now, although terrible small wars continue to break out on the planet, war as a way of solving problems is no longer quite as acceptable as it once was. Considering the historical record, human rights are at the highest priority they have ever been. There was a time when the concept of human rights never even entered people's minds. This gradual enlightenment of the species means there is less room for the dragons to maneuver. Their old familiar territory is gradually being erased by the maturing of the human value system, slow as this may be.

However, as the dragons are pushed out of one arena after another, they will dig in and become more cunning, masquerading as newfound maturity. For example, the greed dragon may manifest not so much as greed for territory, money, or power as greed in relationships. The arrogance dragon, rather than creating a brash display of expensive cars and symbols of wealth, will hide in aloofness and shyness. The sections in previous chapters regarding each dragon's behavior at higher levels of maturity describe where human beings are headed. The adolescent and adult levels of maturity are the focus of the next phase in human history.

This chapter is important because the main thrust of dragon activity in the future will be in relationships between individuals. As individuals struggle to communicate with one another, and try to find connection, the dragons will attempt to block their progress. This becomes the battlefield. Therefore, the more you can learn about and identify dragon behavior, the better armed you will be for this battle, and the better you will be able to guide those around you trying to find their path of truth.

The following are descriptions of the typical activities of dragons in relationships between people. You may see familiar scenarios in which you yourself or your family members, friends, or coworkers have participated. Read these descriptions with a little chuckle rather than getting upset over the scenarios. The dragons do not like you to laugh at yourself. Your detachment tends to ruin their fun. They would rather see you raging, grieving, fearing, self-recriminating, and feeling shame and guilt. So each time you chuckle at your human foolishness, you disentangle your self further from the confusion and struggle that the dragons offer.

There are twenty-eight possible combinations of dragons, and each combination has pitfalls. None of the combinations are good, so none of the following descriptions sound inspiring. They are meant to be stark presentations of dragon activity that show you what to avoid in life. These worst-case scenarios portray the dragon patterns clearly. You may experience much milder versions of these scenarios in your own life, and you may find many people actively working to overcome these destructive exchanges. Use the information to identify patterns in your own relationships and begin to use the tools in this book to erase those patterns in yourself. However, be aware that you cannot clear away your partner's dragon; you can only erase your own.

Every dragon combination can be healed with intention and discipline. The final section of this chapter pertains to dragon-free relationships, the making of essence contact, and where the future lies.

Four Basic Formulas for Dragon Relationships

Formula one

In partnerships, it is common to find one person with a narrow-focused dragon and the other person with a wide-focused dragon. People having the self-destruction, self-deprecation, and martyrdom dragons are likely to pair with people having the greed, arrogance, or impatience dragons. All of them are likely to pair with the stubbornness dragon.

Formula two

In general, parents tend to produce children with the same dragons as themselves because of the role-modeling factor. Stubborn parents often produce stubborn children; greedy parents produce greedy children, and so on. The result is that, in relationships later in life, people often select partners with the same dragon as themselves. People controlled by the greed dragon often partner up with others similarly controlled by the greed dragon.

When two people have the same dragon, they tend to project things onto each other. Since they know the patterns of their dragon so well, even if subconsciously, they tend to see these patterns in their partners and accuse them of their own issues. Thus, they are likely to get into mutual blaming. For example, two stubborn people may accuse each other of being stubborn; this goes nowhere.

Formula three

As described in earlier chapters, there are three pairs of dragons: arrogance and self-deprecation, impatience and martyr-dom, and greed and self-destruction. People in relationships in which each partner has one dragon of a pair also have a tendency to project onto each other. For example, if one party has the self-deprecation dragon and the other has the arrogance dragon, both suffer from lowered self-esteem. They can easily see that low self-esteem in each other and use this perception to blame or attack each other.

Formula four

People are often attracted to spouses, friends, or partners who have the same dragon as one of their parents. This is true for two reasons:

First, the pattern is familiar. Therefore, the people know subconsciously what to expect from their partners. Since they associate some love and affection with this pattern, they expect to find it once again with partners having the same pattern. For example, people with martyrdom are often attracted to people with stubbornness. Why? Because people with martyrdom often had inflexible parents who squashed their sense of independence. Typically, these stubborn parents were at times loving. In their stubborn partners, the martyrs recognize the pattern and figure there will be love there somewhere.

Second, people are always trying to work out unfinished business with their parents or guardians. They subconsciously select friends and spouses who reproduce their dilemmas with their parents so they can heal or fix these dilemmas for all. Unfortunately, this does not always work out.

For example, people with the self-deprecation dragon are often attracted to people with the arrogance dragon because self-deprecators typically had parents with the arrogance dragon. Since arrogant people tend to be highly critical, they often produce children with self-deprecation. In selecting arrogant partners, the self-deprecators feel that this time they will be able to overcome the criticism and finally feel good about themselves as individuals.

Common Parent-Child Dragon Combinations

Following is a list of the parent-child combinations that most commonly arise from the formulas just described. These parent-child combinations are often replicated in adult relationships. These are the most common combinations of dragons. However, any combination of two dragons is possible.

Parents with arrogance:

Children with self-deprecation: Judgmental parents can be highly critical of their children. If the children feel they can never measure up, they become self-deprecating.

Children with martyrdom: Arrogant parents, in additions to being critical, can be demanding to the extreme. Their love can certainly be conditional. These parents do not want their children's behavior to embarrass them, especially in public or at social occasions. The children feel required to deliver good behavior at all times, despite what they feel. This pattern is a golden opportunity for martyrdom.

Children with arrogance: When parents are critical, the children feel they have to measure up. The children may adopt their parents' critical attitudes and strive for perfection, always trying to cover up their weaknesses to prevent detection by their parents. They then become arrogant themselves.

Parents with self-deprecation:

Children with impatience: This scenario is similar to that of impatient children with martyred parents. Chronic self-deprecation in parents can lead children to become frustrated and intolerant of their parents' cowardice. Self-deprecation leads the parents into the smaller world of avoidance. The children feel they have things to do, places to go, and people to meet. They feel trapped and deprived of life experience by their fearful parents. Their rush to get out becomes impatience.

Children with self-deprecation: Parents without self-esteem cannot teach their children to have self-esteem. The parents see themselves as inadequate at parenting. The children then learn to feel inadequate themselves.

Parents with impatience:

Children with stubbornness: Intolerant, impatient parents often rush their children. This is the way children learn to fear change, one of the hallmarks of stubbornness.

Children with martyrdom: Impatient parents model for their children the experience of feeling trapped. This can easily lead to martyrdom in the children, especially if the parents are intolerant and demand good behavior.

Children with impatience: Impatience is easy for children to pick up when it is the behavior pattern both of their parents and their culture at large.

Parents with martyrdom:

Children with impatience: Parents who are martyrs often produce highly impatient children. First, the children learn about feeling trapped from their parents' modeling. Second, they typically get impatient with their martyr parents' complaining and long suffering. They especially get fed up with their parents if they are made to feel guilty all the time. This primes them for the dragon of impatience.

Children with martyrdom: This combination occurs when the children ally themselves with the victim stance of their parents.

Parents with greed:

Children with self-deprecation: Greedy parents tend to blame everyone else for their dissatisfaction and unhappiness. When they blame their children, the children believe them and feel that they are inadequate to make their parents happy. Add to this the fact that greedy parents seldom give praise and the stage is set for serious self-deprecation in the children.

Children with martyrdom: Greedy parents do not give unconditionally. These emotionally hungry parents, besieged by their own needs and cravings, often regard their children as a bother or even as competition for attention. They want the children to demand as little as possible, to be good and obedient. The compliant children will do anything for approval, so they become good victims or martyrs.

Children with self-destruction: Greedy parents often emotionally and physically abandon their children to pursue their own gratification. If corporal punishment is used during the random times they are present, the stage is set for self-destruction in the children. More often, the greedy parents abandon their children to the mercy of abusive substitutes.

Children with greed: Greedy parents cannot give. Instead, they abandon their children in their search for what they crave. Greed thrives on abandonment. In this way, greed is passed on from generation to generation.

Parents with self-destruction:

Children with greed: Because self-destructive parents so often abandon their children physically and emotionally, they set up the perfect conditions for their children to grow up hungry, prime candidates for the greed dragon takeover.

Children with self-destruction: Self-destructive parents who beat, abuse, or abandon their children at random create the perfect environment for the self-destruction dragon in their children.

Parents with stubbornness:

Children with martyrdom: Stubborn parents, with their inability to compromise and their demands that everything be done their way, create trapped atmospheres for their children. The children have no say, or there is a power struggle with the parents that the children cannot win. The children become compliant as a strategy for survival in the face of rigid, immovable parents.

Children with stubbornness: Nothing creates stubbornness in children quite like stubborn parents. First of all, children of stubborn parents have excellent role models for rigidity. In addition, these children have perfect setups for rebellion against too much control. Stubborn people fear authority because of their negative experience with it. Fear of authority creates stubborn people. Thus, stubbornness is passed on through the generations.

Dragon Combinations in Relationships

Arrogance with self-destruction

Arrogant people in relationship with self-destructive people have perfect partners to judge and feel superior to. This pushes the self-destructive people into ever greater feelings of being out of control. Their tendency is to try to prove their control to their arrogant partners, and of course fail. The arrogant people are fairly safe in these relationships because their self-destructive partners are not capable of too much intimacy. Thus, the arrogant people remain emotionally distant and the self-destructive people are abandoned, their worst fear. However, at some point, the arrogant people realize their worst fears because they discover they are not perfect enough to save their partners. Their partners constantly embarrass them with public displays of self-destruction like drunkenness and being arrested. In severe cases these are marriages made in hell.

Arrogance with greed

People with arrogance and greed are often initially attracted to each other because they advertise what the others think they want. Greedy people see distant, arrogant people and decide they want the treasures they think lie there. These aloof, arrogant people often look rich, powerful, or special to them. Later they discover that the arrogant people remain emotionally distant, and they continue to feel abandoned.

The arrogant people see their greedy partners as people who might bolster their public images, especially if the greedy people are wealthy or well known. However, as they get to know the greedy people, they find a nightmare of anger coming from them. The greedy people want to own the arrogant people, and this causes the arrogant people to withdraw and back-pedal more and more. The greedy people then begin to blame and judge the arrogant people heavily, producing the arrogant people's worst fear.

Arrogance with self-deprecation

This is a common pairing. To self-deprecators with fears of inadequacy, arrogant people may appear attractive because they seem so self-assured and confident. Not only that but the self-deprecators often had arrogant parents, so they are familiar with the pattern of arrogance. To the arrogant people, the self-deprecators look attractive because they are not threatening and make them feel more confident. However, the arrogant people cannot refrain from judging and being derisive toward the self-deprecators. This makes the self-deprecators feel more and more inadequate, their worst fear. Often the arrogant people are embarrassed by the cringing and inadequacy of the self-deprecators.

For example, an arrogant husband was mortified when his

self-deprecating wife announced to everybody that they were lost and couldn't seem to follow maps right. He, however, would have driven around for hours before asking anybody for help.

Since both of these types lack self-esteem, they eventually see the ugliness of that in each other. The self-deprecators torture the arrogant people, shaming them by suggesting that their aloofness is a facade. "If you're so great, why can't you get it up in bed?" self-deprecators might say. The arrogant people torture the self-deprecators by criticizing their every act. "You can't do anything right," they might proclaim.

Arrogance with arrogance

This is the marriage of coldness. The two are attracted to each other because they look so good together to the world. She's beautiful and he's handsome. Both are Harvard brains, highly successful in business. Or both are wealthy. Since both of them are terrified of vulnerability, they certainly do not show vulnerability to others who are so critical. Therefore, it is hard to make any progress on the intimacy front.

Individuals in these relationships can hurt each other badly by being critical of each other. They are driven to be more and more perfect in each other's eyes. Inwardly, they grow in contempt for each other, projecting onto each other their critical, internalized parents. These relationships can look more like businesses than close sharing partnerships. There may be many affairs because both people crave warmth and affection but can't get these with their partners. They mutually accuse each other of being aloof and arrogant and project their problems on each other. For the cure, see chapter 3.

Arrogance with martyrdom

This combination bears some similarities to the pairing of arrogance with self-deprecation. The arrogant people feel safe with people in martyrdom because they feel sorry for them or are patronizing of them. The martyrs see the arrogant people as having solved all their problems, which they admire at first. But the arrogant people eventually become derisive, and the martyrs are only too willing to become victims. The martyrs provoke the arrogant people to no end by trying to get them to perform imperfect acts, like hitting them or abandoning them. The arrogant people trying to be perfect, do not oblige and thus torture the martyrs. Nevertheless, these relationships can sometimes come to an uneasy workability because martyrs are not afraid of intimacy. The martyrs can be rather warm and affectionate toward the arrogant people, despite their remoteness. The arrogant people are actually desperate for warmth, so they stick around despite their partners' annoying martyrdom.

Arrogance with impatience

Since both of these dragons are wide focused and fat, people in this combination can make life rather difficult for each other. The people with impatience tend to grow quickly intolerant of the arrogant people's aloofness and criticalness. This makes the arrogant people feel unsafe, so they armor themselves with even more layers of distance. This slows things down in the relationships, making the impatient people feel more and more frustrated. When the impatient people feel criticized, they are stressed. Rather than slowing down, they try to go faster, which only makes matters worse. The people who are impatient have a tendency to fly the coup first.

Arrogance with stubbornness

When arrogant people meet stubborn people, there is often a stalemate. The arrogant people are critical of both themselves and others. The more they try to judge the stubborn people, the more the stubborn ones dig in and refuse to change or acknowledge their arrogant partners, because they rebel against all authority. The stubborn people see the arrogant people as trying to be authorities over them. Thus, arrogant people can help manufacture terrifically stubborn partners over time.

The stubborn people refuse to feed their arrogant partners' egos, and they try to defeat them with passive resistance. The arrogant people then feel more and more alone, something that the dragon wants but not what the people actually need.

Self-deprecation with self-destruction

In these relationships, the people with self-deprecation feel that they do not deserve better in life than the pain of relationships with their self-destructive partners. In fact, they often feel that their partners' binges, drug taking, and self-destructive behavior are their fault. This is a perfect playground for the self-deprecation dragon to frolic in. On the other hand, the self-destructors are reinforced in their beliefs that their lives are not worth living and that no one is capable of controlling them. In worst case scenarios, they can get away with violence toward their self-deprecating partners, something that only reinforces their partners' belief that they are hopelessly inadequate. In these relationships, the self-destructive parties are more likely to step up their self-destructive behaviors because they are rewarded for them.

Self-deprecation with greed

This combination does not last long. The greedy partners do not see what they want in the self-deprecating partners unless they just happen to have inheritance, fabulous looks, or family connections that look attractive. The greedy partners are likely to take what they want and move on. This, of course, only reinforces the self-deprecators' inadequacy.

If the greedy people have addictions, as they often do, the self-deprecators tend to feel responsible and inadequate to cure them. The greedy partners may stick around because they fear abandonment, and the self-deprecators are not likely to leave them. However, the greedy people do not get the feeling that the self-deprecators are strong enough to stop their indulgent behavior. If the greedy people play out deprivation, the couple can be poor indeed, because the self-deprecators do not have the self-esteem to have anything either.

Self-deprecation with self-deprecation

When self-deprecation meets self-deprecation, little can be accomplished. Both people lack the self-esteem to feel they deserve anything. Together, they are rather poor or even recluses. At best, they feel a kind of understanding of one another. More likely, they feel they are stuck with partners they deserve, people whom they perceive to be as inadequate as they are. When one of them makes progress and starts to move ahead, the other feels like an even greater failure. So they do not encourage each other to break out of their pattern of failure. Thus, the failure tends to be mutually reinforcing. Since the partners see themselves in each other, the probability of projecting onto each other is great. There are mutual accusations, each blaming the other for being such a wimp.

Since self-deprecators are often defensive and imagine that they are being put down in every exchange, their communication with one another can deteriorate to nothing. When neither of them says anything, neither of them are hurt, and neither has to deal with the other's defensiveness.

Self-deprecation with martyrdom

Self-deprecation and martyrdom are both narrow-focused dragons. Therefore, people in this combination tend to keep each other small and powerless. The martyrs resent their partners and tend to blame them for the ills in their lives. The self-deprecators are only too willing to accept this blame as personal inadequacy and hang their heads ever lower, even though they tend to be defensive in response. The martyrs get no satisfaction from this response, so they usually arrange illness and other acts of sabotage to act out their martyrdom. The self-deprecators feel sorry for them and try to make life a little better, all the while blaming themselves. Pity only makes the martyrdom worse. These relationships are mutually reinforcing, and neither party is likely to leave the other.

Self-deprecation with impatience

This combination is rather painful because the impatient people are extremely intolerant of the self-deprecators' chronic lack of self-esteem. After trying to bolster them for awhile, they get impatient, give up, and feel like kicking their partners in the pants. This, of course, only reinforces the self-deprecators' view of themselves that they can't do anything right. In return, this behavior reinforces the impatient people's fear that they are losing valuable time. These can be potentially abusive relationships, with the impatient parties acting out their frustrations on their partners. On the other hand, the relationships may not last long because the impatient people have a tendency to bolt.

Self-deprecation with stubbornness

This combination is less toxic than some of the others. At worst, there is blocked energy with not much movement. The self-deprecators are not likely to tell their stubborn partners what to do, so they do not raise rebellion in them. Nor are they likely to create rapid unplanned changes that would scare the stubborn people. The self-deprecators do, however, tend to feel that problems in the relationship are their fault. The stubborn people can exploit this by giving their partners silent treatment when they are displeased.

Martyrdom with self-destruction

This partnership is a classic and common combination. In the self-destructive people, the martyrs find perfect companions. They can be constantly victimized and tortured by the destructive and out-of-control behavior of their partners. Long-suffering spouses are wedded to alcoholics, drug addicts, gamblers, batterers, incesters, criminals, and suicidal partners. The martyrs have much to complain and whine about. The self-destructive people are blamed and provoked endlessly by their partners. This only instigates more fights and drinking rampages. Both parties get worse and worse until the self-destructive people die or are imprisoned. Then the martyrs go out and find other people to take their place.

Martyrdom with greed

The scenario of martyrdom with greed is very similar to the relationship of martyrdom with self-destruction. It is also a common combination. However, with martyrdom and greed there is less violence and suicidal behavior. Instead, the greedy people respond with addictive behavior to the provocations of the martyrs. The martyrs get to be victimized over and over again and, in their resentment, withhold love from their greedy partners. The greedy people feel extreme frustration at not getting what they want from the martyrs. This drives them to gratify their addictions. If the greedy people are oriented toward deprivation, this suits the martyrs just fine. They still feel victimized by the stinginess of their greedy partners. The greedy people are likely to withhold more and more from the martyrs and seek gratification outside the relationships.

Martyrdom with martyrdom

These relationships are slugfests of blame. Initially, the martyrs are attracted to each other because they find a lot in common about how awful they think the world is. However, as the partnership develops, the martyrs all believe they are the victims in the relationships and demand reparations from their partners. None of them are willing to admit to anything. Since they have the same patterns as their partners, they easily project their feelings of victimization onto each other, telling each other not to be such victims.

On occasion, these partners arrange to be martyrs together over outside causes. They are both taken in by used car dealers who sell them lemons. They are both victims of investment scams in which they lose all their money. Even so, they tend to deteriorate into blaming each other.

These households feel dense and hopeless. Since misery loves company, these people do a lot of complaining about the world at large in "ain't it awful" scenarios. The miserable atmospheres drive everyone else away. Of course, this is more food for martyrdom.

Martyrdom with impatience

This is another common combination because both partners share a bit of each other. The people with impatience are driven to high levels of intolerance by their martyred partners. They want to get going, and they feel the martyrs are always sabotaging them by getting sick, experiencing aches and pains, and having things not work out in general. The martyrs feel that their impatient partners are always intolerant of them and pushing them into situations in which they feel trapped and victimized.

> One impatient businessman created such a busy schedule that he had no time to handle the responsibilities of his five children. His wife, with martyrdom, was left to carry the whole load, a burden she never let her husband forget. He tried to make up for this by planning a big busy vacation for the whole family. His wife, knowing that the vacation would be more work, broke her ankle on a curb. The whole family was forced to stay home. Her martyrdom grew, as did her husband's impatience.

Martyrdom with stubbornness

This is another popular combination. The people with martyrdom can make very little headway with their stubborn partners. Instead of feeling guilty, the stubborn people just refuse to hear the martyrs anymore. Stubbornness turns a deaf ear to martyrdom. Thus, the martyrs are sure of getting no relief from their complaints. The stubborn people persist more and more in their fixed patterns and rebel against the martyrs' guilt-inducing authority.

Impatience with self-destruction

The people in this combination are not likely to spend much time together. The impatient people are not inclined to wait around for their self-destructive partners to perpetrate their violence or suicidal behavior. If the self-destructive people threaten suicide, their impatient partners might say, "Well, why don't you just do it, already."

If these people do spend time together, the relationships are apt to be rather inflammatory. People with impatience and self-destruction can have severe fights. Neither dragon offers much in the way of impulse control. The self-destructive people contribute to the impatient people feeling that time is being wasted. The impatient people's intolerance furthers the self-destructive people's belief that life is not worth living anyway. They may think, "Why not speed up the process of destruction. Nobody cares about me anyway."

Impatience with greed

People with these two dragons are alike in many respects because they both fear the loss of something. People with impatience fear the loss of time, while people with greed fear the loss of love symbolized by power, money, food, and the like. When the impatient people rush and lose valuable time by having accidents, the greedy people fear that money or power are lost in the process. When the greedy people engage their addictions, the impatient people fear the loss of time this brings. Thus, they torture each other by raising each other's fears.

The impatient people may become very frustrated if their partners are involved in the deprivation side of greed. For example, the greedy people may decide to move to different locations for greener pastures just when the impatient people feel they are getting ahead.

Impatience with impatience

This combination could be called "frenzy." People with impatience are inclined to rush each other into early graves. They do not know how to slow down and take it easy. They typically take on too much and are frustrated that their partners have failed to accomplish everything on their lists. They are inclined toward impulsive decisions and are likely to make foolish choices because they do not allow enough time to think of all the ramifications. Two impatient people are inclined to incite each other's fears tremendously.

This combination is unfortunately common among Americans who live high-stress, crazed lifestyles. It is the impatient couple yelling at their kids to hurry into the car on their fast-paced, see-it-all vacation to Florida. This is supposed to be relaxing?

Impatience with stubbornness

This is an extremely abrasive combination because of the opposite strategies of the two dragons. People with impatience want to hurry up while people with stubbornness want to slow down. However, at first the two may be attracted to each other. To the impatient people, the stubborn people appear calm and steadfast, an antidote to their perpetual fever of activity. To the stubborn people, the impatient people may seem free of constraint, like colorful blurs of activity, in sharp contrast to their inflexible selves.

However, as they get to know each other, the impatient people become more and more intolerant of the recalcitrance of their partners. The stubborn people just dig in more and more, refusing to budge. They can reach quite a stalemate. The impatient people often just go ahead with their plans and avoid the stubborn people's perpetual naysaying. When the stubborn people find out that changes are forthcoming that they have not been privy to, they go into boiling rages. They may retaliate by canceling all plans, thus sending the impatient people into fits of frenzy. Eventually, the intolerant, impatient people may simple leave these relationships.

Self-destruction with self-destruction

This is one of the most tragically common combinations. Usually, self-destructive people had self-destructive parents. Therefore, they are inclined to be drawn to partners like their parents. However, that is not the only reason they seek other self-destructors. People who are addicts or partners to violence give each other permission to carry on out-of-control behavior. Everyone at a party shooting heroin is likely to be self-destructive.

Violent types find each other through similar activities such as subscribing to mercenary soldier journals or joining extremist groups dedicated to bombing and assassinations. Specific bars are meeting grounds for alcoholics and those who like to fight. Examples of this combination include alcoholic couples who drink themselves to death. They give each other the illusion of being in control, while in reality they are spiraling into chaos. The same is true for drug addicts. They tend to egg each other on to ever greater feats of self-destruction. They do not care about themselves, nor do they care about each other.

Self-destruction with greed

This combination bears great resemblance to the self-destruction with self-destruction combination. The only difference is that, in this combination, the greedy people are likely to take what they want from the self-destructors and then move on, abandoning their partners to die just as they themselves were once abandoned. If the self-destructors die first, the greedy people feel horribly abandoned and indulge their addictions to avoid the pain.

These relationships are highly destructive for both parties. Unfortunately, the self-destructive people often lure their greedy partners to overindulge to the point of death. This is especially true if the self-destructive people have stronger constitutions than their greedy partners. Self-destructive people can sometimes take amazing amounts of punishment while others are killed by the same amount of combinations of drugs.

Self-destruction with stubbornness

This is another combination in which there may be an initial attraction between the dragons. The stubborn people see the self-destructive people as colorful, free, and not constrained by inflexibility. The self-destructive people see the stubborn people as steadfast, grounded, and in control. Eventually, the self-destructive people can wreak havoc in the lives of the stubborn people because their behavior is so erratic and unpredictable. This creates immense fear for the stubborn individuals, and they tend to become less and less responsive in the relationships. As they gradually abandon their self-destructive partners by clamming up, their partners engage in ever-spiraling destructive acts. They mutually destroy the relationships.

Greed with greed

The greed with greed combination has much in common with the self-destruction with self-destruction combination. Both people are hungry for love but sure they are never going to find it. They certainly won't find it with greedy partners. Both blame each other for the lack they feel. Both are highly demanding but have little emotional food to give each other because they are deprived. They are not likely to be faithful to each other. Affairs are assured, because the blame and dissatisfaction grow and grow until they seek greener pastures.

Both people tend to engage in their favorite addictions. If one shops, the other might eat as the stress rises. If their addictions are the same, they just reinforce them in each other. Both may eat themselves into grotesque weights, or they may jointly accumulate money and power with no personal satisfaction. Sometimes, one party is into indulgence and the other is into deprivation. This makes for a parent-child relationship in which one partner disapproves and withholds while the other sneaks to indulge an addiction. For example, a powerful, greedy minister of a church with a wealthy congregation might austerely reprimand his wife for her alcoholism. The more he does so, the more she drinks, and the more austere and depriving he becomes.

Greed with stubbornness

This is a particularly painful combination because the partners are not likely to get anything they want from each other. The greedy people want everything from the stubborn people. The stubborn people do not want demands made, rejecting them as negative authority. The stubborn people clam up and withdraw, and the greedy people feel abandoned. As the greedy people are pushed away, their demands get louder and more shrill. The stubborn people make themselves impossible to reach. Chances are the greedy people then look afield of the relationships to satisfy their needs. This creates unpleasant, sudden changes for the stubborn partners, and they are faced with their worst fears.

Stubbornness with stubbornness

Stubborn people are likely to find each other because in many cases their parents were stubborn and they are familiar with the pattern. This combination could be entitled "lockjaw." It can result in power struggles on a grand scale. Both parties resist the authority of each other and go about trying to prove their independence and power. In some cases this results in cold-shoulder treatment that goes on for years. An example was given previously of a couple whose fight ended with the man on the couch and the woman in the bedroom for five years. In another case, a father and daughter did not speak with each other for six years. Sadly, these are common occurrences for stubborn couples.

If the partners manage to live together, their lives are characterized by very little spontaneity and change. Other people may be driven away by the dullness of their existence or their endless bickering over petty issues. I once witnessed a couple argue for two hours over whether the Halloween candy should be on the table to the right of the door or to the left of the door. It is understandable why the grown children of such couples never want to visit them.

Making Dragon-Free Contact: Essence Communication

The previous section listed all the ways that humans avoid real contact with one another. The dragons create dramas that result in all types of repeated human suffering. However, it is possible for you to relate to others in a totally different way leads to joy, satisfaction, and love. This is called "essence contact." It is a deep intimacy resulting from total acceptance and the absence of conditions.

Essence contact is one of the most profound, exquisite, and spontaneous experiences available to human beings. It is characterized by pure delight and openness. Essence contact involves pure and total honesty between yourself and another person without any effort to control the experience. The experience may be of very short duration because you may tend to fear it and run away from it quickly. Nevertheless, even a short experience of essence contact can be miraculously healing for yourself and the other person.

Simply put, essence contact is your experience of pure, unconditional love with another person. It may or may not be a sexual experience, and it may be with someone of any age, gender, or race. The experience usually happens without warning, when your personality is relaxed or not resisting. You can feel it easily if you hold newborn babies because they are pure essence with no defense and no dragons. They allow you to be temporarily free, also.

Essence contact erases the boundaries that your personality normally perceives, allowing you to experience other people as they exist at the most essential level of their beings. There is no room for judgments, evaluations, considerations, or fear. These essence experiences are often accompanied by pure laughter or tears of joy, but occasionally they occur at times of great intensity such as births, farewells, or the facing of death together. Such experiences are effective because they are one of a kind.

Essence contact is hard to repeat by design. It has to happen naturally. It is a product of your normal, healthy human desire to connect deeply. Unfortunately, for many people, it only happens under extraordinary conditions or when there is nothing left to lose. However, this need not be the case, because essence contact is available to you anywhere, anytime, even under very ordinary circumstances.

Naturally, the dragons react with horror to this kind of experience. They try to deny it, distract you from it, or make you not recognize it when it has a chance of happening. They also try to make sure it never happens again. That is why so often after exceptional closeness, two people tend to fight. I have witnessed this on numerous occasions in marriage counseling after particularly moving or intimate sessions. The dragons try to make you decide that the other person is untrustworthy, unacceptable socially, or a threat to your freedom. You may decide that to see the other person again would distract you from your work or duties. The excuses are endless and often absurd considering the true nature of the experience.

Following are the conditions that promote your experience of unconditional love or essence contact with another person:

First: Your dragon must be either asleep or taken by surprise so that it cannot prevent the experience.

Second: Your personality must be willing to lose control over your emotions, at least for a few moments.

Third: You need to be undefended against the other person, even if only for a short time. You need not have a prior relationship with the other person, but essence contact is more common when you know one another better. Sex may promote essence contact. But then, many people use sex to push other people away or to go to sleep, so this is not always effective. Sometimes more platonic relationships reduce the expectations and dragon play that block intimacy, so they are a good place to start.

Fourth: It is helpful to validate the experience and acknowledge to yourself when it is happening. That way you are less likely to deny the experience or pretend it is not happening. You do not necessarily have to talk about it, however.

Fifth: Focusing all your attention on the other person and being totally present tends to promote essence contact. It also helps to concentrate on what is beautiful about the person.

You know when you are having an experience of essence contact because it feels wonderful. You have no fears, no worries, and no pain. You feel a great sense of expansion and a positive feeling of being without confining boundaries. You are deeply relaxed and aware of great beauty in the other person, in yourself, and in your surroundings. Remember again what it feels like to hold a newborn; it is that feeling but with anyone.

You also know when the experience is over because the dragon comes roaring back with all its fears, considerations, and worries. You might feel chagrined or embarrassed about what happened. You might tell yourself that it was a fluke or that you made it up. You may say that you deceived yourself and that the other person didn't really connect with you after all. You may even go about trying to make sure it does not happen again because it is too painful to experience such a feeling and then be without it.

You might feel disappointed that you could not hang on to the experience and beat yourself up for losing it. However, getting attached to the event surely cuts it off. Essence contact is difficult to sustain, so it is normal for it to cease. If you do not resist its going away, you make it more possible for it to happen again.

Essence contact with another is really essence contact with yourself. While it is happening, you know yourself in a way that is totally authentic and delightful. That is why it is important not to attribute the experience to the other person. Too often people think that they can never feel the same way after their spouses have died or their lovers have left them or their babies have grown. These things are understandably painful, but the emotional disconnection is an illusion. The experience of essence contact is your own. It just happens to occur in the presence of the other person. The truth is, essence contact can occur with anyone, with anything, at any time, and it has the same characteristics because it has to do with you. You can have essence contact with an animal, for example a cat purring on your lap or a dog licking your face. You can have essence contact with the world when you are watching a sunset, walking in the desert, lying on the beach, or listening to music.

The magic of essence contact is that the more you allow yourself to experience it, the more likely it is to occur. Each time it lasts longer. Essence contact can heal your spirit faster than any medicine or treatment available, and it transforms your dragons better than any other approach.

Chapter Eleven

TRANSFORMING THE DRAGONS AND DISCOVERING HAPPINESS

A Formula for Transforming the Dragons

The basic formula for making the difficult work of getting rid of the dragons easier involves using the fact that the dragons work in pairs. If you suffer from greed, you also suffer in a less direct way with self-destruction. This, of course, is also true in reverse. If you are a martyr, you are also in some way impatient. If you are arrogant, you also have some self-deprecation, or vice versa. If you are stubborn, you have elements of all the dragons. The formula involves sliding to the positive pole of the paired dragons.

Following is a visual representation of the formula:

SELF-DESTRUCTION—GREED: positive pole of "appetite"

SELF-DEPRECATION—ARROGANCE: positive pole of "pride"

MARTYRDOM—IMPATIENCE: positive pole of "daring"

GREED/ARROGANCE/IMPATIENCE—STUBBORNNESS:
    positive pole of "determination"
STUBBORNNESS—flexibility, adaptability, change

If you are working on your own dragons, or if you are a counselor assisting people to overcome their dragons, you can use the dragon paired with your primary dragon to help release you from your primary dragon. Sometimes, getting rid of the whole dragon influence at once is too big a challenge. Therefore, for example, if you have a narrow-focused dragon of self-destruction, it is a good idea to harness the wide-focused greed dragon to help you get rid of your primary dragon.

Candace lived a wild existence, drinking, taking drugs, and having indiscriminate sex with a variety of partners who stole from her and beat her up. She was actively suicidal, saw no purpose to her existence, and came to therapy out of desperation. I saw that, even though she was in the firm grip of the self-destruction dragon, the greed dragon was also at work within her personality. She was hungry for love and always thought that her next partner would give her what she wanted. She overconsumed alcohol, another sign of greed: "Maybe this next drink will make me feel full and better inside." She also tended to deprive herself, lived in a little dump of an apartment, and spent all her considerable income before she received her paycheck.

The first major problem Candace confronted in therapy was self-destruction. Through confrontation and discipline, she gradually tackled the drugs and the drinking. But to make her life worth living, her greed had to be redirected toward its positive pole: "appetite." I encouraged her to make a long list of all the things in life she actually wanted but didn't think she could have. With encouragement, the list grew rather long, and we talked about each item on the list. I had Candace select three items from her list that she would concentrate on. They were: better pay for her work; a nicer, more spacious place to live, and travel to Europe. These became goals to satisfy. As a reward for her success in ceasing to drink, I encouraged her to ask for more money at work and agreed to see her on credit, a risky thing to do with this kind of client. She secured the higher pay because, since she had stopped drinking, her work was worth higher wages. She also sought and found a much nicer living space for only a little more rent. She began paying off debts to various people, but I insisted that she put away part of her money for a trip to Europe.

I wanted to encourage Candace's lust for some aspects of living and show her she could have more. At the end of a year and a half, she saved enough money to travel and took off for two months to Europe. She returned a changed woman. She paid me off, got a better job, and began to actively meditate on a daily basis. She started avidly reading philosophy and studying world religions. In the process, she met a good man to relate to. She had gotten rid of the self-destruction dragon, and her appetite (greed) turned to knowledge rather than to drink and deprivation. This was far better than where she had begun. Over time, she could gradually work on releasing herself from the greed dragon altogether.

You can move away from the self-deprecation dragon by seeking activity that is in the arrogant dragon's domain. The positive pole of arrogance is "pride," something that will help you if you are in the grip of self-deprecation. You can learn to take pride in projects or accomplishments. Later, your pride can be dispensed with.

If the martyrdom dragon is in control of you, you can go toward the impatience dragon, using its positive pole of "daring" to break out of your trap. In general it is best to move away from self-destruction toward greed, away from self-deprecation toward arrogance, and away from martyrdom toward impatience, but not to move in the reverse directions. To work with greed, arrogance, and impatience, it is better to move toward the positive pole of stubbornness, "determination." To work with the stubbornness dragon, it is best not to push toward any other dragon but to work on flexibility, adaptability, and the courage to change.

The Most Powerful Dragon Weapons of All

Although each previous chapter has included weapons and exercises to combat the specific dragons, there are two universal approaches that defeat all the dragons powerfully and effectively. They are meditation and mindfulness. Meditation and mindfulness lead you gradually toward the four pillars of life. These four pillars of vitality are true work, true play, true study, and true rest. When you establish balance among these four pillars, you create vitality so powerful that the dragons cannot penetrate. Mindfulness has great power to keep the dragons at bay because it helps you to identify the four pillars of vitality. So armed, you are not only a happier human being, you are a role model and guide for others.

Meditation and Mindfulness

Most powerful dragon weapons of all

Your dragon thrives on the constant chatter that goes on in your mind. If you are still for a little while, you notice that, even though you are not physically moving your body and you may appear calm, your mind is almost always active—remembering, worrying, anticipating, commenting, questioning, and considering its usual activities. It is easy for the dragon to take over and direct this constant chatter. In fact, this is the principle way that the dragon takes over your personality and controls your life. So, to the extent that you cannot control your thoughts, you cannot control your dragon.

The secret is to still your mind. Meditation is the strategy for doing this. However, as a Westerner, you may feel that achieving something means looking active and producing tangible and visible results. Meditation may not be attractive because it appears to be wasting time doing nothing. You might get restless just thinking about it. But the truth is that you do meditate, perhaps unbeknownst to yourself, and the results are quite wonderful.

While at the seashore, you might find yourself following the waves repeatedly crashing on the shore. You have no thoughts at all, simply a feeling of well-being. This often happens in nature when you just sit and listen to wind, rain, or a brook, or when you watch rippling grass, lightning, or trees waving in the wind. What you are doing is focusing one of your senses on something that is repetitive, rhythmical, and beautiful. This produces a calmness and quiets your mind chatter.

The quiet mind offers the dragons no place to play. Therefore, when you meditate, you are freed from them for a period of time. This allows your true self, or essence, to come forward and express itself. This is what real creativity is.

A Meditation

There are many forms of meditation. Following is a simple, tried-and-true meditation method that you can practice.

1. Sit comfortably with your spine straight and your arms, hands, and legs uncrossed. Or, you could use the Eastern method and cross your legs lotus style.
2. Close your eyes or leave them open just a slit to see the ground in front of you.
3. Focus on your breathing. At first, do nothing to alter it; simply watch it.
4. Then, gradually regulate your breathing according to an eight count: Count to seven while breathing in gradually. On the count of eight, cease to breathe. Then, slowly release your breath to the count of seven. On the count of eight, cease breathing again. Continue inhaling and

exhaling in this fashion. Watching your breath and counting gives you a simple structure.

5. Your thoughts may tend to intrude, causing you to forget about your breath and counting. When this occurs, simply notice your thoughts as you would notice falling leaves. That is all they are: temporary events without meaning. They are something to release.

6. Should you become irritated at the exercise or yourself, notice this and persist beyond your irritation. Everything is part of the meditation. And everything that happens is in service of the meditation, even sleepiness. However, it is best to plan your meditation practice when you are fairly awake, not when you are very tired.

At first, you may find this meditation technique difficult— as have millions of human beings before you. However, if you persist you will find that the exercise becomes easier. Eventually, it will become highly desirable, not just because of the benefits but because it in itself becomes pleasurable. I personally nlook forward to my meditation practice because it makes me feel good.

Wakefulness

When you meditate, you may look asleep or appear to be dozing. However, nothing could be further from the truth. Effective meditation is a form of wakefulness, of mindfulness, of being fully present and aware. It is not so much an act of doing as an act of being. When you meditate regularly, this quality of being awake and attentive spreads to your everyday, ordinary activities. Food tastes more delicious, textures feel more intense, and your hearing becomes more acute because you learn to be present for your experience. Rather than the dragons living your life for you, you live your own life. This leads to tranquillity, serenity, and happiness.

The more you erase the dragon's playground, the more

mature your behavior becomes. You regress less into infant or toddler behavior and become less attached to the outcome of events. You begin to enjoy the process of living more than life's ever-elusive results.

Concentration

An alternative practice in mindfulness is to learn the art of concentration. There are four levels at which this can be practiced:

Simple focus: This level involves focusing your attention on a specific experience created by your senses. For example, you isolate a single sound from the environment like the sound of a cricket and stay with that sound for a couple of minutes. Then you shift your attention to a detail in your field of vision like a tree in the distance, and you stay with that. Then you shift to a specific sensation like an itch or the feel of your right thumb. Then you move to an emotion, and so on. This develops your attention into a laserlike focus that can isolate aspects of life.

Soft focus: The next step in concentration is to develop your awareness of the broad spectrum or ground of your experience. Rather than isolating a single sound from the background of noises, you focus softly and listen to all the sounds at once for a time. Then you soft focus your eyes and take in the whole range of your vision without focusing on any details. Then you focus on the sensation of your entire body. Then you feel the mood in the whole room, and so on.

Shift focus: The next level of concentration involves moving smoothly from one type of focus to another, from inner to outer focus, from single focus to soft focus.

Exchange focus: The next step in concentration is to interchange your levels of focus so that, for example, you see the inside of your thumb, then you listen to it and hear its sound, then you feel the tree in the distance, then you hear its inner sound, and so on.

The value of this exercise in concentration is to:

1. increase your ability to focus your attention the way you wish;
2. assist you in taking responsibility for how you use your mind;
3. reduce the capacity for the dragon to take over your undisciplined mind and run it by fear;
4. increase your ability to sense the beauty of yourself and your surroundings;
5. increase your overall vitality, health, and energy levels.

The Four Pillars of Vitality

During the first half of your life, prior to your mid-thirties or early forties, your dragon tends to play havoc with your experiences. By late adolescence, the dragon is usually firmly in place. By your late twenties, you may know that something is not working quite right, and you gain the first insight that there is a dragon to transform. However, this period may slip by, and it may not until you reach thirty-five or so that your real battle to contain the dragon begins. That is why the mid-thirties are so challenging.

If you do not overthrow the dragon at this point, you may allow it to remain with you for life, getting stronger and stronger until you are fearful and irritable in your old age. However, the dragon can be overthrown at any age if you have the adequate motivation. If you are older, this motivation may arise from a catastrophic illness or tragedy that propels you into motion. Or, it may be the knowledge that death is staring you in the face that pushes you to master the dragon before you die.

When you succeed in identifying and challenging your dragon, your work begins. There is progress and there is regression as the battle for your personality rages. Gradually your true self prevails because, in the end, it is more powerful. With perseverance and commitment, the dragon fails because it is only a guest, a parasite, an intruder. When that occurs, a marvelous event unfolds: the four pillars of vitality emerge and become clarified. As mentioned earlier, these four pillars are true work, true play, true study, and true rest.

True Work

True work is the absorbing work that most people discover in the second half of their lives. It is a contribution that makes you feel happy and satisfied while doing it. It is something you have a talent for, that you enjoy doing, and for which you are appreciated by others for doing well. This work is not what you might call a career. A career is an idea made up by modern culture to keep you enslaved. A career easily becomes your master; you become its slave. You have to make career moves that have nothing to do with your true self. Forget the idea of a career. Focus on your true work.

When you begin to do your true work, windows of opportunity open and obstacles clear away as if by magic. Discovering this work or embarking on it is quite difficult as long as the dragon controls your behavior. When you push the dragon out of your life, true work begins to find you. However, you cannot be balanced if all you do is work. You have other needs. That is why it is important to discover the other pillars.

True Play

True play is grounding. It keeps you from becoming scattered, overwhelmed, too serious, and unproductive. In order to be successful at your true work, you must engage in your true play as well. True play can be energetic experiences like riding horseback, playing baseball, or wrestling with the dog. Or it can be playing chess, collecting baseball cards, playing the piano, or exploring the countryside. As with true work, true play is different for every person.

When you are playing, you are totally absorbed and you enjoy yourself immensely. Obviously, you cannot experience true play if the dragon is controlling you; you may look like you are having fun to others, but you won't be enjoying yourself. For example, a skier may curse as he or she fails to come down the slope perfectly enough. That is not play at all. If you do not play, you cannot actualize yourself. You are under the grip of the dragon. Discovering your true play is of major importance if you want to become a balanced human being. But discovering it is not enough; you must set aside plenty of time to do it. The dragon won't like that.

True Study

True study helps you focus yourself and prepares you to perform your true work. It is so absorbing that you may literally forget meals or other activities because it interests you so much. True study may involve anything, from the study of music to the study of the properties of metals when heated. It may be the study of human behavior, philosophy, theology, anatomy, geology, weather, mathematics, investment, or horticulture. You know what your true study is by the way you feel about the subject matter, or by the way you go on and on about it when someone asks you. The key is that it does not feel like work to you. It is fascinating, and it is usually related to your true work. To effectively experience true study, you cannot allow the dragon to be in charge of your personality.

True Rest

True rest restores you and revitalizes you so that you can get around to your true work, true play, and true study. True rest is a rejuvenating activity. It may be reading, walking, meditating, being in the company of a friend, listening to or playing music, napping, contemplating, bathing, humming, getting a massage or manicure, or an endless variety of other experiences. What is restful to one person is not necessarily restful to another. Sleeping is not at all restful to many people.

It is important to learn what is truly restful for you and not just a popular notion of the mass media. Vacations are often not restful at all, as you may know. Yet, they may be needed changes of scene, or related to true play. However, vacations may be simply awful because the dragon is running them.

Your true rest consistently relaxes you and restores you. It is something that most Westerners do very little of, and this lack throws the entire system off balance. True work, true play, and true study are not possible to enjoy without adequate true rest.

These four pillars of vitality lead to a balanced, healthy, satisfying life. When you have these four pillars active and balanced in your life, you are highly attractive to others because you are a sterling example of what a human being can be. You are effective, creative, and productive in your work, good to spend time with, and compassionate toward others. When you exhibit these traits, it is not because you were born this way or because you lead a charmed life. It is because you had severe challenges, faced difficult times, and struggled with your dragon for years. Because you faced your dragon and overcame it, the four pillars became accessible to you. You then found a proper balance among them that was unique to you as an individual.

Keeping Free of Dragons:
The Masculine and the Feminine

To be free of dragons, you must develop and exercise will, or intention. Will is the ability to exercise choice in your life, rather than being controlled by the dragon. When you are run by the dragon, you act more like a puppet or mechanical windup toy. Your behavior is predictable and repetitive, and your life is not your own. Will or volition is one of the necessary ingredients to turn you into a human being who is not predictable or mechanical but spontaneous and creative. Will is that dynamic, laserlike focus that makes things happen in your life. Will is responsible for getting you from here to there, and it is what helps you manifest your vision. Without a vision, you have no hope of transforming the dragon because you do not know where you are going or why you are alive. So, you need will to manifest your vision, and you need vision to get beyond the dragon.

Vision is only possible when you see the big picture of how your actions influence the world around you. The context or background of your life is the ground upon which your will acts. Your will helps you start a business, but the context of your life is what determines whether that business is in harmony with your own and other people's best interests. Just as will represents the masculine qualities of life, the context or background upon which you act represents the feminine or magnetic qualities of life. This magnetic background acts as a support for your will. It is like the soil that the plant grows from.

When will is divorced from the larger context of life, it can be quite destructive. Wars, takeovers, criminal activity, and attacks are all the result of the use of will without consideration of the ramifications in the big picture. This is the unfortunate history of mankind for the last several thousand years. It is the result of the masculine running roughshod over the feminine, without respect for context.

Masculine will is only productive when it works in harmony with the feminine, supportive context of the big picture. By the same token, the context of life is inert unless it is acted upon by the will. Vision is the product of will and context working together.

The necessary ingredient to get will and context to work together is gratitude, also known as recognition. For the masculine will to be truly productive, it must be grateful to the feminine context for serving as its game board. Will cannot truly function without a context, and that context, for human beings, is the planet itself. If will (human action) insults the context (the Earth), the result is destruction of the environment, toxic waste, pollution, poverty, and pain. Gratitude for the Earth brings human will and vision into harmony with it.

In the same way, gratitude for your own life brings your intentions into harmony with your life. In order to be grateful for your life, you must know why you exist. The great spiritual teachers of history have said that the purpose of life is to be a complete human being. They have said that the purpose of life is life itself—to wholly and fully be a reflection of the Creator, or the Tao, as the Chinese put it. It is very difficult, almost impossible, to get rid of the dragons in your life unless you have a meaningful reason for existing. If you are not grateful for being alive, then the dragons have an easy time taking over.

So, the will and vision in your life are totally dependent on the respect you have for your life. The greater respect you have for your life and for all that lives, the greater your possibility of transforming the dragons to live in freedom and joy.

will + context + gratitude = vision of happiness, joy, satisfaction

Will without vision creates chaos. Vision without will never gets realized. Will and vision (dynamic) without gratitude for context (magnetic) can be dangerous and lead to disharmony. When dynamic and magnetic come together in harmony, no dragon can prevail. So, the final equation is:

dynamic (masculine) + magnetic (feminine) + respect = no dragons

Keeping Free of Dragons: Learning Unconditional Love

You can remain dragon free if you remember what feeds the dragons so that you know what to deprive them of. First of all, dragons thrive on fear, and fear comes from perceiving that you are separate. So any kind of alienation, bigotry, prejudice, discrimination, and judgment is dragon food. To judge that you are inferior to others is dragon food. To judge that you are better than others also feeds the dragons. To be judgmental is to separate yourself from others, and when you do that you make your love conditional. You then love people only if they agree with you on everything, or if they are white or Americans, or church-goers, or A students, or rich, or good looking—the list is endless.

You may tend to love only what you can identify with and judge what you find strange or foreign. Yet, natural as that seems, it expands the dragons because it promotes fear, and fear is their favorite food.

The only way to remain dragon free is to unconditionally love yourself and others. The greatest teachers in the world have all taught this basic principle. They have also warned, in their own ways, about dragon behavior and its dire consequences for humankind. In addition, they have given excellent suggestions for how to avoid the dragon claws.

Learning tolerance is a good place to start. Learning unconditional love is a greater challenge. However, there are those sprinkled throughout the human population who show us it can be done. It is good to have a muse, a teacher, or a mentor to inspire you to actualize your aspirations. Personally, I have found Gandhi and Mother Teresa to be such role models. There are countless others. Choose your own and your way will be made easier. You will never regret embarking on this heroic journey. In fact, you have already begun. The journey of transforming your dragons helps the human race to evolve toward its ultimate destiny of integration, peacefulness, and transformation. That destiny begins with you.

Appendix A

THE
SEVEN
DRAGONS
AT A GLANCE

Arrogance Dragon:

the fear of vulnerability as well as the fear of being judged negatively; confusion over self-worth. People with this dragon swing from feeling inflated and special to experiencing puncture and deflation. Their fear pattern includes aloofness, shyness, remoteness, performance, anxiety, false personas, vanity, critical-ness, and narcissism. They attempt to be perfect in others' eyes, and were compared to high standards as children.

Self-Deprecation Dragon:

the fear of being inadequate or poorly equipped for life; low self-esteem, sometimes called an inferiority complex. People with this dragon have a fear pattern that includes cringing, apologizing, shrinking, self-deflation, and inner criticism. They avoid criticism by criticizing themselves first, and were put down as children.

Impatience Dragon:

the fear that time will run out. People with this dragon rush, are intolerant, experience heavy stress, try to do too much in too short a time, and are constantly in future fantasies. They are not present, can be accident prone, and were deprived of experience as children.

Martyrdom Dragon:

the fear of being trapped by circumstances or outside forces. People with this dragon complain, whine, act "poor me," and are oriented toward being victims. They are excellent at creating guilt in those around them, and were forced to be constantly obedient as children.

Greed Dragon:

the fear that there is not enough to go around. People with this dragon have a fear pattern that expresses itself in addictive behavior, hoarding, coveting, amassing, or depriving themselves and others. Their greed tends to fixate on food, power, sex, wealth, or something specific. They were abandoned as children.

Self-destruction Dragon:

the fear of losing control. People with this dragon are addictive, violent, and suicidal. They exhibit wild behavior or desperate self-sabotage. They may not live long because they cannot find meaning to life. As children, they were abused and abandoned.

Stubbornness Dragon:

the fear of authority and sudden change. People with this dragon have a fear pattern that is expressed in rebelliousness, rigidity, obstinacy, argumentativeness, hardheaded behavior, a refusal to listen, and a refusal to submit. They try to slow down events to buy time. As children, they were given no options and were forced to do what they were told.

Appendix B

STAGES OF MATURITY AND THE SEVEN DRAGONS

Stages of Maturity					
Dragon					
	Infant	Toddler	Child	Adolescent	Adult
Arrogance	biggest gorilla	petty bureau-crat	high status	shy	philo-sophical arrogance
Self-Depreca-tion	cringing savage	pawn	phobic about age and appear-ance	social misfit; misunder-stood	low confi-dence
Impatience	ruthless gratifi-cation	bigoted irritabil-ity	fast track haste	impatience at self and system	vision-ary impa-tience
Martyrdom	extreme victim	social sheep and pawns	controls with money	political martyr	mild victim-ization

Dragon					
	Infant	**Toddler**	**Child**	**Adolescent**	**Adult**
Greed	ruthless savage survival-ism	addiction and local corrup-tion	hoarding amassing flouting	jealousy and hunger for love	spiritual material-ism
Self-Destruc-tion	criminal insanity	wanting to get caught; gangs	short life in the fast lane	suicide	self-sabotage
Stubborn-ness	autism and catatonia	skinheads, reaction-aries; the far right	good old boys; the Mafia	radical leftists rebels	self-defeat; internal rigidity

Appendix C

THE
DRAGONS
AND BOUNDARIES

Each of the dragons alters people's boundaries in specific, significant ways. Boundaries are psychological edges or limits that help people identify what they are and what they are not. People with strong boundaries know who they are, what they need and want, and what they will and will not accept. People with weak boundaries let others walk all over them because they are confused about their spaces and don't really know when and where to say "no." People with rigid boundaries have no flexibility when it comes to others. The dragons cause people's boundaries to go out of balance and harmony; the boundaries become brittle, weak, too rigid, or too sloppy. Maturity level also affects boundaries.

Arrogance

Arrogant people create rigid boundaries around themselves to wall themselves off from hurt and criticism. When they are in doubt about their self-worth, or if they are shy, they retreat from others. They can also fall into intrusiveness when they assume too much importance and disregard the boundaries of others. This is especially true when they are critical and demeaning.

Self-Deprecation

People with self-deprecation are notorious for their lack of boundaries. They are in doubt about their value and their right to be alive, so they tend to omit necessary boundaries, letting others do as they please with them. Their primitive form of boundary is a brittle defensiveness that falls apart easily. They hardly ever intrude on others' boundaries.

Impatience:

Impatient people push through others' boundaries in order to hurry them up. They also tend to have a very poor sense of where they are. Their boundaries can be elusive but are by no means completely absent.

Martyrdom:

Martyred people are calculating about how they allow others to intrude upon them. They appear to have no boundaries at all, but they actually have more control than they show. They make a business out of relinquishing their boundaries.

Greed:

Greedy people are famous for intruding on others and failing to respect others' boundaries. However, they defend themselves against receiving and place too many rigid boundaries on themselves. That is the deprivation side of greed.

Self-Destruction:

Self-destructive people have a dual approach to boundaries. They are difficult to reach and have rigid defenses against intimacy. However, they tend to be sloppy about respecting others' boundaries, and they intrude on others in violent ways.

Stubbornness:

People with stubbornness have rigid, inflexible boundaries. They draw their lines in the sand over arbitrary issues that are typically fears of oppression projected onto others. If others crash through their brittle boundaries, they can become deeply depressed or overwhelmed with despair. Stubborn people do not necessarily invade others' boundaries; they are more protective of their own.

Appendix D

MENTAL AND EMOTIONAL DYSFUNCTIONS RESULTING FROM THE ACTIVITIES OF THE DRAGONS

This is a partial list of the dysfunctions listed in the *Diagnostic and Statistical Manual of Mental Disorders*, and the dragons that are typically related to them. There are exceptions to these associations, of course. Some dysfunctions are not listed because any dragon can be associated with them. In many cases, a given dysfunction is the result of the combination of dragons listed. However, sometimes the dysfunction is the result of just one of the dragons.

1. Pervasive developmental disorders—
   Autistic disorder: stubbornness

2. Specific developmental disorders—mostly stubbornness and impatience

3. Disruptive behavior disorders—
   Attention deficit hyperactivity disorder: impatience
   Conduct disorders: mostly self-destruction
   Oppositional defiant disorder: stubbornness

4. Anxiety disorders of childhood or adolescence—
   Separation anxiety disorder: greed, self-deprecation
   Avoidant disorder: arrogance, self-deprecation
   Overanxious disorder: self-deprecation, impatience

5. Eating disorders—
   Anorexia nervosa: greed, self-destruction
   Bulimia nervosa: greed, self-destruction
   Pica: greed

6. Gender-identity disorder—mainly stubbornness and
   martyrdom

7. Tic disorders (including Tourette's syndrome)—
   impatience and stubbornness

8. Elimination disorders—
   Encopressis and enuresis: stubbornness, impatience

9. Speech disorders— mostly impatience and stubbornness

10. Psychoactive substance-use disorders—
    alcohol, cocaine, amphetamines, and so on:
    self-deprecation, greed, self-destruction

11. Schizophrenia—
    Catatonic: stubbornness
    Paranoid: arrogance, sometimes with martyrdom,
    stubbornness

12. Delusional (paranoid) disorders—
    Grandiose type: arrogance
    Jealous type: self-deprecation
    Persecutory: martyrdom

13. Psychotic disorders—
    Schizoaffective disorder: self-deprecation, arrogance
    Schizophreniform disorder: self-deprecation, arrogance

14. Mood disorders—
    Mixed: self-deprecation, arrogance
    Manic: arrogance with impatience

Depressed: self-deprecation with martyrdom
Cyclothymia: self-deprecation and arrogance

15. Bipolar disorder— self-deprecation and arrogance, or impatience and martyrdom

16. Depressive disorders—
Dysthymia (depressive neurosis): self-deprecation, martyrdom
Depressive disorder: greed, self-deprecation, arrogance, martyrdom

17. Anxiety disorders—
Panic disorder w/agoraphobia: martyrdom
Panic disorder w/out agoraphobia: impatience
Agorophobia: martyrdom, arrogance
Social phobia: martyrdom, arrogance
Obsessive compulsive disorder: arrogance; self-deprecation; greed; impatience, stubbornness
Generalized anxiety disorder: impatience

18. Somatoform disorders—
Conversion disorder (hysteria): martyrdom
Hypochondriasis: martyrdom
Somatization disorder: martyrdom, impatience
Somatoform pain disorder: martyrdom

19. Dissociative disorders—
Multiple Personality Disorder: self-destruction, greed
Psychogenic fugue: self-destruction
Psychogenic amnesia: self-destruction

20. Sexual disorders—
Parafilias:
Exhibitionism: greed
Fetishism: greed, arrogance
Frotteurism: greed, arrogance
Pedophilia: greed, arrogance
Sexual masochism: martyrdom

Sadism: self-destruction
Voyeurism: greed, arrogance

21. Sexual dysfunctions—
Hypoactive sexual desire disorder: greed
Sexual aversion disorder: stubbornness, arrogance
Female sexual arousal disorder: impatience, stubbornness;
arrogance
Male erectile disorder: impatience, stubbornness,
arrogance
Inhibited orgasm: stubbornness, martyrdom
Premature ejaculation: impatience

22. Sleep disorders—
Insomnia: impatience, martyrdom

23. Factitious disorders—martyrdom

24. Impulse control disorders—
Intermittent explosive disorder: self-destruction, greed
Kleptomania: self-destruction, greed
Gambling: self-destruction, greed
Pyromania: self-destruction, greed

25. Personality Disorders—
A. Paranoid: arrogance, martyrdom
   Schizoid: self-deprecation
   Schizotypal: arrogance, self-deprecation
B. Antisocial: self-destruction
   Borderline: self-destruction, arrogance, self-
   deprecation, impatience, greed
   Histrionic: greed
   Narcissistic: greed, arrogance
C. Avoidant: self-deprecation
   Dependent: self-deprecation
   Obsessive compulsive: arrogance, stubbornness
   Passive-aggressive: stubbornness, martyrdom

Appendix E

THE
HEALTHY
PERSON

From the description of the seven dragons comes a clear picture of dysfunction and unhealthy habits that prevent happiness. Here is a list of the qualities of healthy human beings who are free from the dragon's control.

A healthy person displays:

Unconditional acceptance of self and others regardless of race, age, sex, and belief systems.

The ability to accept mistakes as a form of learning.

Vulnerability and accessibility, yet with a firm sense of personal boundaries: "No, you can't walk on my head."

The courage to be honest with self and others without cruelty.

The capacity to be real, authentic, genuine, and consistent with others.

The ability to say "no" when necessary.

Confidence with regard to assertiveness and willingness to take reasonable risks for the sake of discovery, stretching, and learning.

The resourcefulness to accept criticism as a guide to learning and growth.

The facility to let go of control and accept spontaneity and the novel turns of life.

The ability to make intimate contact with others.

Acceptance of situations impossible to change.

The courage to ask for help when it is needed.

The power to face emotional pain, experience it, and let it go.

The capacity to forgive one's self and others.

Simplicity with regards to material and emotional needs.

Generosity with love and material things.

Kindness and respect toward one's body.

The ability to make decisions and act on them.

Silence of mind and word unless intentionally engaged.

Grace, rhythm, pace, and natural timing.

Responsibility for thought and action without blaming one's self or others.

The ability to be direct and brief with anger without the intent to harm.

The facility to wait peacefully.

The capacity to say "yes" to more of life.

The ability to listen intently and respond truthfully.

Flexibility and adaptability of mind and behavior.

The courage to apologize when necessary.

The capability to accept and enjoy differences in others.

The facility to feel, think, and act with equal proficiency.

A good sense of humor.

Respect for all living things and the resources of the planet.

Glossary

Action Dragons: Dragons that stop constructive action: martyrdom and impatience.

Adolescents: People undergoing puberty and the aftermath; they range in age from eleven years to twenty years. Refers to all people fixated at the adolescent developmental level, characterized by confusion, intensity, relationships, and broader outlook.

Adults: People who are developmentally grown up and sophisticated in thought, emotional response, and deed. The adult level is a level of detachment.

Affirmation: A simple positive statement in the present tense that assists people to overcome dragons or fear patterns.

Arrogance: Personality fear pattern (dragon) wherein the fear of vulnerability and criticism causes people to protect themselves with aloofness, criticalness, and inflation.

Assimilation dragon: The dragon that stops absorption of information: stubbornness.

Concentration: The ability to focus attention on inner, outer, detailed, and background phenomena.

Dragon: From the Greek word drakan, meaning "the seeing one." Metaphor for seven personality fear patterns that act as obstacles to happiness and that create human suffering. Dragons do have vulnerable spots but must be faced directly to overcome them.

Elders: People who have gained wisdom throughout their lives and have erased all personality fear patterns or dragons. Their focus is mentoring and being of service. Elders are all people who display these characteristics, no matter what their ages.

Expression dragons: Dragons that stop expression: self-destruction and greed.

Essence-self: The true personality at the core of each person, without the influence of any dragon.

Gratitude: Recognition and respect. Gratitude is the catalyst that brings the dynamic and magnetic aspects of life into harmony. It is essential for remaining free of the dragons or fear patterns.

Greed: Personality fear pattern (dragon) wherein the fear of lack is so strong that it produces severe cravings or deprivation behavior, often leading to addictions, hoarding, and amassing.

Impatience: Personality fear pattern (dragon) wherein there is a dread of lack of time, resulting in chronically rushed or hurried behavior.

Infants: People at the stage of human development characterized by total helplessness and the need for protection and nurturance. Infants are all people who behave in infantile ways and display extremely primitive behavior patterns devoid of basic values.

Inspiration dragons: Dragons that stop inspiration: self-deprecation and arrogance.

Intention: The use of will to achieve a specific goal. Intention has male dynamic qualities and can be highly destructive if it is not harmonized with female magnetic qualities.

Martyrdom: Personality fear pattern (dragon) wherein the fear of being trapped by circumstances ironically causes people to act like chronic victims.

Masters: People at the climactic stage of human development, including avatars and teachers at the level of Jesus Christ, Buddha, Krishna, and Lao Tzu. Masters have no personal agenda or ego. They are dedicated to complete service and have special abilities.

Maturity stages: Stages of human development characterized by different abilities and values. These stages refer to the levels at which people are fixated later in life.

Meditation: Ancient, effective process for quieting the mind of all its constant chatter. Meditation is essential for effectively keeping the dragons out of people's lives.

Narrow-focused dragons: Personality fear patterns (dragons) that narrow people's sphere of influence: martyrdom, self-deprecation, and self-destruction.

Negative pole: The most destructive aspect of each fear pattern or dragon. This pole creates the most suffering.

Pillars of vitality: The four activities in life that are required for healthy living. Health and happiness depend on their being in balance and harmony. They are: true work, true play, true study, and true rest.

Positive pole: The least destructive aspect of each personality fear pattern or dragon. This pole helps people find the way out of the pattern. It is not truly positive in the long run, however.

Self-deprecation: Personality fear pattern (dragon) wherein people suffer from major fears of inadequacy. This pattern tends to reduce opportunity in life; it has a shrinking quality.

Self-destruction: Personality fear pattern (dragon) wherein people suffer from dread of being out of control. This fear paradoxically makes the people act out of control much of the time, leading to violence or death.

Stubbornness: Personality fear pattern (dragon) that causes people to fear and rebel against authority and to fear sudden change. This pattern makes people rigid and uncompromising.

Transform: To take the energy of something and use it for something else more desirable. Transforming drains the energy out of the fear patterns or dragons and releases it to increase vitality and personal power.

Toddlers: People at a developmental stage approximately between one year and three years of age. These young people discover their independent mobility and strive for autonomy. Toddlers are also those adults who are fixated at the toddler level. They have a need for authority and they experiment with breaking the rules.

True play: One of the four pillars of vitality. True play is specific fun activity that prevents scattering.

True rest: One of the four pillars of vitality. True rest is specific relaxing activity that restores people after intense play, work, or study.

True study: One of the four pillars of vitality. True study is a specific, interesting focus of learning that helps people become informed in relation to their true work.

True work: One of the four pillars of vitality. True work is a specific vocation that is totally absorbing and provides complete fulfillment and satisfaction to a person. It is often not discovered until midlife, and it may or may not be salaried.

Vision: The ability to see the long-range picture without sacrificing the total picture. Vision includes the ability to see some of the major steps along the way.

Wakefulness: The state of being totally present and conscious in the human body. Wakefulness implies having presence, which is necessary to keep all the dragons at bay.

Wide-focused dragons: Personality fear patterns or dragons that have a bigger impact on the environment and increase the sphere of dragon influence in a damaging way: greed, impatience, and arrogance.

Will: The facility that mobilizes energy toward the achievement of a particular focus.

Recommended Reading

Ajaya, S. *Psychotherapy East and West*. Honesdale, PA: The Himalayan Institute, 1983.

Aurobindo, S. *The Adventure of Consciousness*. Pondicherry, India: Sri Aurobindo Ashram Press, 1968.

_____. *The Destiny of the Human Body*. Pondicherry, India: Sri Aurobindo Ashram Press, 1975.

_____. *The Future Evolution of Man*. Wheaton, IL: The Theosophical Publishing House, 1971.

Brown, I. *Understanding Other Cultures*. Englewood Cliffs, NJ: Prentice Hall, 1963.

Bugental, J. *The Search for Authenticity*. New York: Irvington Publishers, Inc., 1981.

_____. *Psychotherapy and Process*. Menlo Park, CA: Addison Wesley Publishing Co., 1978.

Bynner, W., trans. *The Way of Life According to Lao Tzu*. New York: Capricorn Books, 1962.

Chaudiri, H. *The Evolution of Integral Consciousness*. Wheaton, IL: The Theosophical Publishing House, 1977.

Cirlot, J. E. *A Dictionary of Symbols*. New York: Philosophical Library, 1962.

Coleman, et al. *Abnormal Psychology and Modern Life*. Seventh edition. Palo Alto, CA: Scott Foresman and Company, 1984.

Crum, T. *The Magic of Conflict: Turning a Life of Work into a Work of Art*. New York: Simon and Schuster, 1987.

Dhiravamsa. *The Middle Path of Life*. Surrey, England: The Gresham Press, 1974.

Diagnostic and Statistical Manual of Mental Disorders. Third edition, revised. Washington DC: American Psychiatric Association, 1987.

Dundes, A. *Everyman His Way: Readings in Cultural Anthropology*. Englewood Cliffs, NJ: Prentice Hall, 1968.

Dychtwald, K. *Body-Mind*. New York: Jove Publications, 1977.

Erikson, E. *The Life Cycle Completed*. New York: W.W. Norton Co., 1985.

Fischer, L. *The Life of Mahatma Gandhi*. New York: Collier Books, 1950.

Fraiberg, S. *The Magic Years: Understanding and Handling the Problems of Early Childhood*. New York: Scribner's Sons, 1959.

Frankl, V. *Man's Search for Meaning*. New York: Washington Square Press, 1963.

Fromm-Reichman, F. *Principles of Intensive Psychotherapy*. Chicago: University of Chicago Press, 1960.

Golas, T. *The Lazy Man's Guide to Enlightenment*. NewYork: Bantam, 1972.

Hall, E. *The Silent Language*. New York: Doubleday, 1973.

Hall, M. *The Secret Teachings of All Ages*. Los Angeles: The Philosophical Research Society, Inc., 1975.

Hanh, Thich Nhat. *Peace Is Every Step*. New York: Bantam, 1992.

Huber, J. *Through an Eastern Window*. New York: Bantam, 1965.

Huber, R. *Treasury of Fantastic and Mythological Creatures*. New York: Dover Publications, Inc., 1981.

Isherwood, C., ed. *Vedanta for Modern Man*. New York: Collier Books, 1962.

Jabes, G. *Dictionary of Mythology, Folklore, and Symbols*. New York: Scarecrow Press Inc., 1961.

Jung, C. G. *Analytical Psychology*. New York: Random House, 1968.

_____. *Man and his Symbols*. Garden City: NY: Doubleday, 1964.

_____. *Symbols of Transformation*. Princeton, NJ: Princeton University Press, 1976.

Kaplan, A. *The New World of Philosophy*. New York: Random House, 1961.

Krishnamurti, J. *Talks with American Students*. Berkeley: Shambala, 1970.

Liebert, R., and M. Spieglar. *Personality: Strategies and Issues*. Homewood, IL: Dorsey Press, 1984.

Lowen, A. *Bioenergetics*. Baltimore: Penguin Books, 1975.

_____. *Depression and the Body*. Baltimore: Penguin Books. 1972.

_____. *The Language of the Body*. New York: Macmillan Publishing Co., 1958.

_____. *Love and Orgasm*. New York: New American Library, 1965.

_____. *Pleasure*. Baltimore: Penguin Books, 1975.

Mahler, M., et al. *The Psychological Birth of the Human Infant*. New York: Basic Books, 1975.

Mascaro, J., trans. *The Bhagavad Gita*. New York: Penguin, 1962.

McGowan, T. *Encyclopedia of Legendary Creatures*. San Francisco: Rand McNally and Co., 1981.

Merton, T. *Gandhi on Non-Violence*. New York: New Directions, 1964.

_____. *Zen and the Birds of Appetite*. New York: New Directions, 1968.

Metzner, R. *Know Your Type*. Garden City, NY: Doubleday,1979.

Miller, A. *Prisoners of Childhood*. New York: Basic Books,1981.

Mills, B. *Wokini*. Fair Oaks, CA: Feather Publications, 1990.

Neumann, E. *Art and the Creative Unconscious*. New Jersey: Princeton University Press, 1959.

Ouspensky, P.D. *The Fourth Way*. New York: Random House, 1957.

_____. *In Search of the Miraculous*. New York: Harcourt Brace and World Inc., 1949.

_____. *A New Model of the Universe*. New York: Random House, 1971

Palmer, H. *The Enneagram: The Definitive Guide to the Ancient System for Understanding Yourself and the Others in Your Life*. San Francisco: Harper and Row, 1992.

Pearce, J. *Magical Child*. New York: E.P. Dutton, 1977.

_____. *Magical Child Returns*: New York: E.P. Dutton, 1985.

Polhemus, T. *The Body Reader: Social Aspects of the Human Body*. New York: Pantheon, 1978.

Rama, S. *Yoga and Psychotherapy*. Glenview, IL: Himalayan Institute,1976.

Reich, W. *Character Analysis*. New York: Farrar, Straus, and Giroux, 1949.

Reps, P. *Zen Flesh, Zen Bones*. Garden City, NY: Doubleday, no date listed.

Riso, D. R. *Personality Types: Using the Enneagram for Self-Discovery*. Boston: Houghton Mifflin, 1987.

Scheflan, A. *How Behavior Means Exploring the Contexts of Speech and Meaning, Kinesics, Posture, Interaction, Setting, and Culture*. New York: Doubleday, 1974.

Schiller, H. *Communication and Cultural Domination*. White Plains, NY: International Arts and Sciences Press, 1976.

Shah, I. *The Way of the Sufi*. New York: E.P. Dutton, 1970.

Smith, H. *Forgotten Truth*. New York: Harper and Row, 1976.

_____. *The Religions of Man*. New York: Harper and Row, 1986.

Standard Dictionary of Folklore, Mythology, and Legends. New York: Funk and Wagnalls, 1950.

Stevens, J. *Earth to Tao*. Santa Fe, NM: Bear & Co., reprinted 1993.

_____. *Tao to Earth*. Santa Fe, NM: Bear & Co., reprinted 1993.

Stevens, J., and L. Stevens. *Secrets of Shamanism: Tapping the Spirit Power Within You*. New York: Avon, 1988.

Stevens, J., and S. Smith. *The Michael Handbook*. Orinda, CA: Warwick Press, 1990.

Stevens, J., and J.P. Van Hulle. *Personality Puzzle: Solving the Mystery of Who You Are*. Orinda, CA: Affinity Press, 1990.

Sullivan, H. S. *The Interpersonal Theory of Psychiatry*. New York: W.W. Norton, 1953.

Suzuki, S. *Zen Mind, Beginner's Mind*. New York: Weatherhill, 1973.

Talbot, M. *The Holographic Universe*. New York: Harper Collins, 1991.

Thompson, W. *The Time Falling Bodies Take to Light.* New York:
   St. Martin's Press, 1981.
Tzu, Lao. Translation by V. Mair. *Tao Te Ching.* New York:
   Bantam, 1990.
Watts, A. *The Way of Zen.* New York: Penguin, 1958.
Wellwood, J. *The Meeting of the Ways.* New York: Schocken
   Books, 1979.
White, J. *The Highest States of Consciousness.* New York:
   Doubleday, 1972.
Wilber, K. *The Atman Project.* Wheaton, IL: The Theosophical
   Publishing House, 1980.
Yarbro, C.Q. *Messages from Michael.* New York: Playboy
   Paperbacks, 1979.
_____. *More Messages from Michael.* New York: Berkeley
   Publishing Group, 1986.

More Information and Resources

Pivotal Resources, Inc., founded by José Stevens and his wife, Lena, sponsors personally-designed retreats, vision quests, lectures, educational seminars, and workshops in Santa Fe, New Mexico, and in many other locations around the world. Pivotal Resources has 800 acres of pristine land in northern New Mexico for its wilderness retreats. If you would like to be on their mailing list for a calendar of events and travel schedule, send your name and address.

Private sessions and consultations with José Stevens are available by phone or in person. Contact Pivotal Resources at 505-982-8732, or Fax: 505-989-4626. Consultation services include:

Individual and couples counseling
Personality profile
Organizational development and team building
Legal consultation and jury selection.

You can subscribe to the Pivotal Resources quarterly newsletter, which contains up-to-the-moment articles about the changing times, world events, life issues, shamanism, prosperity, channeled articles, and many topics. The newsletter also includes a schedule of upcoming events. A subscription for four issues is $12 USA and $20 foreign. Please send your name, phone number, and subscription to:

Pivotal Resources, Inc.
P.O. Box 6691
Santa Fe, New Mexico 87502

About the Author

José Stevens, Ph.D., received his doctoral degree in counseling from the California Institute of Integral Studies in San Francisco and his Masters Degree in Clinical Social Work at the University of California, Berkeley. In addition to extensive travel in the United States, Asia, Europe, and Africa he has pursued post graduate training in both traditional psychotherapy and in alternative intuitive methods. Dr. Stevens taught for over eight years in the Psychology Graduate School and the Department of Transpersonal Counseling at John F. Kennedy University in Orinda, California.

A psychotherapist with more than twenty years of experience, Dr. Stevens, successfully uses the principles outlined in *Transforming Your Dragons* with his individual clients and in consultation with organizations.

With his wife Lena, he coauthored the classic *Secrets of Shamanism: Tapping the Spirit Power Within You*, now translated in six languages. In addition, he is the coauthor of *The Michael Handbook*, and *The Personality Puzzle*, and is the sole author of two books, *Tao to Earth* and *Earth to Tao*.

Dr. Stevens lectures internationally, focusing on the Seven Dragons and topics related to personality, vitality, and balanced living. Currently he is a consultant and team builder with the Sol y Sombra Foundation, a nationally recognized center in Santa Fe, New Mexico, focusing on community building and showcasing permaculture.

He has been interviewed on local, national, and foreign radio and television networks and has been featured in several European magazines.

BOOKS OF RELATED INTEREST
BY BEAR & COMPANY

ACCEPTING YOUR POWER TO HEAL
The Personal Practice of Therapeutic Touch
by Dolores Krieger, Ph.D., R.N.

BREAKING OUT OF ENVIRONMENTAL ILLNESS
by Robert Sampson, M.D., and Patricia Hughes, B.S.N.

BRINGERS OF THE DAWN
Teachings from the Pleiadians
by Barbara Marciniak

EMBRACING DEATH
Riding Life's Transitions into Power and Freedom
by Angela Browne-Miller, Ph.D.

LIQUID LIGHT OF SEX
Kundalini Rising at Mid-Life Crisis
by Barbara Hand Clow

TRANSFORMATION THROUGH BODYWORK
Using Touch Therapies for Inner Peace
by Dan Menkin

VIBRATIONAL MEDICINE
New Choices for Healing Ourselves
by Richard Gerber, M.D.

Contact your local bookseller

~ or ~

BEAR & COMPANY
P.O. Box 2860
Santa Fe, NM 87504
1-800-WE-BEARS